MW00379644

HOLMAN
Old Testament
Commentary

HOLMAN *Old Testament* Commentary

Daniel

GENERAL EDITOR

Max Anders

AUTHOR

Kenneth O. Gangel

NASHVILLE, TENNESSEE

Holman Old Testament Commentary

Bible versions used in this book:

Unless otherwise stated all Scripture citation is from the HOLY BIBLE, NEW INTERNATIONAL VERSION®. Copyright © 1973, 1978, 1984 by International Bible Society. Used by permission of Zondervan Publishing House. All Rights Reserved. The "NIV" and "New International Version" trademarks are registered in the United States Patent and Trademark Office by International Bible Society. Use of either trademark requires the permission of International Bible Society.

The American Standard Version

The King James Version

Scripture passages marked MLB are taken from The Modern Language Bible, The New Berkeley Version. Copyright 1945, 1959, © 1969 by Zondervan Publishing House. Used by permission.

Scripture passages marked NASB are taken from Scripture taken from the NEW AMERICAN STANDARD BIBLE, © Copyright The Lockman Foundation, 1960, 1962, 1963, 1968, 1971, 1972, 1973, 1975, 1977, 1995 Used by permission. Scripture passages marked NRSV are taken from the New Revised Standard Version of the Bible, copyright © 1989 by the Division of Christian Education of the National Council of Churches of Christ in the United States of America Used by permission. All rights reserved.

Scripture passages marked RSV are taken from the Revised Standard Version of the Bible, copyrighted 1946, 1952, © 1971, 19?3.

Verses marked TLB are taken from The Living Bible. Copyright © Tyndale House Publishers, Wheaton, Illinois, 1971. Used by permission.

Scripture taken from THE MESSAGE. Copyright © 1993, 1994, 1995, 1996, 2000. Used by permission of NavPress Publishing Group.

ISBN-13: 978–0–8054–9476–1

ISBN-10 0–8054–9476–6

Dewey Decimal Classification: 224.507

Subject Heading: BIBLE. OT. Daniel

Library of Congress Card Catalog Number: 2001043404

Gangel. Kenneth O.
Daniel / author, Kenneth O. Gangel.
p. cm. — (Holman Old Testament commentary)
Includes bibliographical references. (p.).
ISBN 0-8054-9476-6
1. Bible. O.T. Daniel—Commentaries. I. Title. II. Series.
BS1555.53 .G36 2002
224'.507—dc21 2001043404

6 7 8 9 10 11 12 13 16 15 14 13 12

To those whose classes and books taught me about prophecy and the importance of the Lord's return—

Alva J. McClain

J. Dwight Pentecost

John F. Walvoord

John C. Whitcomb Jr.

Contents

Editorial Preface

Today's church hungers for Bible teaching, and Bible teachers hunger for resources to guide them in teaching God's Word. The Holman Old Testament Commentary provides the church with the food to feed the spiritually hungry in an easily digestible format. The result: new spiritual vitality that the church can readily use.

Bible teaching should result in new interest in the Scriptures, expanded Bible knowledge, discovery of specific scriptural principles, relevant applications, and exciting living. The unique format of the Holman Old Testament Commentary includes sections to achieve these results for every Old Testament book.

Opening quotations stimulate thinking and lead to an introductory illustration and discussion that draw individuals and study groups into the Word of God. "In a Nutshell" summarizes the content and teaching of the chapter. Verse-by-verse commentary answers the church's questions rather than raising issues scholars usually admit they cannot adequately solve. Bible principles and specific contemporary applications encourage students to move from Bible to contemporary times. A specific modern illustration then ties application vividly to present life. A brief prayer aids the student to commit his or her daily life to the principles and applications found in the Bible chapter being studied. For those still hungry for more, "Deeper Discoveries" take the student into a more personal, deeper study of the words, phrases, and themes of God's Word. Finally, a teaching outline provides transitional statements and conclusions along with an outline to assist the teacher in group Bible studies.

It is the editors' prayer that this new resource for local church Bible teaching will enrich the ministry of group, as well as individual, Bible study, and that it will lead God's people truly to be people of the Book, living out what God calls us to be.

Holman Old Testament Commentary Contributors

Vol. 1, Genesis
ISBN 978–0-8054-9461-7
Kenneth O. Gangel
and Stephen Bramer

Vol. 2, Exodus, Leviticus, Numbers
ISBN 978–0-8054-9462-4
Glen Martin

Vol. 3, Deuteronomy
ISBN 978–0-8054-9463-1
Doug McIntosh

Vol. 4, Joshua
ISBN 978–0-8054-9464-8
Kenneth O. Gangel

Vol. 5, Judges, Ruth
ISBN 978–0-8054-9465-5
W. Gary Phillips

Vol. 6, 1 & 2 Samuel
ISBN 978–0-8054-9466-2
Stephen Andrews

Vol. 7, 1 & 2 Kings
ISBN 978–0-8054-9467-9
Gary Inrig

Vol. 8, 1 & 2 Chronicles
ISBN 978–0-8054-9468-6
Winfried Corduan

Vol. 9, Ezra, Nehemiah, Esther
ISBN 978–0-8054-9469-3
Knute Larson and Kathy Dahlen

Vol. 10, Job
ISBN 978–0-8054-9470-9
Steven J. Lawson

Vol. 11, Psalms 1-72
ISBN 978–0-8054-9471-6
Steven J. Lawson

Vol. 12, Psalms 73-150
ISBN 978–0-8054-9481-5
Steven J. Lawson

Vol. 13, Proverbs
ISBN 978–0-8054-9472-3
Max Anders

Vol. 14, Ecclesiastes, Song of Songs
ISBN 978–0-8054-9482-2
David George Moore and Daniel L. Akin

Vol. 15, Isaiah
ISBN 978–0-8054-9473-0
Trent C. Butler

Vol. 16, Jeremiah, Lamentations
ISBN 978–0-8054-9474-7
Fred M. Wood and Ross McLaren

Vol. 17, Ezekiel
ISBN 978–0-8054-9475-4
Mark F. Rooker

Vol. 18, Daniel
ISBN 978–0-8054-9476-1
Kenneth O. Gangel

Vol. 19, Hosea, Joel, Amos, Obadiah, Jonah, Micah
ISBN 978–0-8054-9477-8
Trent C. Butler

Vol. 20, Nahum, Habakkuk, Zephaniah, Haggai, Zechariah, Malachi
ISBN 978–0-8054-9478-5
Stephen R. Miller

Holman New Testament Commentary Contributors

Vol. 1, Matthew
ISBN 978–0-8054-0201-8
Stuart K. Weber

Vol. 2, Mark
ISBN 978–0-8054-0202-5
Rodney L. Cooper

Vol. 3, Luke
ISBN 978–0-8054-0203-2
Trent C. Butler

Vol. 4, John
ISBN 978–0-8054-0204-9
Kenneth O. Gangel

Vol. 5, Acts
ISBN 978–0-8054-0205-6
Kenneth O. Gangel

Vol. 6, Romans
ISBN 978–0-8054-0206-3
Kenneth Boa and William Kruidenier

Vol. 7, 1 & 2 Corinthians
ISBN 978–0-8054-0207-0
Richard L. Pratt Jr.

Vol. 8, Galatians, Ephesians, Philippians, Colossians
ISBN 978–0-8054-0208-7
Max Anders

Vol. 9, 1 & 2 Thessalonians, 1 & 2 Timothy, Titus, Philemon
ISBN 978–0-8054-0209-4
Knute Larson

Vol. 10, Hebrews, James
ISBN 978–0-8054-0211-7
Thomas D. Lea

Vol. 11, 1 & 2 Peter, 1, 2, 3 John, Jude
ISBN 978–0-8054-0210-0
David Walls and Max Anders

Vol. 12, Revelation
ISBN 978–0-8054-0212-4
Kendell H. Easley

Holman Old Testament Commentary

Twenty volumes designed for Bible study and teaching to enrich the local church and God's people.

Series Editor	Max Anders
Managing Editor	Steve Bond
Project Editor	Dean Richardson
Product Development Manager	Ricky D. King
Marketing Manager	Stephanie Huffman
Executive Editor	David Shepherd
Page Composition	TF Designs, Mt. Juliet, TN

Introduction to

Daniel

On October 30, 1992, the Associated Press reported a story from Seoul, Korea. Reverend Chang Man-Ho, a pastor in Seoul, had predicted that the world would end on Wednesday, October 28, 1992. When it did not, Pastor Chang calmly announced to his followers, many of whom had sold possessions and given up everything because of his predictions, "Nothing has happened. Sorry. Let's go home."

Pretentious ignorance still prompts well-meaning but ill-advised people to predict the return of the Lord and other end-time events. The New Testament clearly warns against this kind of dangerous behavior, but perhaps some are encouraged by the accuracy of prophecy in Old Testament books like Daniel. Although the shortest of the major prophets, Daniel is referred to in New Testament prophetic passages more than any other Old Testament book. It also contains more fulfilled prophecies than any other book in the Bible.

A prophet of the exile, Daniel wrote from the heart of Babylon. The Northern Kingdom, Israel, had been captured by Assyria in 722 B.C. Just over one hundred years later the Babylonians took the Southern Kingdom, including its capital Jerusalem. God had put up with disobedience and rebellion from Israel for five hundred years, but now judgment had fallen. Although Daniel deals often with history throughout these chapters, his book primarily focuses on prophecy and the prediction of future events. Remember, too, that chronological arrangement is not a major concern of either the historical or predictive sections of this book.

Before we look at some keys to the Book of Daniel, let's remember that this commentary series emphasizes expository and practical treatment of the text. For scholarly foundational material readers are referred to Gleason Archer's fine work in *The Expositor's Bible Commentary* series or Stephen R. Miller's excellent introduction to Daniel in *The New American Commentary.*

Both deal with canonicity, languages, and other special problems, matters on which we will touch only lightly.

AUTHORSHIP

Like most ancient authors, Daniel frequently refers to himself in the third person. Nevertheless, throughout the book he clearly identifies himself (9:2,20; 10:2) and Jesus talks about "the prophet Daniel" in Matthew 24:15. Ezekiel also comments on Daniel (his contemporary) by saying, "Even if these three men—Noah, Daniel and Job—were in [the rebellious land], they could save only themselves" (Ezek. 14:14,20).

Virtually no one put forth significant attack on the authorship of Daniel until more than two thousand years after the book was written. Even then it arose largely from those who question the integrity and inspiration of Scripture. Many have argued that the book is actually fictional, a claim which rests on the rejection of the miracles and predictive prophecy so essential to Daniel's work. They attempt to get around the obvious historicity of the book by claiming that since no one can predict future events, the book must have been written much later, years after everything Daniel describes had already happened.

But since several of the prophecies in Daniel (and their fulfillment) could not have taken place by the second century B.C., the prophetic dynamic of the book cannot be denied. As Miller points out: "Furthermore, if the writer of Daniel could not have foretold events in the second century B.C., he could not have predicted the person and work of Jesus Christ in the first century; and he certainly could have had nothing to say concerning Christ's second coming. Such a position would, of course, be contrary to the plain teaching of the New Testament and Christ Himself (e.g., Luke 24:25–27,44–46)" (Miller, p. 32).

DATE OF WRITING

The question of dating is important because it affirms the prophetic reality of Daniel's work. Gleason Archer speaks to this with authority and clarity: "As to the date of the composition of Daniel, the narrative of the prophet's earliest experiences begins with his capture as a hostage by Nebuchadnezzar back in 605–604 B.C. And according to 1:21, he continues certainly until the first year of Cyrus (about 537 B.C.), in relation to his public service, and to the third year of Cyrus (535 B.C.), in relation to his prophetic ministry (Dan. 10:1). Daniel seems to have revised and completed his memoirs during his retirement sometime about 532 or 530 B.C., when he would have been close to 90 years old (assuming his birth about 620 B.C.). The appearance of Persian-derived governmental terms, even in the earlier chapters composed in Aramaic, strongly suggests that these chapters were given their final form after Persian had become the official language of government" (Archer, p. 6).

PURPOSE

Although historical and moral in content and tone, Daniel is primarily a book of prophecy. As we have seen, Jesus himself referred to "Daniel the prophet" (Mark 13:14, KJV). The theme of Daniel clearly centers in the sovereignty of God. Perhaps more than any other Old Testament writer, Daniel clarifies for us a basic proposition of truth—there are no heroes in the Bible except God. This is not a biography of Daniel's life, not a book about the history of Israel, and not a theology of the Hebrews. It purposes to predict future events and, as such, was surely of great hope and encouragement to the Jews who returned to restore the temple and rebuild the city some years later. But it also contains great encouragement and hope because it holds the key to understanding the Olivet Discourse in Matthew 24–25 and serves as a sister book to Revelation. Neither book can be properly understood without the other.

Both Daniel and Revelation are apocalyptic books, so called because of their use of supernatural visions. The Greek word *apokalupsis* means the unveiling of truth which had been previously unknown or deliberately concealed by God. Most evangelical scholars would place the following books in that category: portions of Ezekiel (notably chs. 40–48); most of Daniel; most of Zechariah; and Revelation.

As Walvoord reminds us: "The fact that a book is apocalyptic does not necessarily mean that its revelation is obscure or uncertain, and conservative scholarship has recognized the legitimacy of apocalyptic revelation as a genuine means of divine communication. If close attention is given to the contextual interpretive revelation, apocalyptic books can yield solid results to the patient exegete" (Walvoord, *Daniel*, p. 14).

LANGUAGES

Daniel offers his book in two languages—Hebrew (chs. 1; 8–12) and Aramaic (chs. 2–7). These two languages are also used in Ezra, but that does not answer the key question—why would these men write in two languages? Actually, the answer is more simple than one might first imagine. In Daniel the Hebrew sections deal with concerns unique to God's people of the old covenant, the Jews; the Aramaic chapters deal with matters related to the wider populations of the Babylonian and Persian empires.

We should remember too that though the Jews of the early Old Testament spoke Hebrew, by the time of Jesus they were speaking Aramaic (also called Chaldee or Syriac). Interestingly, in dialogues which appear in Genesis, Jacob speaks Hebrew, but his uncle Laban speaks Aramaic.

Actually, identification of the Aramaic is helpful in deciding the date of Daniel. If Daniel used "official Aramaic," the book would come from the sixth or fifth centuries B.C. A later form of Aramaic would date the book around the second century, which is what critics insist upon. The Dead Sea Scrolls are very helpful in this analysis, and much has been written about their impact. The Job Targum found in Cave 11 at Qumran offers Aramaic language even younger than that of Daniel. The editors of the Job Targum date it some time in the second half of the second century.

Significant time passed between the earlier Aramaic of the Book of Daniel and the Job Targum, pointing to an earlier date for this prophecy than critical scholarship has been willing to acknowledge. Conservative scholars clearly place the writing sometime before 500 B.C., possibly a completion date of about 530 B.C. after the capture of Babylon by Cyrus in 539 B.C.

CANONICITY

Critics of Daniel like to point out that the old Masoretic arrangement of Old Testament books included Daniel with the Writings and not the Prophets. Evangelical scholars have taken the position that this interesting phenomenon occurred because Daniel's book is of a different character, the proclamations of a pagan government official rather than a preacher commissioned to proclaim God's message to Israel. We must remember that the Writings were hardly considered any less inspired than other Scripture, nor was their collection identified with any particular date. By the time of the Septuagint (LXX), Daniel was included with the prophets.

Almost all the arguments against Daniel—its date, its authenticity, its arrangement in collections of Old Testament books—arise from the efforts of critics to deny the credibility and reality of predictive prophecy. When one can cross that hurdle, the details fall comfortably into place.

THEME AND THEOLOGY

The Book of Daniel centers in the sovereignty of God. Daniel writes at a time when Israel had every reason to think that all the old promises had been broken and all the old covenants shattered. Paganism had triumphed twice (Assyria and Babylonia), and the cause of the Jews was clearly lost.

Arising from those ashes comes the clarion call that the affairs and outcomes on earth, the deliberations of kings and the victories or defeats of their armies, rest in the hands of God. If Daniel could have gotten his hands on the music, he might have spent a great deal of time singing "He's Got the Whole World in His Hands."

In addition to Daniel's central character—the omnipotent God—he also teaches us about angels, naming both Gabriel and Michael in his book. Clearly the doctrine of human depravity arises in Daniel, and the constant need to make moral choices appears to both Daniel and the pagan kings he served. The doctrine of the resurrection (as old as Job 19) appears in Daniel 12, reminding us of Isaiah 26 and Ezekiel 37. Daniel, finds complete harmony with the rest of the Old Testament in focusing on the general progressive revelation of Scripture and laying a foundation for the eschatology of the New Testament.

As Walvoord observes: "In many respects, the Book of Daniel is the most comprehensive prophetic revelation of the Old Testament, giving the only total view of world history from Babylon to the Second Advent of Christ and inter-relating Gentile history and prophecy with that which concerns Israel. Daniel provides the key to the overall interpretation of prophecy, is a major element in premillennialism, and is essential to the interpretation of the Book of Revelation. Its revelation of the sovereignty and power of God has brought assurance to Jew and Gentile alike that God will fulfill His sovereign purposes in time and eternity" (Walvoord, *Daniel*, p. 27).

STRUCTURE

Those who would attempt to impose a rigid structure (such as one finds in Romans) on the historical/prophetic work of Daniel will likely find only frustration. With some minor exceptions the only proper way to look at this book is in its twelve separate but related chapters. This commentary appears in more than twelve chapters because it attempts to provide a more reader-friendly approach; we do not suggest that the division of the chapters in this work reflects some specific division in Daniel.

We have already noted the linguistic distinction in the book, but we can also observe a dividing line right down the middle in terms of content. In chapters 1–6 Daniel interprets the visions of others, while in chapters 7–12 he receives his own. The first six chapters are primarily historical, the last six primarily prophetic. Apart from that, no good can come from forcing some kind of external structure on this vibrant and dynamic book. As we tackle the task before us, we will look first at the chapters and then at the paragraphs within the chapters, usually making our way along the path verse by verse.

Some merit can be found in the outline utilized by the *NIV Study Bible* which calls chapter 1 the prologue and notes that chapters 2 through 7 deal with the destinies of the nations of the world and 8 through 12 with the destiny of the nation of Israel. Others will appreciate Miller's ten-point outline complete with multiple subpoints (Miller, p. 52).

INTERPRETATION

The interpretation (hermeneutic) used in the approach to Daniel will determine not only the handling of the text but also the way the text is applied. We have already assumed an early date, authenticity in the canon, and the authorship by Daniel, a prophet/statesman in Babylon. We have noted that the work is somewhat historical, mainly prophetic, and distinctly eschatological. These matters all deal with our interpretation of the book.

Furthermore, Daniel offers us some keys to interpretation by internal connections such as the confirmation of chapter 2 in chapter 7. We face little problem in recognizing Babylonia, Persia, Greece, and even Rome in this book. The problem comes in the extension of the Roman Empire to deal with events yet future, including the coming of Christ and the final days, particularly Israel's role in God's prophetic plan.

This commentary approaches Daniel with a premillennial perspective. It assumes that an earthly kingdom of Christ still awaits the future and that this promise rests squarely on Old Testament texts (particularly in Isaiah and Daniel) and the promises of Christ himself (Matt. 11:2–6; Luke 1:31–33). The millennium, however, is only a part of the kingdom age, not the kingdom itself. The millennium lasts only one thousand years, but the kingdom, already present in the hearts of those who trust the King, lasts forever.

Here is a helpful paragraph from the work of Robert D. Culver:

> Premillennialists believe that at the second coming of Christ there will be a resurrection of the saints only, that at His coming He will destroy the wicked living, that the righteous will enter the Millennium to people the earth during the Millennium and that the glorified saints of former ages shall join with the restored Israel in ruling the world during the Millennium. At the close of the Millennium the resurrection and final judgment of the wicked will take place (Culver, p. 46).

All readers understand that a work of this extent requires strong support for the author. My sincere appreciation, therefore, flows to my wife Betty for manuscript reading and to Ginny Murray my faithful and competent manuscript typist. This is now my third Holman Commentary volume and working with Max Anders and Steve Bond has been a genuine delight.

Daniel 1:1–21

Lessons from Kidnapped Children

I. INTRODUCTION
Emergency Interruption

II. COMMENTARY
A verse-by-verse explanation of the chapter.

III. CONCLUSION
Courage for Public Service
An overview of the principles and applications from the chapter.

IV. LIFE APPLICATION
Prioritizing Parenting
Melding the chapter to life.

V. PRAYER
Tying the chapter to life with God.

VI. DEEPER DISCOVERIES
Historical, geographical, and grammatical enrichment of the commentary.

VII. TEACHING OUTLINE
Suggested step-by-step group study of the chapter.

VIII. ISSUES FOR DISCUSSION
Zeroing the chapter in on daily life.

Quote

"Judge of the Nations, spare us yet,
lest we forget—lest we forget!"

Rudyard Kipling

PERSONAL PROFILE: JEHOIAKIM

- Son of Josiah who reigned in Jerusalem from 607 to 597 B.C.
- An oppressive and wicked king whose name was changed from Eliakim by the king of Egypt
- Died in disgrace while a captive (Jer. 22:19)
- Followed by Jehoiachin his son (2 Kgs. 24:8)

PERSONAL PROFILE: NEBUCHADNEZZAR

- Ruled the Neo-Babylonian Empire from 605 to 562 B.C.
- Mentioned in Kings, Chronicles, Ezra, Nehemiah, Jeremiah, Ezekiel, and Daniel
- His name means "Nabu, protect the boundary" and is sometimes seen with the spelling Nebuchadrezzar
- One of the greatest monarchs of the ancient world whose empire extended over Egypt, Syria, and Palestine

GEOGRAPHICAL PROFILE: BABYLON

- The name, likely derived from the Akkadian, means "gate of God"
- Most important city of the Babylonian Empire
- Situated in central Mesopotamia on the Euphrates River about fifty miles south of the contemporary city of Baghdad in Iraq

- May have been twenty-four hundred years old before Daniel arrived

GEOGRAPHICAL PROFILE: JERUSALEM

- According to the Roman historian Pliny, "By far the most famous city of the ancient Orient"
- The name is built on the Hebrew word *salem* which means "peace"
- The name *Jerusalem* occurs six hundred times in the Old Testament
- Captured by David approximately one thousand years before the birth of Christ, it became David's capital

GEOGRAPHICAL PROFILE: JUDAH

- The fourth son of Jacob from whom a tribe of the same name descended
- A member of the tribe of Judah, David united the entire Israeli kingdom, a union that stayed in place during the reign of Solomon
- After Solomon the nation split into two parts, commonly called the Northern Kingdom, Israel, and the Southern Kingdom, Judah
- The Southern Kingdom, Judah, was approximately half the size of the Northern Kingdom and also held approximately half the population (about three hundred thousand)

IN A NUTSHELL

Wherever life takes us, whatever it brings us, however difficult our problems, we must remain faithful to God.

Daniel 1:1–21

Lessons from Kidnapped Children

I. INTRODUCTION

Emergency Interruption

When I agreed to write this commentary on Daniel, I had no idea that the opening verses of the first chapter would be prepared in the surgical waiting room of our local hospital. But here I sit, separated from the Coke machine by about twenty yards of pale gray carpet, the outdated magazines arranged neatly on a table to my right. Down the hall and around the corner a team of surgeons and nurses perform major surgery on my wife of forty-four years—a large mass in her uterus must be removed, and we will learn today whether it is malignant and how that will change our lives. Four days ago she was a vibrant, healthy woman, busily preparing a dinner party for eighteen people from our church which was scheduled for this evening. Then a 3:00 A.M. rush to the emergency room realigned all the priorities in our lives.

How could this happen so quickly? Why did we not see symptoms earlier? What does one say to one's wife as the anesthesia is injected and she begins to drift slowly out of consciousness? Her last words before closing her eyes formed a question: "Do you have anything to say to me before I go to surgery?" Such a moment calls for no platitudes or plaque rhymes, no Christian clichés or technical theology. I simply said, "Yes, I do. I love you, and God is in control of everything."

The Book of Daniel is not about Daniel. Like Abraham, Moses, and Joshua, Daniel was God's vessel, a tool in his hands to accomplish his eternal purpose on earth. In the Pentateuch and historical books, God's sovereignty appears as the backdrop, an assumption about the God of the universe. In Daniel it becomes the central theme, a message to be shouted to God's people Israel and to the pagan nations surrounding them: *There is a God, and he is in charge of his world.* We'll explore sovereignty in greater theological depth later in this book, but here let's just define it very simply by saying *God knows what he's doing, and he's doing it.*

II. COMMENTARY

Lessons from Kidnapped Children

MAIN IDEA: *God's people, whether Israel or the church, always stand as the countercultural opponents of the systems of this world. Never was that reality more poignantly lived out than in the Old Testament captivity and exile, and particularly the dominance by Babylon. That national struggle will emerge early in our book, but the first chapter primarily teaches us that righteousness begins with a firm commitment to God.*

 Attack by Babylon (1:1–2)

SUPPORTING IDEA: *God's plan is often accomplished in ways his people do not understand such as through oppression, suffering, and captivity.*

1:1. Throughout this book we should expect a high level of scholarly writing since Daniel was one of the most educated people of the Bible. When we think about the New Testament, the apostle Paul rises to the surface among intellectual Christians. In the Old Testament we think of Moses and Solomon, but Daniel would probably hold no lower than third place in the ranks of those thoroughly trained for God's role for them in history and ministry.

Daniel begins by telling us when he first went to Babylon—**in the third year of the reign of Jehoiakim king of Judah**. Scholars agree that this was 605 B.C., and we see parallel accounts in 2 Kings 24:1–2 and 2 Chronicles 36:5–7. It helps us to remember that there were three distinct deportations—this first one in 605 when Daniel and a few others were taken captive to Babylon; the second in 598 B.C. when Jehoiachin and the royal family were captured along with Ezekiel and all the treasures of the temple (2 Kgs. 24:10–17); and the third in 587 B.C. when Jerusalem and the temple were destroyed and Judah ceased to be the Southern Kingdom (2 Kgs. 25:1–21).

Critics love to point out what appears to be a discrepancy between Daniel's account and a statement of Jeremiah (Jer. 25:1) which seems to indicate the first year of Nebuchadnezzar was in the fourth year of Jehoiachin. But this problem is easily solved by observing that Daniel used Babylonian reckoning whereas Jeremiah used Egyptian reckoning. The Babylonians considered the first year of a king's reign the year of accession and the second year would be the official "first year."

Indeed, there are many more elaborate arguments and even different options offered for this explanation (see Leupold and Keil). Walvoord reminds us that "the evidence makes quite untenable the charge that the chronological information of Daniel is inaccurate. Rather, it is entirely in keeping with information available outside the Bible and supports the view that Daniel is a genuine book" (Walvoord, *Daniel*, 32).

Because of his prominence throughout this book, we must explore further this giant ruler, **Nebuchadnezzar king of Babylon**. Some years later this name was spelled Nebuchadrezzar, but we find it with the "n" in Kings, Chronicles, Ezra, and parts of Jeremiah. Different spellings of ancient names hardly present a stumbling block, especially when one considers the transliteration of Babylonian cuneiform into either Hebrew or Aramaic. Actually his name was Nabu-kudurri-usur, which means something like, "Nabu, protect the boundary."

But some will ask, was Nebuchadnezzar really king at this time? After all, his father Nabopolassar was not yet dead. Both Jeremiah 27:6 and extra-biblical sources call him king, and almost every reputable scholar agrees that the two men shared the throne for some years before Nabopolassar's death.

To get a better handle on the kingdom of Babylon, let's go back to the year 625 B.C., likely the year of Daniel's birth (though Archer chooses 620 B.C.). In that year Ashurbanipal, the last great king of Assyria, died, and his son Ashuruballit attempted to continue the kingdom. But the power of Assyria passed to the king's viceroy, and Nabopolassar took all of Babylonia out of the Assyrian Empire. Daniel was a young teenager during the fall of Nineveh in 612 B.C., an event which gave Babylon control of western Asia. At the end of his teen years, Daniel was taken captive to Babylon, and the great story of our book begins.

But before we leave this first verse, let's remember that the godly influence on Daniel took place very early in his life. The great and good king Josiah had already reigned for fifteen years when Daniel was born, and for the next sixteen the revivals he brought to Judah surely touched the young man's life. We can assume the godliness of Daniel's parents, and history shows us the godliness of the national leadership he enjoyed.

W. A. Criswell captures the downward spiral after that fateful day of Josiah's death at the hands of Pharaoh-Necho at Megiddo in the Valley of Jezreel: "Following Josiah's death and the plunging of the nation into rampant idolatry, he [Daniel] formed attitudes of faithfulness to God that never changed. The sudden and extreme contrast now introduced into his political and moral surroundings made the decision to serve God the more meaningful in his life. As the kingdom of Judah reeled dizzily in want and idolatry and wickedness, Daniel girded himself to withstand rather than to drift with the current of his time. The great revival may have been lost upon the wicked Jehoahaz and Jehoiakim and Zedekiah and Jehoiachin, but the revival found a glorious response in the hearts of Daniel and Hananiah and Mishael and Azariah" (Criswell, p. 111).

1:2. Daniel wastes no time getting to his theme—the sovereignty of God. How was the nation of Israel lost? **The Lord delivered Jehoiakim king of Judah into his hand**. Most commentators do not elaborate this phrase, primarily because they seem to be caught up in the historical detail and the battle over authenticity and authorship. But I propose that Daniel introduces the primary theme of his book right here. The captivity of 605 B.C. was not a victory for Nebuchadnezzar any more than the crucifixion was a victory for Satan. The God of creation decided that year that a new chapter would open in his personal "world book," so he sent Jehoiakim to defeat and Daniel to Babylon.

Daniel's mention of **some of the articles from the temple of God** lays the foundation for the reappearance of these and other vessels (2 Chr. 36:18) in the fascinating story of Belshazzar's feast in chapter 5. Carrying worship vessels from one nation to another, from one god to another, was common practice for the ancient kings. We need not get symbolic here. In the fourth century A.D. Jerome wrote: "By these vessels we are to understand the dogmas of truth. For if you go through all of the works of the philosophers, you will necessarily find in them some portion of the vessels of God. . . . [They] combine truth with error and corrupt the good of nature with many evils, for that reason they are recorded to have captured only a portion of the vessels of God's house, and not all of them in their completeness and perfection" (Jerome, p. 20).

What the venerable theologian says of truth and philosophy surely pertains as well today, but finding that kind of significance in this verse creates unnecessary word pictures from the text.

But two phrases still await our attention before we leave verse 2. The first is **Babylonia** or the "land of Shinar." Most scholars suggest that the name refers to a wider area of Mesopotamia of which Babylonia was a part. Normally it carries theological implications as a place opposed to the message and spirit of God. Here we find the Tower of Babel (Gen. 11:2), and here also we see the banishment of evil (Zech. 5:11).

When Nebuchadnezzar brought the vessels back to Babylon, he put them in **the temple of his god**. Daniel tells us that twice in one verse, indicating its importance. He wants us to understand that this is not only a battle between nations but also a battle between deities—God against Marduk, great god of the Babylonians. We have here one historic pinpoint in the battle of the ages, the eternal struggle between heaven and earth, light and darkness, truth and error.

Veldkamp says it well: "Jerusalem versus Babel is the great opposition that has dominated world history throughout the ages. It is the colossal struggle between the Kingdom of God and the kingdom of Satan, the Church and the world, the Christ and the Antichrist. Whereas John tells us in Revelation of the final battle and ultimate triumph of Christ, Daniel describes one of the many phases in the struggle (Dan. 1:9–10)" (Veldkamp, p. 9).

B Training in Babylon (1:3–7)

SUPPORTING IDEA: *Every Christian who wants to serve God effectively in the wider world would do well to show aptitude for every kind of learning.*

1:3. Sometimes kidnapped children can rise to prominence in an alien land. It happened to Joseph, and now it would happen to Daniel. Many have questioned the name **Ashpenaz** in this verse, challenging its historicity, but it does appear in the Aramaic text and Cuneiform records with a slightly different spelling. There is no reason to concern ourselves about the name's derivation. Once we affirm Daniel's authorship of the book, we can simply accept that he knew this man well and recorded his name accurately.

We need to pay more attention, however, to this man's office, called in the NIV **chief of . . . court officials**. The KJV calls him "master of . . .

eunuchs," a phrase which carries interesting implications for the four Hebrew boys. Isaiah had prophesied the loss of temple vessels to Babylon (2 Kgs. 20:12–17) and also said, "Some of your descendants, your own flesh and blood, that will be born to you, will be taken away, and they will become eunuchs in the palace of the king of Babylon" (2 Kgs. 20:18). The Hebrew word *saris* normally designates a castrated male, but a metaphorical use certainly had become common by Daniel's day.

Most earlier Hebrew works believe we should take *eunuchs* in its literal physical sense; that includes Josephus upon whom we depend for so much information. Actually, however, *saris* can mean "court officer," and it is certainly not necessary to require the physical interpretation here. Some turn away from *eunuch* on the basis of the phrase "without any physical defect" in verse 4. But at this point in the book, that phrase could refer to precastration. As Walvoord says, "Ultimately the choice is left to the interpreter, although, as indicated above, some favor the thought of 'court officer'" (Walvoord, *Daniel*, p. 34).

Nebuchadnezzar's strategy here can also be viewed from different perspectives. We could see it as brainwashing, a deliberate attempt to purge out any earlier religious, sociological, or cultural influences and make these boys thoroughly Babylonian. On the other hand, he knew he had his hands on gifted young men of royal lineage, and one could view his behavior as highly logical by the most modern understanding of leadership principles. Find gifted people, train them, and take advantage of their skills. These boys were, we might say, the cream of the crop, the "royals" of their own nation. It would be a waste of talent for Nebuchadnezzar to use them as slaves or hostages.

1:4. Any university in America would be ready to sign scholarship papers for these four—they met and exceeded all the qualifications. How young were they? We cannot be sure, since this word was used in the Old Testament for Rehoboam at about forty, Benjamin somewhere near the age of thirty, and Joseph at about seventeen. Most scholars agree they were in their teens, and that fits nicely with the obvious parallel we see between the Joseph and Daniel narratives.

As Miller notes: "Young points out that according to Plato . . . 'the education of Persian youth began in their fourteenth year,' and it is reasonable to assume that the Babylonians commenced the training of young people at about the same age of the Persians. Daniel then would likely have been about fourteen or fifteen years of age when he was taken into captivity and began his training" (Miller, p. 60).

They were strong, physically fit, good-looking, bright, well-read, and, in a word, **qualified**. We should not be surprised at this resume since in their own country they would have had the best of education, no small matter in a kingdom that could boast Solomon and Josiah among its leaders.

Royalty of one kingdom prepared to serve royalty of another kingdom—it makes sense. But what they did not know was **the language and literature of the Babylonians**. The word **Babylonians** is actually *Chaldeans,* as we have noted earlier, and this was the language of Abraham. In chapter 2 Daniel uses this word to describe a certain class of scholarly philosophers (*kasdim*), but the use of the word for the whole nation is not unusual. The *NIV Study Bible* sums up their curriculum quite nicely: "The classical literature [was] in Sumerian and Akkadian Cuneiform, a complicated syllabic writing system. But the language of normal communication in multi-racial Babylon was Aramaic, written in an easily learned alphabetic script" (p. 1300).

1:5. We know something of the curriculum in this training program; now we learn the time involved—**three years**. This was probably not a Bible institute undergraduate pattern, but more like the current master of divinity programs in seminaries. It is interesting that much of our education still revolves around three-year patterns, once one finishes high school and a baccalaureate degree. One can earn a doctorate three years beyond the baccalaureate, or study for law, medicine, or ministry in three-year chunks. Given the intellectual preparation these young men had already received back in Judah, Ashpenaz designed a program of graduate study.

But what about this **food and wine from the king's table**? Later we learn it was unacceptable, but there is no reason at this point in the text to believe that Nebuchadnezzar or Ashpenaz had anything but the best intentions in providing royal food and drink for the new recruits. Anyone who has visited a foreign country, particularly in the Third World, understands that when folks from other cultures get out their most special foods, they might be very different from the culinary delights of Western culture. I remember eating seashell soup in Japan with the shells still in it and a delicacy or two in India, the derivation of which I still do not care to know. Nebuchadnezzar wanted nothing but the best for these trainees—the best training, the best food, and the best coaching his kingdom could provide.

1:6. Up to this point Daniel has not named the elite quartet, so he introduces them here. **Daniel** means "God is judge" and is used elsewhere in the Bible of other people (1 Chr. 3:1; Ezra 8:2; Neh. 10:6). Ezekiel mentions our Daniel in 14:14,20,23. The name **Hananiah** means "Jehovah is gracious," and this name also appears elsewhere in the Old Testament (1 Chr. 25:23; 2 Chr. 26:11; Jer. 36:12 to name a few). **Mishael** literally means "Who is what God is?" implying that the God of the Hebrews has no equal, an important theological point in a land of idolatry. **Azariah** means "The Lord helps," and this name (as well as Mishael) appears elsewhere in the Old Testament.

We should not miss the key lesson here. These young men were named by godly parents, people who selected names reflecting their spiritual commitments. This the ancients did commonly, especially the Hebrews, but Christians of the twenty-first century have strayed somewhat from this pattern. Certainly one would not measure parents' commitment to Christ by what they name their children. But in this post-modern time I always wonder when I hear Josh or Zach or Adam shouted out on a soccer field whether the parents deliberately selected a biblical prototype. Apparently in name selection it's possible to be hip and old-fashioned at the same time.

The assigning of new names to transplanted people is hardly unusual in Old Testament times (Gen. 17:5; 41:45; 2 Sam. 12:24–25; Esth. 2:7). So Nebuchadnezzar's motive might not have been anything more than general practice, although many Bible students believe there was a direct and even sinister effort to purge out all references to previous religious commitments and to replace them with paganism. Criswell says, "The attempt is made to wipe out every memory of the God of their fathers. In each new heathen name a favorite god in Nebuchadnezzar's pantheon of idols is exalted" (Criswell, p. 16).

1:7. Daniel now tells us that **the chief official gave them new names**. Daniel's new name, **Belteshazzar**, was identical to Belshazzar and offers an appeal to the Babylonian god Bel (Marduk) to watch over the one who bears his name. We could translate it, "May Bel protect his life" (Dan. 4:8). Obviously, Bel reminds us of Baal, the chief god of the Cananites. Hananiah becomes **Shadrach**, the name of the Sumerian moon god that we might translate "command of Aku." Ashpenaz became very creative with Mishael, changing his name from "Who is what God is?" to **Meshach**, "Who is what Aku is?" We cannot be entirely certain about this one since some scholars think Meshach means "salvation by Aku."

Yet another pagan god comes into play with Azariah's new name—**Abednego**, "servant of Nebo." The traditional pronunciation of these three new names has given birth to the amusing picture of children eating cookies at the kitchen table and saying, "My snack, your snack, and to bed we go."

Names are important, especially to people of faith. Veldkamp reminds us that we all received a new name as Christians and we are also members of a new royal household in which we serve. He offers a paragraph of practical advice to parents raising children and young people in a pagan society like twenty-first-century North America.

> But how in the world are our children to become confessors of God's name and bearers of His banner if even their parents teach them the wisdom and letters and language of the Chaldeans? We push our children to get a top-notch education so that they will be able to find a good job and carve out a place for themselves in society! We make them study all sorts of things and read all kinds of books. Yet we don't bother to find out whether they read the Book of books, whether they understand the language of faith or whether they know that the fear of the Lord is the beginning of wisdom. We have little time for youth work or for the church's instruction in the faith. Where are you to look for the modern-day Nebuchadnezzar who entices your children away from serving God? Have you looked for him in your favorite chair in front of the TV set? (Veldkamp, p. 13).

C Commitment in Babylon (1:8–14)

SUPPORTING IDEA: *When God's people respond to adversity with courage and courtesy, God may melt the hearts of the adversaries.*

1:8. Daniel decided that **the royal food and wine** carried defilement. Readers of this text should not assume that the alcoholic content of the wine was at issue here. Actually, the boys faced double defilement. First, the food was not kosher (Lev. 3:17; 7:26; 17:10–14; 19:26). Second, this food might have been offered to idols, a problem that we encounter in the New

Testament as well. Commonly in ancient pagan religion, portions of food and wine were first offered to household deities. The eating and drinking of that food implied some recognition of those deities. Exodus 34:15 clearly forbids this, and Hosea predicted that citizens of the kingdom of Israel would face this problem (Hos. 9:3–4), a prophesy Ezekiel himself experienced (Ezek. 4:13–14).

But if we spread new covenant theology back into the old, we might conclude here that Daniel's attitude was an even more important issue than his diet. He **resolved not to defile himself**, and he requested that this wish be granted. But why did he object to the food while showing no concern for the name change or the pagan education? Most likely because the latter two did not directly defy Jewish law. No rebellion. No hunger strike. Breeding shows through as Daniel courteously asked for a special exemption. In this verse, very early in our book, we see this great prophet/statesman display the courage of his convictions.

According to Campbell: "Daniel could discern the fact that the Babylonian culture was in conflict with the Word of God, and he had the maturity and moral courage to say a firm no to culture pressures. Involved in this is the clear implication that Daniel was a keen student of the Scriptures and that he had the ability to apply what he knew to the problems of his daily life" (Campbell, p. 14).

1:9–10. For the second time in our book, the sovereignty of God controls Daniel's situation. First he delivered Judah to Babylon; now he works in the heart of Ashpenaz to produce kindness (*hesed*) and **sympathy** (*rahamim*) toward Daniel. This latter word could very well take the English expression of the KJV, "tender love."

However, when one serves a pagan king, one does not change the rules at a whim. Kindness is one thing; risking one's head for that kindness is quite another. Asphenaz's fear was well-grounded as we learn in chapter 3. It turns out that he had not determined the diet (although he apparently issued the names), but the menu came directly from the throne. His logic was flawless given the information he had: If Daniel and his buddies showed up at some future inspection looking weak and pale, it was his head on the block (or some Chaldean equivalent).

Since we noticed Daniel's attitude, let's not miss the changed heart of Ashpenaz. Surely he could have simply turned down the request by saying,

"Rules are rules." But he explained to Daniel why he thought this might not be a good idea for any of them. How often in Scripture we see that God raises up friends and protectors from unusual places. Certainly Joshua hardly expected his spies to find aid in the house of a harlot any more than Balaam anticipated God's revelation from his braying donkey. In Daniel's case, we should probably assume that the initial request was not granted.

1:11–12. Well, Daniel tried; now it was probably time to shut up and get with the program. Not likely—that was not Daniel's style. He simply moved to Plan B, a test run on a vegetarian diet. This appeal did not go to Ashpenaz but **to the guard whom the chief official had appointed**. The KJV gives him the name Melzar, but almost all scholars now agree that is not a proper name but simply the word for *steward*. But not just any steward; the definite article (unusual for Hebrew proper names) identifies him as *the steward*.

The Hebrew text for **vegetables** refers to food grown in the ground. Calvin suggests that Daniel may have had a special revelation from God to propose this particular request. Obviously, this is no proof text for a vegetarian diet. On the other hand, those of us who have adventured on occasion into no-star restaurants know that a salad is considerably safer than the blue-plate special.

1:13–14. Any legitimate assessment requires verification of the results. Daniel, considerate of Ashpenaz's concern, invited a direct comparison with those who ate the specialty of the house. Daniel had no fear that God would not honor his stand on defiled food, and he fully expected to do well during exam week. The text does not tell us that God worked in the steward's heart as well, but certainly he took as great a risk as Ashpenaz since it would be no trick to trace any failure in this project directly back to him.

Jerome spelled it out for us in the fourth century: "His faith was so incredibly great that he not only promised he would be in good flesh by eating the humbler food, but he even set a time-limit. Therefore it was not a matter of temerity but of faith, for the sake of which he despised the sumptuous fare of the king" (Jerome, p. 22).

D Blessings in Babylon (1:15–21)

SUPPORTING IDEA: *Knowledge and understanding come from God. These four young men incarnate the mental, physical, and spiritual qualities commended so often in Proverbs.*

1:15–16. No surprise here. When people take a stand for God and follow the principles of his Word, they will always pass the test with flying colors. Let's not insert a miracle here since one is hardly required. Virtually any nutritionist today would probably verify that a diet of vegetables and water would beat red meat and alcohol in any culinary schedule. Now the experiment becomes the norm, and the steward takes the royal fare back to the chef.

As we rejoice in God's blessing on Daniel and his three friends, we also have to wonder why we learn of no other resistance to pagan defilement. Certainly it is possible that others followed Daniel's example, but the first chapter does not suggest that kind of conclusion, nor does the rest of the book smoke out any other champions of faith. We don't need to wait until the section on application to recognize the lesson here: Christians need the courage to resist worldliness.

As Veldkamp observes:

> The danger is this, that we derive the norms for our thought and conduct *not* from the Scriptures but from the "world." These two sets of norms are completely opposed to each other. Forgiving our neighbors again and again, regarding our brothers and sisters as better than ourselves, praying for our enemies and business competitors, treating others as we would have them treat us—all these things are the dietary regulations of the church; they are the bread and water on which the church subsists (Veldkamp, p. 20).

1:17. Physical blessing is following by intellectual blessing. I live on a college campus, and it's not difficult to imagine some struggling freshman finding a verse like this and praying, "God, please do it again." Imagine the sweeping mental achievement of this verse—**knowledge and understanding of all kinds of literature and learning**. This reminds us of Moses' education in Egypt, although the text seems to imply that Daniel enjoyed greater discernment between truth and error. If that is true, we can account for it by the age at which each of these great men was torn away from his godly parents.

Yes, all four had superior intellectual skills, but only Daniel **could understand visions and dreams of all kinds**. Since Daniel wrote these words, we might take them as a personal boast, but later in the book we learn about his genuine meekness. No, this is not arrogance, just history. Furthermore, this was not an automatic ability, not the option to throw a basketball down into the hoop because you stand over seven feet tall. He was not limited in the types of dreams and visions he could handle, but as we will quickly learn in chapter 2, the specific interpretation of certain dreams came only by God's revelation, and that after much prayer.

Blending the theology and culture of Jerusalem with the worldly wisdom of historic Babylon gave these four young scholars a holistic view of learning. Their understanding and wisdom rested on the centrality of God's revelation, the genuine core curriculum of any serious Christian education at any level in our day.

Campbell offers an interesting quote from the British educator Sir Walter Moberly on this very point:

> If you want a bomb, the chemistry department will teach you how to make it; if you want a cathedral, the department of architecture will teach you how to build it; if you want a healthy body, the department of physiology and medicine will teach how to tend it. But when you ask whether and why you should want bombs, or cathedrals, or healthy bodies, the university is dumb and silent. It can help and give guidance in all things subsidiary but not in the attainment of the one thing useful (Campbell, p. 17).

1:18–19. When we read a phrase like **at the end of the time**, we wonder what Daniel had in mind. Surely our best choice is the end of the three years of training, since all the candidates were presented to the king. And let's not miss the importance of being handpicked by the king himself. Imagine how many employees of the Ford Motor Company or IBM are handselected by the CEO. Quite possibly only the vice presidents or important leaders of corporate units within those companies. It gives us some key to the significance of this training and selection process, a matter which we see repeated many times throughout the book.

We certainly would not go wrong to apply the principles of this chapter to our own relationship to the King of Kings and our responsibilities in his service. He selects us, he equips us, he clears away barriers to our service, and he rewards and blesses our obedience to the principles of his Word.

1:20. How interesting that we see the number ten again. But let's not be drawn into some kind of numerological mysticism. These are numbers which we might use today, even in casual conservation—a test of **ten** days, someone performing ten times better than expected (or better than others). God's blessing, not the achievement of the boys or the exam scores, is the focus here.

As Walvoord puts it:

> Even this praise . . . is mentioned in such a matter-of-fact way and so evidently due to the grace of God that Daniel is delivered from the charge of boasting. Their straightforward character and honesty, as well as the deep insight of these young men into the real meaning of their studies, must have stood in sharp contrast to the wise men of the king's court, who often were more sly and cunning than wise. Nebuchadnezzar, himself an extraordinarily intelligent man as manifested in his great exploits, was quick to respond to these bright young minds (Walvoord, *Daniel,* p. 42).

Some have used this verse to challenge the veracity of Daniel by suggesting that if this superiority surfaced so early, the king would have asked these four and not his traditional advisors for the interpretation of his dream in chapter 2. But no one should argue that the chronology of Daniel is exacting. Possibly that section of chapter 2 occurred before the end of the training period and the statements of 1:19–20.

1:21. Here we have a much debated textual issue, although hardly a problem. The reference to **the first year of King Cyrus** seems out of sync with the reference to the third year in Daniel 10:1. But saying that Daniel remained to the first year does not negate the possibility of staying to the third, fourth, or fifth years. The text merely emphasizes that the same Daniel who started with Nebuchadnezzar served in the court for the full forty years until Cyrus arrived. In other words, his work spanned several monarchs. From the earliest days of the Babylonian captivity to the preparation for the release by Cyrus, God's man Daniel **remained**. Nebuchadnezzar was gone; Belshazzar was gone; but Daniel remained.

In retrospect we can be a bit more specific. Daniel served the court in Babylon until about 539 B.C. and possibly considerably longer. Whether this verse indicates that Daniel held official position until the first year and then served in an emeritus capacity, we do not know. Certainly no character of the Old Testament (apart from Joseph in Egypt) ever exerted influence in the affairs of pagan nations to the extent that Daniel did.

Veldkamp challenges us to adopt a similar courageous and aggressive posture in witnessing to our own times:

> In the first chapter of Daniel, we see something of the dynamic, the saving power of the gospel. We see believers defending themselves and then taking the offensive. We see them refusing to defile themselves by eating food from the king's table. In other words, we see them taking pains to keep themselves unspotted from the world. But we also see them using their power in a quiet but forceful way to make the people of the court to bow before the majesty of God's Word (Veldkamp, p. 27).

MAIN IDEA REVIEW: *God's people, whether Israel or the church, always stand as the countercultural opponents of the systems of this world. Never was that reality more poignantly lived out than in the Old Testament captivity and exile, and particularly the dominance by Babylon. That national struggle will emerge early in our book, but the first chapter primarily teaches us that righteousness begins with a firm commitment to God.*

III. CONCLUSION

Courage for Public Service

We find it difficult to find a modern equivalent of the experiences described in this chapter. Certainly we have seen people committed to Christ rise to high office; the faith of Jimmy Carter was evident before, during, and after his presidency. We also know great leaders who have served in a country whose culture and language were not their own; Henry Kissinger reminds us of this every time we hear him speak. But the rise of the four kidnapped children (teenagers) from capture to prominence stirs our hearts and minds to wade further into the stirring ocean of this book. Up to this point Daniel had no way of knowing that his courage would lead to political power; he simply chose truth and right as he understood them.

> Then to side with Truth is noble when we share her wretched crust,
> 'Ere her cause bring fame and profit, and 'tis prosperous to be just;
> Then it is the brave man chooses, while the coward stands aside,
> Doubting in his abject spirit 'til his Lord is crucified,
> And the multitude make virtue of the faith they had denied.
>
> (James Russell Lowell, "The Present Crisis")

PRINCIPLES

- God's covenant people often live in an alien environment.
- Remnant people are always a minority.
- We never know where God will use us.
- God honors the obedience of his people.
- Believers must obey even when they are tempted to disobey.

APPLICATIONS

- Christian parents should prepare their children for serving God in any situation.
- Christians must learn to resist evil even when it seems innocent and without major consequences.
- Christians must know when and how to say no.
- Christians need perseverance and determination to thrive spiritually in a world which wants them to fail.

IV. LIFE APPLICATION

Prioritizing Parenting

The statistics inundate us to the point of despair. Fourteen million American children live in poverty. More than one-half of American children live with only one parent. The school dropout rate stands at 25 percent overall, and 50 percent for Blacks and Hispanics; many urban districts report dropout rates as high as 65 percent. Daniel Patrick Moynihan, recently retired senator from New York, once claimed that we may be the first generation of Americans whose children are worse off than their parents. Beyond the obvious problems of divorce, adultery, wife and child abuse, drug and alcohol abuse, and a general tone of immorality, there exists this subtle but real influence of a society that encourages accountability to no one.

To be sure, the two major themes of this first chapter center in the sovereignty of God and the courage of Daniel. But silently standing in the background is this argument from silence, this overwhelming sense of what the parents of these four young men had accomplished in the years before they became kidnapped children. Christian parents do not teach their children responsibility just to make it through the teen years, but to produce godly adult leaders for new families and for the broader body of Christ.

For years my wife and daughter, both kindergarten teachers, have told stories about how the behavior of children in class mirrors their home environment and parental training. That is precisely the point we see here, again in chapter 3 and yet again in chapter 6. By focusing on these displaced young men, these "kidnapped children" as I have called them, we see how our own children can behave long after being removed from the influence of their homes, their churches, and perhaps even their native land. Mentioning my wife reminds me that I did not finish my hospital story which began the chapter. The malignant mass was removed, and God granted complete healing.

V. PRAYER

Father, grant us the courage and wisdom of Daniel. May we be obedient and faithful in any situation into which your providence might take us. Grant that our uncompromising spirituality will be evident to all who know us so that they will be drawn to our Savior. Amen.

VI. DEEPER DISCOVERIES

A. The Chaldeans (1:4)

The NIV uses the term *Babylonians,* but the original text actually uses the more ancient word *Chaldean.* Many critics of Daniel have used the appearance of this word in this book to argue that it could not have been written as early as the sixth century. They focus particularly on its use to describe the astrologers in 2:2. The argument claims that the word *kasidim* was unknown in the Assyrian/Babylonian language and only appeared after the end of the Babylonian Empire. Therefore, Daniel could not have used it in the sixth century, and the book must have been written later.

Furthermore, outside Daniel the Scriptures never use this word to denote an entire people. Daniel uses it both ways, and in the Hebrew section (4:1) and the Aramaic section (5:30). And Daniel uses it several times to describe this special priestly class (1:4; 2:4–5,10; 3:8; 4:7; 5:7,11–12). Robert Dick Wilson has given extensive space to this argument. Those who wish to pursue it in its archaeological detail would be advised to consult his scholarly work.

B. Babylon (1:1)

The name goes all the way back to the Tower of Babel (Gen. 11), and we find brief mention of "a beautiful robe from Babylonia" in Joshua 7:21. But not until the major prophets does Babylon catapult to its prominence in Old Testament history. The written history of the city begins about 2800 B.C., describing a significantly advanced civilization in the Mesopotamian Valley. Sargon the Magnificent stretched the Babylonian kingdom from Persia to the Mediterranean Sea between 2360 and 2180 B.C.

Then came the Elamites and after them the Ammorites and the period that scholars call "old Babylonian" (1830–1550 B.C.), which included the reign of the famous Hammurabi (1726–1686 B.C.). Discovered on an eight-foot-high column of black diorite at Susa, the Code of Hammurabi contained 282 paragraphs on criminal law. From this amazing document scholars learned a great deal about ancient Babylonian civilization and the Akkadian language.

For the next eleven hundred years dynasties came and went until the rise of Tiglath-Pileser, who became king of Babylon in 729 B.C. This famous king who figures so prominently in the virgin prophecies of Isaiah 7 was conquered by the Assyrian Sennacherib in 689 B.C. and Babylon went once again into a tailspin.

The Neo-Babylonian Empire began with Nabopolassar, who took charge in 625 B.C. His victories over Nineveh and the great Pharaoh-Necho of Egypt built the kingdom that he handed over to his son Nebuchadnezzar.

This brief introduction by no means disposes of our study of Babylon. It appears throughout this book and, along with many of Daniel's prophecies, skips to Revelation, which describes the still future days of this ancient pagan capital. According to Walvoord:

> Through the centuries the influence of Babylon has been that of satanic perversion of biblical religion. This will continue until the end of time. Babylon's influence in Revelation 17 and 18 is the subject of final prophecy. Revelation 17 portrays Babylon as a wicked woman astride a scarlet-colored beast, thus describing the final form of the apostate church in the end time. Revelation 18 pictures Babylon as the capital city of the end time which is destroyed by the gigantic earthquake of Revelation 16:19 (Walvoord, *Major Bible Prophecies*, p. 142).

C. Dates of the Captivity

Difficult and at times confusing as it may be, the chronology of the captivity is extremely important as a foundation for Daniel's prophecy. Nebuchadnezzar's conquest of Palestine actually took place in three phases. The first, described at the beginning of this chapter, took place in 605 B.C., the second in 597 B.C., and the third and final one in 587 B.C. The captivity lasted seventy years until the first exiles returned to the land, led by Zerubbabel. The importance of the seventy-year time frame comes from Jeremiah 29:10: "This is what the LORD says: 'When seventy years are completed for Babylon, I will come to you and fulfill my gracious promise to bring you back to this place.'"

But, one could argue, would not seventy years require that the captivity began in 606 rather than 605? That all depends on whether one looks at the beginning or the ending of Nebuchadnezzar's project. Captivity doesn't take place in a weekend. Specifically the siege began in the month of Nisan in 606 B.C. and ended in the month of Adar in 605 B.C. In emphasizing the importance of this exacting period, Sir Robert Anderson writes, "By the test of chronology, therefore—the severest test which can be applied to historical statements—the absolute accuracy of these Scriptures is established" (Anderson, *Critics*, p. 22).

VII. TEACHING OUTLINE

A. INTRODUCTION

1. Lead Story: Emergency Interruption
2. Context: Daniel forms the bridge between the major and minor prophets and also takes on many of the characteristics of the historical books. It enfolds the broadest biblical vision of the future of the world as well as the future of nations immediately following Daniel's time. This first chapter offers appropriate introduction to the book by establishing Daniel's reason for being in Babylon and how God would use him and his companions to advance his cause on earth, especially among pagan peoples.
3. Transition: The lessons of morality, courage, obedience, and faithfulness in Daniel 1 establish the foundation for the rest of the book. This first chapter also shows us how God's priorities are often different from ours. Only one verse touches on the fall of Jerusalem and one more on the professional education of the four young men. Half the chapter emphasizes a discussion over what many might call a miniscule religious law. But two enormous principles emerge from the discussion: that God can cause his people to survive and even thrive in an alien environment and that he always blesses those who courageously follow his Word.

B. COMMENTARY

1. Attack by Babylon (1:1–2)
2. Training in Babylon (1:3–7)

3. Commitment in Babylon (1:8–14)
4. Blessings in Babylon (1:15–21)

C. CONCLUSION: COURAGE FOR PUBLIC SERVICE

VIII. ISSUES FOR DISCUSSION

1. How would you answer someone who argued that Daniel did not write this book?
2. What can we do in today's churches and families to prepare young leaders like these four?
3. In a sentence or two, describe your understanding of the statement, "God is sovereign."

Daniel 2:1–23

Monarchical Monument

I. INTRODUCTION
Outfoxing the Faculty

II. COMMENTARY
A verse-by-verse explanation of the chapter.

III. CONCLUSION
Any Dream Won't Do
An overview of the principles and applications from the chapter.

IV. LIFE APPLICATION
Stranger at the Door
Melding the chapter to life.

V. PRAYER
Tying the chapter to life with God.

VI. DEEPER DISCOVERIES
Historical, geographical, and grammatical enrichment of the commentary.

VII. TEACHING OUTLINE
Suggested step-by-step group study of the chapter.

VIII. ISSUES FOR DISCUSSION
Zeroing the chapter in on daily life.

Quote

"When God wills or purposes a thing, no man or a group of men can countermand or interdict God's sovereign judgment."

W. A. Criswell

PERSONAL PROFILE: NEBUCHADNEZZAR

(See page 10)

PERSONAL PROFILE: ARIOCH

- Commander of the king's guard in Babylon
- The name also appears in Genesis 14:1 to identify a king of Ellasar

Daniel 2:1–23

IN A NUTSHELL

All knowledge and wisdom, even the mysteries of the human mind, are known only by the God of heaven.

Monarchial Monument

I. INTRODUCTION

Outfoxing the Faculty

Twice in my forty-year career in Christian higher education, I served as a dean of faculty, once at the undergraduate level and again at the graduate level. Now lest any reader think I have been besieged by illusions of grandeur, let me say that I am fully aware that no legitimate comparison exists between being an academic dean and ruling Babylon, or for that matter, ruling at all.

We deans have collected a sack full of humorous stories about our position, one of which tells about a president who had accepted a speaking engagement at some kind of luncheon but whose schedule required him to cancel. The woman arranging the luncheon event asked if he could send a substitute from the college, but she assured him she wanted "no one lower than a dean." To which the president quickly responded, "Madam, there is no one lower than a dean."

With that anecdotal backdrop, we move on to encounter in this chapter Nebuchadnezzar's "faculty" of philosophers, theologians, astrologers, and the like. We should not view these magicians, enchanters, sorcerers, and astrologers as some group of pseudoscientific crackpots who pronounced incantations over the entrails of a slaughtered animal.

One could call them the savants of the ancient world, scientists of a type, and certainly university-level philosophers and professors. To be sure they had no grasp on real truth, but one could hardly expect that in the pagan darkness of their cultural surroundings. Indeed, that picture emerges clearly in the first half of Daniel 2—darkness versus light, error versus truth, ignorance versus knowledge, and human wisdom versus divine revelation. We'll visit them at faculty meeting in just a moment.

II. COMMENTARY

Monarchial Monument

MAIN IDEA: *Daniel 2 is one of the most important chapters in the Bible and one of the longest. It provides information on God's master plan for all time by introducing the Rock of Ages and the kingdom that will never be destroyed. It provides evidence of the truth we find in Ephesians 1:10–11: "To be put into effect when the times will have reached their fulfillment—to bring all things in heaven and on earth together under one head, even Christ. In him we were also chosen, having been predestined according to the plan of him who works out everything in conformity with the purpose of his will."*

A Sleepless in Babylon (2:1–4)

SUPPORTING IDEA: *God can use his gifted servants, even in the most difficult and unexpected situations.*

2:1. Daniel now takes us back to **the second year** of Nebuchadnezzar's reign, so we know the time frame falls between April 603 and March 602 B.C. Nebuchadnezzar is hardly the first national leader to receive revelation from God through a dream or vision (Pharaoh in Gen. 41; Abimelech in Gen. 20; Pharaoh-Necho in 2 Chr. 35 and 2 Kgs. 23). By this time readers of the Old Testament have well in mind Joseph's experience with Pharaoh's dreams, so Daniel 2 looks like déjà vu all over again, as Yogi Berra might put it.

Hundreds of pages have been written to reconcile the chronology of early Daniel, but such scholarly detail is beyond the purview of this commentary series. We have already observed in the first chapter that the dream probably occurred during Daniel's three years of training, his "senior" year, the final of the three-year graduate course. Those wishing to pursue the most expert explanation of such matters should consult the four-volume series by Robert Dick Wilson.

We should not miss the fact that the word **dreams** appears in the plural, implying this was something of a pattern for the king. Walvoord picks up the pluperfect tense of this verb to emphasize again the issue of chronology: "This would imply that the dream took place somewhere in the sequence of events in chapter 1 but is only now being detailed. Hence, it allows for the conclusion that the dream was interpreted before Daniel's graduation at the end of his three years of training. Commentators generally have been so occupied with the plural of *dreams* that the verb has been neglected" (Walvoord, *Daniel*, p. 46).

We also learn that the king was **troubled and he could not sleep**. Insomnia is hardly an unknown annoyance for people with great responsibilities, but we soon learn in this chapter that stress was not the issue—this was a God-induced problem.

2:2. College professors are often accused of lecturing in "grocery list" fashion, and Daniel showed some of that tendency himself (2:2,36,38; 3:2–3,5,7,10). Here we have four groups of professors, and in 2:27 another group called "wise men" appears. The "faculty" become big players throughout this book, showing up in chapters 2, 4, and 5. What academic disciplines did these gentlemen represent?

The **magicians** take their name from a Hebrew word related to a pen or writing instrument which hints at scholarship in some written mode. We're quite familiar with the term *scribes* in the Bible, people who work with books, perhaps religious literature, which at that time would have been in the Sumerian language unknown to ordinary citizens of Babylon.

The **enchanters** *(ashapim)* bring the hint of spiritism connected with the history of this word. They came from their post in the wizardry department, most likely interrupted from important research related to foretelling the future by analyzing the stars. They probably dealt with matters of death and perhaps communication with the dead, clearly the experts in pathological curriculum.

The name **sorcerers** comes from a word used for the act of cutting, suggesting that they may have worked with pharmaceutical ingredients. This is bolstered by the use of the word *pharikoi* in the Septuagint, the foundation word for our term *pharmacist*.

The NIV translators chose **astrologers** as the fourth category, but these are the *kasdim* we have already met in chapter 1. Again it is important to distinguish between these Chaldeans and the use of that term to designate an entire race of people who lived in southern Babylonia. They become the spokespeople in verse 4, and we surely can assign them the prominent role among this interesting faculty. Here they assemble, ready to put their collective brilliance at the disposal of their king.

2:3. The word *dreamed* in verse 2 takes the singular, so Nebuchadnezzar targets one particular dream among the various dreams mentioned in verse

1. But the request is clearly twofold: the king insisted they **tell him what he had dreamed** and **what it means.** Nebuchadnezzar had not become ruler of his world through ignorance. Concocting some wild interpretation would have been child's play for this crowd. Telling the king what he had actually dreamed presented a considerably more formidable task.

2:4. Here we see our first language switch, from Hebrew to Aramaic, the most well-known and convenient language. All the written text of Daniel from this point to the end of chapter 7 appears in Aramaic for reasons we have already discussed (although the Chaldeans likely addressed the king in Akkadian).

To this point the faculty are still most optimistic about the day and their contribution to the kingdom as they hail their monarch by saying, "Live forever!" The British still say it only in a slightly different form—"Long live the king!"

Dream interpretation was a no-brainer for this faculty; they could create a fanciful tale out of nothing. But a shocking surprise would soon explode in the king's bedroom. In a variation of a modern cliché, they would say, "The difficult we can do immediately, the impossible we can't do at all."

Criswell believes Nebuchadnezzar's actions were quite contemporary in style: "He turned to the intellectuals of his day. These are the men who are high in state. He called for the Magi, the Chaldeans. They were the elect. They were the select. They were the men of books. They were the brain trusters. They had all the answers, just as some of contemporary intelligentsia arrogate to themselves modern omniscience. The wisdom of God is spurned, repudiated, scoffed at, derided, laughed at, scorned. The intelligentsia of our world today say: 'We have all the answers. Ask us, we know'" (Criswell, p. 49).

B Clueless in Babylon (2:5–11)

SUPPORTING IDEA: *The people of the Lord should understand the past, live vibrantly in the present, and show great interest in the future.*

2:5. One can find vast differences between the KJV and the NIV at a number of points in the text of Scripture, but rarely as divergent as this. The phrase "the thing is gone from me" presents a completely different idea from **this is what I have firmly decided.** This takes particular importance when one interprets the KJV phrase to mean the king had forgotten the dream (or at least said he did). For example, Jerome says, "If they should be unable to tell the king what he in his mental confusion could not recall, they would also lose claim to trustworthiness in the interpretation they might give" (Jerome, 25).

Working from the same text, some scholars who hold to the KJV translation take a different interpretation, namely, that the king did not forget the dream but merely said he did. Like modern politicians, Nebuchadnezzar would not have been held to a rigid standard of integrity and morality, so he could say anything he wished. Others claim that the king surely had forgotten the dream because if he had not he would quickly have told the wise men to assist them in their interpretation.

Dogmatism on this point is unwarranted, but the NIV seems to have captured the best choice—an absolute monarch can demand anything, and it is not the business of the faculty to question the boss. We do not know whether the king remembered his dream or not, and he had no intention of telling his wizards the answer to that question. Theirs was not to reason why; theirs was but to do or die. Literally.

One hardly needs exegetical nuances to understand the latter part of verse 5. Perhaps we should note that these threats did not represent routine Babylonian execution. How they would be dismembered the text does not tell us. But, to borrow a line from Camelot, "From fore to aft they would feel a draft." Furthermore, their property would not be confiscated but rather obliterated. The barbaric cruelty of ancient kings surfaces at numerous points throughout the Old Testament.

2:6. That was the bad news. The good news is that **gifts and rewards and great honor** awaited satisfactory explanation and interpretation. We have seen this kind of treatment in the lives of Joseph and Mordecai. It seems like a fair test; if they had the ability they claimed to stay in touch with supernatural powers, retelling and interpreting the dream should be duck soup. But a great deal was at stake here because if these men were failures, they were also frauds.

2:7–9. When one realizes he is on shaky ground like this, it may be worth one more appeal—but not with Nebuchadnezzar. The question of whether the king remembered the dream surfaces again where the KJV also repeats the phrase, "the thing is gone from me." To paraphrase, "You guys are stalling because you know I have forgotten the dream, but it's not going to do you any good. Your fate is already decided; get on with it."

The NIV suggests a different paraphrase: "You guys are stalling for time because you know I am serious about my threats; get on with it." The **one penalty** had already been pronounced, and the stalling led the king to suspect a devious conspiracy.

But what did Nebuchadnezzar mean when he accused them of **hoping the situation will change**? Perhaps a good night's sleep would assuage their moody king's anger. Perhaps if they had a few days, they could come up with a plan to extricate themselves from this dilemma. Baldwin says: "The king suspects that the interpreters of dreams are imposters who have secretly agreed to fob him off with mere words *till the times change,* until the crisis has passed and the king has forgotten the incident. If they can relate the dream this will authenticate their claim to be able to interpret it" (Baldwin, p. 88).

2:10–11. Here come the backup excuses:

- No one on earth can do what you ask.
- No king has ever asked this before.
- Only the gods have this information, and they never share it with human beings.

Some see humility in these appeals, others just sheer terror. After all, these fellows were paid to interpret dreams, read the stars, and predict the future. Why did the gods whom they represented all of a sudden desert them? The professors were in over their heads, and they knew it. They could have said **no one can reveal it to the king except** God (which some expositors claim), but in this idolatrous empire that interpretation seems unlikely.

Let's close this section with a somewhat lengthy but helpful quote from Joseph Seiss, depicting this scenario.

> Here was a full-grown heathenism of more than a thousand years. Here were the combined strength and wisdom of the most noted schools at the highest acme of their glory. Whatever abilities existed in priest or savant, astrologer or necromancer, wise man or magician, apart from the anointed servants of the God of Israel, were here concentrated and embodied. If these men failed, it was the laying prostrate of all the wisdom, power, and art of man. . . . When I read these words, formally given out by the very chiefs in the name

of them all, and sorrowfully pronounced in the audience of the imperial majesty of the earth as the utmost they could do to save themselves from summary destruction, I see a veil of darkness drawn over all the wisdom, strength, and science of man which makes me shudder as I gaze. . . . It proves to me, in brief utterance, that all the religions, arts, sciences, philosophies, attainments, and powers of man, apart from God's inspired prophets, and all-glorious Christ, are but emptiness and vanity as regards any true and adequate knowledge of the purposes and will of Jehovah or of the destinies of man (Seiss, pp. 47–49).

C Helpless in Babylon (2:12–16)

SUPPORTING IDEA: *Calm, cool dignity always offers the believer's best choice, even in times of life-threatening emergency.*

2:12–13. Our word **furious** comes from a word similar to a word we find in Genesis 40:2 and 41:10 describing the wrath of Pharaoh. But the real issue in verse 12 is the extent of the decree. The king could have limited his judgment to the Chaldeans who were doing all the talking. Or he could have included all four groups named in verse 2. Since barbaric excess was a cultural norm in ancient kingdoms, we should probably assume that all the **wise men** in the city of Babylon fell under the curse. Nebuchadnezzar intended to execute the entire faculty!

Passages like this in both Testaments remind us of God's great gift of democracy to countries of the Western world. The old cliché is true despite its age and familiarity: "Power corrupts, and absolute power corrupts absolutely." No congress, no supreme court, no public opinion polls, no appeals to the press. Nebuchadnezzar held life-and-death control over every subject in the Babylonian kingdom.

2:14–16. In his concern for detail, Daniel contacted **Arioch, the commander of the king's guard**, as he did Asphenaz in chapter 1. The latter was a political servant, Arioch clearly a military man. Notice that he also served as chief executioner.

When Arioch came to Daniel's house, the prophet spoke to him with **wisdom and tact.** Not a bad idea in view of the situation. Translators render these two words in various ways—"counsel and wisdom" (KJV); "prudence and discretion" (RSV)—but the nuances of difference add nothing to our understanding. Daniel (in contrast to Elijah and Elisha) always spoke with wisdom and tact.

Nor should we conclude Daniel's choice of the word **harsh** ("hasty," "severe") as incompatible with his **tact.** In fact, the decree was harsh. Arioch obviously understood that because he took time to explain everything to Daniel. Daniel already had the king's ear, so to speak, since Arioch displayed no hesitation in taking him directly into the royal presence. His request of Nebuchadnezzar sounds a good bit different from the ones the king had already heard. Yes, he would interpret the dream; he just needed some time. Time for what? Time for prayer. Time to share his problem with his friends whose lives were also at stake. Time to see what the Almighty God would do when all other gods had failed.

Gleason Archer offers a strong paragraph describing the moment: "The stage was now set to show the reality, wisdom, and power of the one true God—Yahweh—as over against the inarticulate and impotent imaginary gods the magicians worshiped. It is the same general theme that dominates the remainder of the book and serves to remind the Hebrew nation that despite their own failure, collapse, and banishment into exile, the God of Israel remains as omnipotent as He ever was in the days of Moses and that His covenantal love remains as steadfast toward the seed of Abraham as it ever had been" (Archer, p. 42).

D Guiltless in Babylon (2:17–23)

SUPPORTING IDEA: *When things are hopeless, pray. When things are darkest, pray. When you have no idea what to do next, pray.*

2:17–18. Daniel's friends needed to be warned, but more importantly, they needed to pray. Their strategy was flawless: **plead for mercy from the God of heaven.** The text does not tell us that they actually prayed together, although most scholars assume that. Nor does it tell us what they said, although their motive is hardly hidden—**that he and his friends might not be executed with the rest of the wise men of Babylon.** We hear so much about intercession that sometimes we feel a little guilty praying for ourselves. But that is exactly what these young men did on this occasion.

The terminology **God of heaven** is literally "God of the heavens," used first in Genesis 24:7 and found frequently elsewhere throughout the Bible

(Ezra 1:2; 6:10; 7:12,21; Neh. 1:5; 2:4; Ps. 136:26). Their prayer issued from pure hearts; they were indeed guiltless in Babylon.

Should we conclude from verse 18 that the rest of the wise men were already dead and only the four remained? Possible, but not probable. Most likely the effect of Daniel's prayer spread like a blanket across the rest of the Chaldeans, sparing them as well, although that is only inference, not explanation of the text.

The word for **mystery** in this verse represents one of nearly twenty Persian words which appear in the Aramaic text of Daniel. The word itself *(raz)* shows up again in 2:19,27–30,47; 4:9. The word appears commonly in the Greek text of the New Testament to describe God's divine strategy which he reveals only to his chosen servants (Rom. 11:25). Here the meaning of the word is no mystery; Daniel needs to know the dream and what it means.

2:19–20. In contrast to Nebuchadnezzar's dream, Daniel received a **vision**, a supernatural revelation which unfolds during the remainder of the chapter. We are tempted to consider the vision a more important medium than the dream, but that would be a mistake. God frequently used dreams to make known his word. The Revealer, not the means, is at issue in this communication.

In verse 20 prayer turns to praise, appeal to appreciation. Two of God's attributes initiate this beautiful praise poem—**wisdom and power**. The entire prayer is psalm-like, probably demonstrating Daniel's close familiarity with the Psalms. Daniel praised **the name of God** as David frequently did in his psalms. Griffith Thomas tells us, "The *name* stands in Holy Scripture for the nature or revealed character of God, and not a mere label or title. It is found very frequently in the Old Testament as synonymous with God Himself in relation to man. . . . In the New Testament the same usage is perfectly clear" (quoted in Walvoord, *Daniel*, p. 56).

2:21–22. We need to keep in mind here that Daniel already knew the meaning of the dream before he prayed, even though we don't read it until later in the chapter. Consequently, the wording of these verses reflects God's control in human events. The idea that the God of heaven **sets up kings and deposes them** forms a major part of the fabric of this book. God not only possesses infinite wisdom; he chooses to share it with people who are wise and discerning—qualities we already know Daniel possessed. Parallel theology appears in Psalms 103 and 113.

This great God also reveals secrets, even **deep and hidden things.** God dwells in light but has full knowledge of anything that happens in darkness (Pss. 36:9; 139:12).

2:23. Thanksgiving is very much a part of prayer and praise. Daniel was about to display wisdom and power far beyond human ability, and he humbly recognized that it comes not from him, but from God. Some suggest that the wording **God of my fathers** indicates that Daniel saw himself as the recipient of God's mercy in a way that many other saints had in the past. Notice too that Daniel did not place himself above his companions but talked about receiving **what we asked of you** and said, **you have made known to us the dream of the king.**

According to Baldwin: "This little psalm is a model of thanksgiving. No word is merely repetitive; each of the first nine lines extolling God's greatness makes its contribution to the paean of praise, yet none is unrelated to Daniel's experience. . . . The symmetry and beauty of the poetry make their own contribution to the praise of God" (Baldwin, p. 91).

MAIN IDEA REVIEW: *Daniel 2 is one of the most important chapters in the Bible and one of the longest. It provides information on God's master plan for all time by introducing the Rock of Ages and the kingdom that will never be destroyed. It provides evidence of the truth we find in Ephesians 1:10–11: "To be put into effect when the times will have reached their fulfillment—to bring all things in heaven and on earth together under one head, even Christ. In him we were also chosen, having been predestined according to the plan of him who works out everything in conformity with the purpose of his will."*

III. CONCLUSION

Any Dream Won't Do

In the brilliant Andrew Lloyd Webber musical *Joseph and the Amazing Technicolor Dream Coat,* lyricist Tim Rice gives the title character a frolicking final song with clever words. Reflecting on all that has happened to him, Joseph sings:

> May I return to the beginning;
> The light is dimming, and the dream is too.

The world and I, we are still waiting,
Still hesitating.
Any dream will do.

Great romantic poetry; bad theology. Christians are commonly haunted by the strange idea that our Western culture has gone completely secular. To the contrary, modern society obsesses over the supernatural in one form or another, demons and angels attracting the most popularity. Ancient culture was like that as well. From Joseph to Daniel to John in Revelation, dreams and visions form an important part of God's revelation to humankind.

These verses, like all of Daniel, emphasize that all earthly gods are false, all prophets of those gods have no credibility, and only the God of heaven can grant wisdom, power, knowledge, and discernment. Let's remind ourselves again that this book is not about Daniel; it's about Daniel's God.

PRINCIPLES

- The wisdom of the world is neither sufficient nor satisfactory.
- Human prophets cannot, of their own ability, explain the mysteries of God's hand in the world.
- God protects his people from the wrath of powerful evil rulers.
- God controls every part of his world, even those who sit on thrones and win elections.

APPLICATIONS

- Sometimes it helps to remember that God often gives his greatest revelations to people in difficult and dangerous circumstances.
- We need to pray with other people, especially with those who struggle with the same problems we have.
- When God answers prayer, never forget to thank him and praise him.
- Don't be afraid to pray for yourself; God knows your anguish, but he wants to hear it from you.

IV. LIFE APPLICATION

Stranger at the Door

One night during the Civil War, a stranger came to the home of the famous pastor, Henry Ward Beecher. When he knocked, Mrs. Beecher went to see who was there. Opening the door just a bit, she found a tall stranger, covered in wraps up to his eyes against the cold weather. He asked to see Pastor Beecher but refused to give his name.

Beecher's life had been threatened more than once during those days, so Mrs. Beecher closed the door and returned to their upstairs room, leaving the visitor standing in the cold. When Beecher learned that someone was at his door, he at once climbed down the stairs and welcomed the man into his home. Some time later when her husband rejoined her in the bedroom, Mrs. Beecher learned that the muffled stranger was the president of the United States, Abraham Lincoln. He was facing a crisis, and he needed prayer.

A hymnist once wrote, "Prayer is the soul's sincere desire unuttered or expressed." Very likely most of us pray silently in our hearts more frequently than we pray aloud either individually or in groups. Maintaining a spirit of prayer at all times reflects the New Testament command to "pray continually" (1 Thess. 5:17).

But sometimes it helps to pray aloud, and often it helps to pray with other people. Just as Daniel went to his companions, and Lincoln consulted Beecher, we should look for opportunities to pray with other people at home, at church, on the job, or at informal times when our hearts need the corporate support that comes from praying in concert.

V. PRAYER

Father, with Daniel we praise and thank you for being the God of heaven. In our uncertain times when evil seems so strong and moral confusion abounds, we acknowledge that you are in control of your world, that you know what lies in the darkness of our times, and that you are still the Father of light. Amen.

VI. DEEPER DISCOVERIES

A. Witchcraft (2:2)

Since witchcraft is so much alive and even thriving in our own day, it may be worth another look. The word *kasdim* which the NIV translates "astrologers" comes from the Hebrew word *kashaph,* commonly used in the Old Testament for witchcraft or divination. It seems to arise from the performance of various religious rites with special emphasis on communicating with otherworldly beings. The practice usually applies to women, though (as here) we see male sorcerers in Egypt (Exod. 7:11) and Jewish sorcerers in Jeremiah 27:9 and Malachi 3:5. Witchcraft invariably opposes the truth of God and often represents the work of demons.

Girdlestone says:

> Superstition is the natural complement to materialism. The mind of man, having once become warped in religious matters, does not cling with unerring sagacity to the truth that there is a God but goes aside into bypaths, sometimes resting in that which is material, and seeking to exclude the idea of spiritual existence altogether from the mind; at other times oscillating in the direction of what is now called *spiritualism,* a system known in earlier days by the ruder name of *witchcraft.* . . . They are all abominable (Deut. 18:10–12), and are to give way before the simple voice of the inspired prophet (Girdlestone, p. 321).

B. Wisdom (2:20–21,23)

In the secular language of the ancient world, the word *hokmah* arises from the professions of law and medicine. It means the same thing in 1:20 as in the verses here in chapter 2, although in the former context Nebuchadnezzar focused only on the wisdom of the world. In biblical usage the word almost always points ultimately to God as the Creator and controller of his universe. It describes how people tuned to heaven to handle knowledge and information, make decisions, and conduct their lives.

In the New Testament, wisdom becomes *sophia,* somewhat different because of the Greek context out of which that word arose. According to Archer,

> The Hebrew *hokmah* was primarily concerned with living responsibly before God and coping successfully with every problem or task confronting [the] servant of God. Especially in the matter of prudence in business and in the area of human relations (the aspect most frequent in Proverbs), a *hokmah* that proceeded from the fear of the Lord played a decisive role. In the management of armies in time of war or the administration of government in times of peace—i.e., the knowledge of the right thing to do under the circumstances—or for wise policies to follow in dealing with men, *hokmah* was essential (Archer, p. 38).

VII. TEACHING OUTLINE

A. INTRODUCTION

1. Lead Story: Outfoxing the Faculty
2. Context: There is no geographic switch from Daniel 1 to Daniel 2 and a time shift of only two years. We're still in Babylon, the focus still centers on Nebuchadnezzar and his power, and Daniel, Hananiah, Mishael, and Azariah are still in the training stage.
3. Transition: Daniel clearly makes a chronological transition between 1:21 and 2:1, but the real transition of the chapter will come in our next study when Daniel interprets the dream.

B. COMMENTARY

1. Sleepless in Babylon (2:1–4)
2. Clueless in Babylon (2:5–11)
3. Helpless in Babylon (2:12–16)
4. Guiltless in Babylon (2:17–23)

C. CONCLUSION: ANY DREAM WON'T DO

VIII. ISSUES FOR DISCUSSION

1. How do we develop sufficient confidence in our faith to face the greatest horrors of life with a dependence on prayer?
2. How do we see God setting up and deposing kings (and politicians) in our day, and how do we respond to what we see?
3. Name some ways and places we pray with other people besides the familiar public prayer sessions at church.

Daniel 2:24–49

Dreamworks, Inc.

I. INTRODUCTION
Intentional Accidents

II. COMMENTARY
A verse-by-verse explanation of the chapter.

III. CONCLUSION
"Ode to a Water Fowl"
An overview of the principles and applications from the chapter.

IV. LIFE APPLICATION
Statue of Bondage
Melding the chapter to life.

V. PRAYER
Tying the chapter to life with God.

VI. DEEPER DISCOVERIES
Historical, geographical, and grammatical enrichment of the commentary.

VII. TEACHING OUTLINE
Suggested step-by-step group study of the chapter.

VIII. ISSUES FOR DISCUSSION
Zeroing the chapter in on daily life.

Quote

"Don't bother to give God instructions; just report for duty."

Corrie ten Boom

Daniel 2:1–24–49

IN A NUTSHELL

All earthly power, even that exercised by the greatest of human rulers, will ultimately fall before the God of gods and Lord of kings.

Dreamworks, Inc.

I. INTRODUCTION

Intentional Accidents

As the story goes, a west Texas cowboy applied for life insurance and was asked by the agent if he had ever had any accidents. The dialogue sounded something like this:

> "No, never had an accident."
>
> "You mean nothing has ever happened to you? You've never been hurt?"
>
> "Oh sure," said the cowboy. "Once I was bitten by a rattlesnake, and a bucking bronco threw me and broke my arm."
>
> "And you wouldn't call those accidents?"
>
> "Certainly not," said the cowboy. "They did it on purpose!"

There are no accidents with God. He does everything intentionally as part of the divine plan. This biblical doctrine of sovereignty, sung so often in dozens of hymns, finds support throughout all of Scripture. We have already noted (and we shall see many times again in our study of this book) that God knows what he is doing and that he is doing it. Boice reminds us that "the doctrine of the sovereignty of God is no mere philosophical dogma devoid of practical value. Rather it is the doctrine that gives meaning and substance to all other doctrines. It is, as Arthur Pink observes, 'the foundation of Christian theology . . . the center of gravity in the system of Christian truth—the sun around which all the lesser orbs are grouped.' It is also, as we shall see, the Christian's strength and comfort amid the storms of this life" (Boice, p. 150).

Daniel, of course, had been taught this doctrine since his childhood. Nebuchadnezzar, on the other hand, had always considered himself the primary force of the universe. Now he was in for a shock.

II. COMMENTARY

Dreamworks, Inc.

MAIN IDEA: *God is in control of his world and all the people in it from the first moment of Creation to the final hour of human history.*

A Preparation of the King (2:24–28)

SUPPORTING IDEA: *When human wisdom fails and we cannot understand the confusing issues of life, we turn to the God of heaven.*

2:24–25. We should not let Arioch's kindness to Daniel diminish our understanding of his role in Nebuchadnezzar's fortress. One Spanish translation calls him "captain of the cutthroats." Writing in Greek, the early church father Theodotion used the word for "chief butcher." Since he had arranged Daniel's response to the king, he handled the message. Here we learn that Arioch had not previously named Daniel, or perhaps he just did not know that Daniel and the team had talked personally with Nebuchadnezzar (1:19). A typical bureaucrat, Arioch took credit for having **found a man among the exiles**.

Earlier we wondered whether the rest of the wise men had been executed, but now we know that Daniel's intervention saved their lives. By this point Daniel was hardly just another nameless, faceless exile; he was about to graduate *cum laude* from the Royal Academy of Babylonian Arts and Sciences.

2:26. Assuming Daniel was just another of the wise men who already stood under the king's execution order, Nebuchadnezzar asked (we suspect with some amazement) whether Daniel could really repeat the dream and then explain it. Daniel inserted his Babylonian name here, taking us back to 1:7.

2:27–28. Daniel began by affirming that no clergyman, philosopher, or scientist on earth could solve the mystery and put the king's mind at rest. This answered the king's question about whether Daniel would provide the interpretation. He would not. **But there is a God in heaven who reveals mysteries**. And not only can this God accomplish such a feat; he has chosen to do so for Nebuchadnezzar, who was about to find out **what will happen in days to come**.

This phrase, rendered "in the latter days" by the KJV, has intrigued expositors and theologians for centuries. It appears fourteen times in the

Old Testament and inevitably refers to the end of time, well beyond the days of Nebuchadnezzar. Culver has specialized in this particular focus:

> An examination shows that while many events previous to eschatological times are within the scope of the prophesies limited by the expression "latter days," not once is the conclusion of all human history and the consummating events connected with the yet future establishment of the Messianic Kingdom on earth out of sight. Otherwise, the events would be only in *future time,* not necessarily in "the latter days" (Culver, p. 107).

Let's remember that the latter days for Israel would not be the same as the latter days for the church, though this distinction would hardly have meant anything to either Daniel or Nebuchadnezzar. We also should not connect this phrase in 2:28 with Daniel's discussion of the end times in 11:35. Here it seems best to assume that the dream about to be explained covered a time period from approximately 600 B.C. to the still future second coming of Christ to the earth. The prophet will describe four great world empires and their complete destruction by the final empire, the kingdom of heaven.

B Description of the Statue (2:29–35)

SUPPORTING IDEA: *God's Word provides revelation, not mystery. He wants his people to understand how he works in the world and sometimes even gives that information to pagan monarchs.*

2:29–30. How does the old line go? "Uneasy rests the head that wears the crown" (or something like that). Now the absolute monarch of Southwest Asia, Nebuchadnezzar was lying in bed at night wondering, "What next?" These two verses are not about the dream, but rather the king's state of mind which God used as an opportunity to answer his ponderings. Daniel's reference to God as **the revealer of mysteries** offers yet another description of the heavenly monarch.

Once again Daniel hammered home his theme of God's control—**this mystery has been revealed to me, not because I have greater wisdom than other living men**. Indeed, the vision was not to Daniel at all, but rather to Nebuchadnezzar so that he might have God's answer to the piercing question, "What next?"

2:31–33. The shape of the statue was not particularly unusual, but its size and appearance was **large . . . enormous, dazzling . . . awesome**. Let's not make the mistake of thinking this statue an idol. It was a divine representation of how Nebuchadnezzar viewed himself, a giant force in the world. As Baldwin puts it, "In his dream the statue stood for the king, with his huge empire that he could scarcely hold, and symbolized his inadequacy in the face of threats from break-away factions. He feared he had over-reached himself and would fall" (Baldwin, 92).

The polymetallic statue displayed numinous terror and splendor at the same time, with its gold head, silver chest and arms, bronze belly and thighs, iron legs, and iron-clay feet. Several observations are immediately obvious:

1. The quality of the metal declines from the head to the feet.
2. The weight declines from the head to the feet.
3. The metal increases in strength from the head to the feet, with the exception of the clay portion, presumably in the toes.

2:34–35. Up to this point nothing has moved as Nebuchadnezzar stared in awe at the statue. Now all of a sudden a supernaturally formed rock smashed the image on its iron-clay feet and pulverized them. Its feet disabled, the entire statue crumbled and became **like chaff on a threshing floor in the summer**. Every particle of the statue blew away in the wind, but the rock **became a huge mountain and filled the whole earth**. We learn in 2:45 that the stone came *from* a mountain before it *became* a mountain.

As Criswell points out: "The seer was saying that the political sovereignty and the political leadership and power of this world that was vested first in Babylon, then Persia, then in Greece, then in Rome, then scattered among the proliferating nations of the earth, shall be finally vested in the great Shadu-Rabu, the great mountain, the Stone, the Lord God, the Christ of glory" (Criswell, p. 80).

But we get ahead of the story.

C Elaboration of the Four Kingdoms (2:36–43)

SUPPORTING IDEA: *We talk often about superpowers and like to boast that America is the only superpower left in the world. But we are yet to see the full meaning of that concept when God breaks apart modern kingdoms just as he did ancient kingdoms.*

2:36–38. Nebuchadnezzar, scarcely able to breathe much less interrupt, must have just sat staring intently at Daniel's face as he realized the accuracy of the details. So Daniel moved immediately to interpretation. We find here an interesting plural (**we**) and should probably chalk it up to nothing more than the common editorial pronoun. Clearly Daniel was not talking about himself and his three companions, and most assuredly he was not talking about how God and he would handle this dream. Although we hardly use it in common expression, in ancient times this choice would express the characteristic humility we see throughout this book.

Was Nebuchadnezzar really **the king of kings**? Though we often apply that appellation only to God or Christ, in the context of the Babylonian kingdom, Daniel not only described his loyalty to God accurately, but he also used the same language Ezekiel employed in 26:7. Certainly Nebuchadnezzar would have agreed with the title and assumed everyone knew he had risen to power by his own strength and cunning. But Daniel exploded that myth immediately when he said, **the God of heaven has given you dominion and power and might and glory**. The point of saying **you are that head of gold** seems to rest in the identification of a kingdom with its ruler.

According to Archer:

> The first of the four world-empires, then, was the Neo-Babylonian Empire of the Chaldeans that Nebuchadnezzar, whose reign began in 605 B.C., was to rule over for about forty more years—till 562 or 560 B.C. But his empire did not last more than twenty-one years after his death. His son Evil-Merodach . . . reigned two years only (560–558). . . . Neriglissar reigned four years (560–556) and Labashi-Marduk only one (556). Nabonidus engineered a *coup d' etat* in 555 and ruled until Babylon fell to the Persians in 539 (Archer, p. 46).

2:39. Having paid tribute to the great king, Daniel dismissed the next two kingdoms in two brief sentences. All conservative scholars agree that the silver kingdom is Medo-Persia which began with Cyrus the Great in 539 and lasted for more than two centuries. Many suggest that the two arms and two sides of the chest represent the duality of the Medo-Persian Empire.

But we have to ask how one could consider Persia inferior to Babylon. The kingdoms actually gained more territory as we make our way down the statue. But as always in God's design, size is not the issue. Quality outranks quantity almost any time, and that seems to be the point of the change in metals. Babylon exceeded Persia in its political organization, its cultural life, and the absolute authority of the king (a positive attribute in ancient thinking).

Daniel even commented on the wider geography of the third kingdom (Greece) which **will rule over the whole earth**. Alexander the Great began invading Persia in 334 B.C. and finished the job three years later. His was the largest empire of the ancient world, but only eight years after his defeat of the Persians he was killed in battle and Greece became four smaller kingdoms. The Greeks made one final attempt to preserve their unity at the battle of Ipsus in 301, but it failed miserably. Within less than three hundred years, it had all faded into the control of the iron empire.

2:40–43. According to Daniel, **iron breaks and smashes everything**, and that is precisely what happened when Rome ruled the world. But notice how quickly Daniel cut to an explanation of the **feet and toes** and here we find the interpretive controversies. The word for "baked clay" is *hasap,* commonly used for some kind of pottery. So the feet were composed of one of the strongest metals known to humankind (**iron**) and one of the most vulnerable, **baked clay**, that can be broken just by hitting it with one's hand. Furthermore, these two elements do not commonly bind or blend with each other. One can find many interpretations of this strange mixture. Some see the intermarriage of the ancient kings and the weakening of families thereby; others see different kinds of government such as an attempt to blend dictatorship with democracy.

Miller says:

> In summary, shortly before the second coming of Christ, ten (a literal or symbolic number) kingdoms (or nations) of unequal strength will unite to form a coalition that will rise out of the ruins of the ancient Roman Empire. Since Rome is part of Europe and the activities of that ancient empire centered in Europe, it is reasonable to assume that this area of the world will play a leading role in this future regime. In Dan. 7 the prophet indicates that from this empire will come the evil world leader of the last days commonly known as Antichrist (Miller, p. 99).

Surely the confusion and frustration in the interpretation of the toes stems at least in part from attempting to force Daniel's prophesy into the history of the ancient world. Premillennial expositors almost uniformly take the passage to mean the separation, division, and diversity of western European nations in our day. At this point, however, we must enforce the rubric against pushing details, since many have been led astray by attempting to identify ten NATO countries as the ten toes of Nebuchadnezzar's image. This perverse practice comes to naught every time a nation joins or withdraws from that organization.

As Walvoord points out:

> Probably the best solution to the problem is the familiar teaching that Daniel's prophecy actually passes over the present age, the period between the first and second coming of Christ or, more specifically, the period between Pentecost and the rapture of the church. There is nothing unusual about such a solution, as Old Testament prophecy lumps together predictions concerning the first and second comings of Christ without regard for the millennia that lay between (Lk 4:17–19; cf. Is 61:1–2) (Walvoord, *Daniel,* p. 72).

D Prediction of the Future (2:44–49)

SUPPORTING IDEA: *Sometimes when we serve God faithfully and speak for him truthfully, even pagan people will say, "Surely your God is the God of gods and the Lord of kings."*

2:44. Surely this verse is the crux of the chapter and the pitfall of many serious Bible students. We find the key phrase early in the verse—**the God of heaven will set up a kingdom that will never be destroyed**. We also learn that this will happen **in the time of those kings**. This fifth kingdom arose from the rock and smashed the first four. Almost all evangelical expositors identify this as the kingdom of God, but what form that takes provides fodder for much discussion.

The metaphor of God (Father or Son) as stone goes back to Genesis 49:24 and continues throughout both Testaments (Ps. 118:22; Isa. 28:16; 1 Cor. 1:23; 1 Pet. 2:4–7). To Israel, Jesus Christ was a stumbling stone and a rock of offense, but to Christian believers he becomes the cornerstone of faith. To Nebuchadnezzar and the heads of the other three pagan nations, the kingdom of God centered in Jesus Christ the Son becomes a smashing stone of warfare and destruction. Jesus said, "He who falls on this stone will be broken to pieces, but he on whom it falls will be crushed" (Matt. 21:44). Some have chosen to identify this passage as a prophecy of the first coming of Christ and see the kingdom arising from the stone as the church. Usually this interpretation leads to either amillenniallism or postmillenniallism, the views that there will be *no* earthly kingdom, or that the earthly kingdom occurs in some form now.

Premilleniallists link Daniel 2 and 7 with Revelation 20 and expect the coming of Jesus to precede one thousand years of peace during which he reigns on earth. **Those kings**, therefore, likely refers to present or future rulers in the iron/clay toes rather than to any of the leaders of the four major kingdoms.

No smashing of earthly kingdoms has ever taken place in the church which overcomes the world not by physical destruction but by its message of love, peace, and redemption. Archer says, "Parallel passages leave us in no doubt that this fifth realm is the kingdom of God, ruled over by Christ and enduring eternally, even after its earthly, millennial phase is over" (Archer, 48). The interpretation of this verse hardly affects one's eternal salvation, but it plays an enormous role in a proper understanding of end-time events, a major theme in Daniel.

Miller reminds us: "What a comforting passage this is. In this present world of injustice, wars, and crime, it is reassuring to know that Christ is coming; and when he comes, all of the evils of this age will end. There is indeed coming a day when 'the earth will be filled with the knowledge of the glory of the LORD, as the waters cover the sea' (Hab. 2:14), for Messiah's reign of righteousness will extend to the ends of the earth" (Miller, p. 102).

2:45. Daniel tells us what we had already assumed, namely, that the kingdom emerges from the rock which destroyed the image. The phrase **not by human hands** appears again as it did in verse 34 to emphasize God's control over the destruction of worldly kingdoms. At the risk of belaboring a point, let me say again that the rock "struck the statue on its feet of iron and clay" (2:34) and thereby destroyed the entire statue, including "the iron, the clay, the bronze, the silver and the gold" (2:35).

Daniel's conclusion is similar to his introduction, and Nebuchadnezzar can count on this rendering because it comes not from some wizard of the court but from **the great God**.

So when we pray, "Your kingdom come . . . on earth as it is in heaven" (Matt. 6:10), we had better understand the violence with which that kingdom arrives (Ps. 110:1,5–6; Mal. 3:1–5). It will also be highly visible, as we hear (or sing) every Christmas in *Messiah* (Isa. 45). Here are the words of my own mentor, on this important subject:

> It is true that Daniel speaks of the coming of the kingdom as a stone which is cut out of the mountain "without hands" (2:34,45). But in the symbolic dream of the Babylonian king, as confirmed by the prophet, the *stone* was seen; the *cutting* act was seen; also it *falls* and [Daniel observes] the consequent *destruction* of the image. The words "without hands" are intended to indicate the supernatural origin of both the king and his kingdom. Although tangible to men, no human or natural means have any part in the ushering in of this kingdom (McClain, p. 177).

2:46–47. In the superstitious extremism for which Nebuchadnezzar was famous, he swung from an order to execute all the wise men to an act of worship to one of them. Surely Daniel refused this worship, since he has already indicated that he was only God's instrument in this process (2:30). Nebuchadnezzar hardly experienced conversion on this occasion, but he did acknowledge that Daniel's God was **the God of gods and the Lord of kings**, obviously admitting his greatness over Marduk and Nabu. Like Abraham before him and Esther after him, Daniel was elevated to a place of respect by powerful pagan leaders and used in that position by God to care for his people. Daniel's God was a great mystery to Nebuchadnezzar, but the king had taken the first step toward acknowledging his greatness over all other worshiped deities. There may be a warning here for us as well.

According to Laney:

> Too often budding theologians analyze God to such an extent that they attempt to remove the mystery of His divine being. Unfortunately they end up with something that is far less than God. They end up with a mini-god, a god who is limited by their own finite

understanding. As Christians, we must pursue our knowledge of God. But at the same time we must take care that our theological analysis does not diminish the mystery of His divine being (Laney, p. 82).

2:48–49. Can one serve at high levels in government without compromising Christian faith? Certainly. Joseph did it and so did Daniel. He served at court as well, ruling **the entire province of Babylon**. Furthermore, he became dean of the faculty, **in charge of all its wise men**. Daniel wisely requested the political advancement of his three friends, and Nebuchadnezzar wisely granted it. For a lowly Jew, a kidnapped captive, to be honored in such a way should call forth an immediate recognition of God's hand in the appointment.

MAIN IDEA REVIEW: *God is in control of his world and all the people in it from the first moment of creation to the final hour of human history.*

III. CONCLUSION

"Ode to a Water Fowl"

One cold December day a brilliant young man walked across a field in western Massachusetts. At the age of eight, he had begun to write poems, and at thirteen he published a satire on Thomas Jefferson. On this particular day, however, he seemed lonely and a bit sad. As he walked, he saw a wild duck fly across the sky, heading south to a more proper home for the winter. At that moment he knew that the same God who cared for ducks also cared for him. That evening William Cullen Bryant wrote "To a Water Fowl," once called by Matthew Arnold "the most perfect brief poem in the language."

Henry Wadsworth Longfellow, Edgar Allan Poe, and Walt Whitman all admired and imitated Bryant's poetry. Before he died in 1878, Bryant's eulogies of famous Americans were known around the world. He was also influential in the formation of New York's Central Park and Metropolitan Museum of Art.

Like Daniel, Bryant was recognized and honored in the halls of human power. Like Daniel, he also knew that God controls those halls. Here is the last stanza from "To a Water Fowl":

He who, from zone to zone,
Guides through the boundless sky thy certain flight,
In the long way that I must tread alone,
Will lead my steps aright.

PRINCIPLES

- We should always acknowledge that skills, ability, and wisdom come from God.
- God maintains control of earthly kingdoms no matter how evil they might seem to us.
- The kingdom of God, ruled by our Lord Jesus, will one day be established on earth.
- Obedience to God and his truth can often bring promotion and honor in unusual places.

APPLICATIONS

- The faithful witness of God's humble children can even bring about change in the hearts of arrogant and powerful people.
- God reveals the future to those who seriously and openly study his Word.
- God puts us in places where he wants us to serve and then expects us to serve well.

IV. LIFE APPLICATION

Statue of Bondage

In 1884 the nation of France gave to the United States a monument entitled *Liberty Enlightening the World.* The French donated about $250,000 for the statue itself, and citizens of the United States provided $280,000 for the pedestal on which it stands. We all know the image well—the proud stance of a free women, her right arm holding high that great torch and her left arm grasping a tablet which contains the date of the Declaration of Independence.

The statue is made of more than three hundred thin sheets of copper and weighs about one hundred tons. That wonderful poem by Emma Lazarus was inscribed on the pedestal in 1903, some nineteen years after the statue itself was erected.

> "Keep ancient lands, your storied pomp!" cries she
> With silent lips. "Give me your tired, your poor,
> Your huddled masses yearning to breathe free,
> The wretched refuse of your teeming shore.
> Send these, the homeless, tempest-tossed to me,
> I lift my lamp beside the golden door!"

Nebuchadnezzar's dream contains no Statue of Liberty. This was a statue foretelling bondage. Probably no nations in the history of the world—not Genghis Kahn's Mongols, Hitler's Germans, Stalin's Russians, or the Communist purge of China—created more death and destruction than did the combined powers of Babylon, Persia, Greece, and Rome. When the New Testament was written, some sixty million slaves lived in the Roman Empire, many of them teachers, doctors, and artisans. Our awareness of the cruelty and perversity of human leadership in the world from Nebuchadnezzar to the present hour should help us to pray with sincerity, "Thy kingdom come!"

V. PRAYER

Father, we thank you for the great wisdom you gave Daniel and for the way you protected and blessed him in Babylon. We thank you for the revelation of your work in the world, much of it still ahead of us, and we do pray with great sincerity, "Thy kingdom come!" Amen.

VI. DEEPER DISCOVERIES

A. The Purpose of Prophecy

We all agree that the early books of the Old Testament (what scholars call *Law* and *History*) were written to inform us of God's dealings with Israel from the call of Abraham to the return from captivity described in Ezra and

Nehemiah. We see in the Psalms great comfort and cause for praise, and in the Proverbs pithy wisdom for daily living. But why prophecy? Certainly that question arises earlier in the Bible, but it comes to great poignancy in these twelve chapters of Daniel. Let's attempt a few answers to the question.

1. Prophecy shows us that God intended his Word to be revelation, not some mystical code. In Barton Payne's mammoth work *Encyclopedia of Biblical Prophecy,* he writes:

> Both OT and NT teach that the inscripturated language of the prophets possesses an authority equivalent to that of the words of God Himself. . . . A final OT prophet could look back both upon "the law, and the words which Yaweh had sent by His Spirit by the former [preexilic] prophets" and find them equally authoritative (Zech. 7:12). Even so, the modern reader who would enter into a sympathetic understanding of biblical prophecy is called upon, by Christ Himself, for vital faith in Scripture as the Word of God written and therefore inerrant in its autographs (Luke 24:25,44) (Payne, p. 6).

2. Prophecy teaches us that history is linear, not cyclical. We love to say, "What goes around comes around," but in history that is not the case. Daniel 2 drives home the point that the Almighty God works through the kingdoms of earth to accomplish his will and, in time, will destroy them all and establish his own kingdom. As rough and bumpy as the process may seem to us, history is moving toward the final goal that God ordained before the creation of the world.

3. Prophecy leads us to righteousness. Invariably the prophets of the Old Testament tell the nation of Israel that their dilemma and suffering were caused by disobedience and idolatry but that God would deliver them when their hearts turned to him. From Genesis (17:7) to Revelation (21:3) the Heavenly Father says, "I will be their God, and they shall be my people." The covenant is unbroken, and the promises of God will be fulfilled, old covenant promises to Israel and new covenant promises to the church. Jesus Christ is the heart of prophecy and his coming, the hope of the church. So John can write, "Dear friends, now we are children of God, and what we will be has not yet been made known. But we know that when he appears, we

shall be like him, for we shall see him as he is. Everyone who has this hope in him purifies himself, just as he is pure" (1 John 3:2–3).

4. Prophecy provides us comfort and confidence. How many times have other nations virtually obliterated Israel, and how many times have the Jews rebounded from the dust and death of destruction! Today that tiny fragment of ground on the eastern shore of the Mediterranean Sea figures in world news headlines on a daily basis. Criswell writes, "That is why God wrote the prophecy. . . . God wills that we have assurance and quietness of heart, and be without fear or apprehension, whatever the future may bring" (Criswell, p. 100).

B. The God of Gods and the Lord of Kings (2:47)

Reading Nebuchadnezzar's words to Daniel almost makes it sound like Christmas in Babylon. How familiar that language from Handel's *Messiah*: "The kingdom of this world is become the kingdom of our Lord and of His Christ; and He shall reign forever and ever, King of Kings, and Lord of Lords. Hallelujah!" The text is taken from Revelation 11:15 and 19:16 where we read, "On his robe and on his thigh he has this name written: KING OF KINGS AND LORD OF LORDS." This is the rider on the white horse, the one who is called Faithful and True, carrying the name, the Word of God.

Of course, Nebuchadnezzar knew nothing of such matters. He was merely extolling the greatness of Daniel's God over all other gods. The phrase "Lord of kings" appears in the Letter of Adon to Egypt, actually dated in the early years of Nebuchadnezzar's reign. The letter was sent to Pharaoh and begins, "To the Lord of Kings." Lesser luminaries in the Seleucid and Ptolemaic dynasties also applied the term to themselves. While praising God for the opportunity he has given us to connect Daniel and Revelation, let's acknowledge the limitations of Nebuchadnezzar's theology. In the words of Baldwin, "The king is not committing himself to the notion of one true God, as Daniel no doubt realized. As a polytheist he can always add another to the deities he worships" (Baldwin, p. 95).

VII. TEACHING OUTLINE

A. INTRODUCTION

1. Lead Story: Intentional Accidents

2. Context: Since we have divided chapter 2 of Daniel into two parts in this study, the context of the second half of the chapter (dream and interpretation) spins directly from the first half in which we learned that the king had a dream, that no one could repeat or explain it, and that the entire faculty faced execution for their failure. The end of chapter 2, however, sets up the rest of the book, since Daniel now holds official position at the royal court and his friends also serve as administrators over the province of Babylon.
3. Transition: We are now ready for the next arrogant act of the great Nebuchadnezzar of whom Yogi Berra might have said, "He was a legend in his own mind."

B. COMMENTARY

1. Preparation of the King (2:24–28)
2. Description of the Statue (2:29–35)
3. Elaboration of the Four Kingdoms (2:36–43)
4. Prediction of the Future (2:44–49)

C. CONCLUSION: "ODE TO A WATER FOWL"

VIII. ISSUES FOR DISCUSSION

1. Where and how can we find courage to act as Daniel did in this chapter?
2. In what ways can we benefit from the study of prophecy?
3. How should we respond when others attempt to praise and honor us for what God may have done through us?

Daniel 3:1–30

Nebuchadnezzar's Ragtime Band

I. INTRODUCTION
"Hail to the Chief!"

II. COMMENTARY
A verse-by-verse explanation of the chapter.

III. CONCLUSION
The Madness of King George
An overview of the principles and applications from the chapter.

IV. LIFE APPLICATION
Faith to Leap
Melding the chapter to life.

V. PRAYER
Tying the chapter to life with God.

VI. DEEPER DISCOVERIES
Historical, geographical, and grammatical enrichment of the commentary.

VII. TEACHING OUTLINE
Suggested step-by-step group study of the chapter.

VIII. ISSUES FOR DISCUSSION
Zeroing the chapter in on daily life.

Quote

"You cannot run from a weakness;

you must sometime fight it out or perish;

and if that be so, why not now and where you stand?"

Robert Louis Stevenson

GEOGRAPHICAL PROFILE: PLAIN OF DURA

- Mentioned only here in Scripture
- Possibly the Tells of Dura near the city of Babylon or just a word meaning "walled enclosure"
- The location of Nebuchadnezzar's great gold image

Daniel 3:1–30

IN A NUTSHELL

When God chooses to use people, he often puts them through difficult, frustrating, and life-threatening experiences to burn the dross from their lives and refine their character.

Nebuchadnezzar's Ragtime Band

I. INTRODUCTION

"Hail to the Chief!"

James Knox Polk, born near Pineville, North Carolina, in 1795, was elected governor of Tennessee in 1839 and president of the United States in 1844. During Polk's four years of service (he died in 1849), the American flag was raised over the area which now forms nine western states, and Texas became a member of the Union. It is said of his accomplishments, that of all American presidents, only George Washington had a stronger record of success in office.

On the bright side, the country acquired land at a rapid rate, and gold was discovered in California. Meanwhile, however, factories employed small children and immigrants suffered in poverty while slavery continued throughout the South. His critics saw Polk as cold and withdrawn, and when he did not seek a second term, much of the nation shed no tears.

Polk's wife, the former Sarah Childress, became the first presidential wife to serve as her husband's secretary. A strict Moravian, she banned dancing, cardplaying, and all alcoholic drinks from the White House. Another matter also perturbed her. Polk was five feet six inches tall, and he would often enter a room full of dignitaries, perhaps even at the White House, and go unnoticed for several minutes until someone would say, "The president is here."

In an effort to solve this problem of disrespect, Sarah Polk requested the selection of a song to be played each time the president entered the room in order to announce his presence. Someone chose what we now call "Hail to the Chief," composed by James Sanderson in 1828. We only hear this as an instrumental piece, although its words reflect the "Boat Song" in Sir Walter Scott's *Lady of the Lake*. Since the days of Polk, it has announced the presence of every president.

Nebuchadnezzar's musicians might have used "Hail to the Chief" had the charts been available, but nevertheless a variety of musical instruments made up a grand Chaldean orchestra which called people to worship the great king of Babylon. National leaders of all kinds and all ages spend a great deal of effort and money to call attention to themselves, and this chapter is one more ugly example. But once again the Most High God intervened and interfered with the plans of the powerful king in order to deliver three of his chosen people from a horrible death and to promote them in their leadership post within a pagan empire.

II. COMMENTARY

Nebuchadnezzar's Ragtime Band

MAIN IDEA: *Verse 18 provides the key to an understanding of Daniel 3. The young men believed God would deliver them and testified, "Even if he does not, we want you to know, O king, that we will not serve your gods or worship the image of gold you have set up." Spiritual courage trusts and obeys God to the death.*

A Erection of the Golden Image (3:1–7)

SUPPORTING IDEA: *Satan often uses the threat or promise of power to entice God's people to sin, a trick he even used with Jesus.*

3:1. Daniel 3 contains no prophecies, but this simple and well-known narrative of faith has challenged millions for millennia. Christian martyrs by the thousands have been burned at the stake over the centuries, and this is the first record of servants of God thrown into fire as an execution. Perhaps the writer of Hebrews had them in mind when he spoke about heroes of faith who "quenched the fury of the flames" and then after his list of suffering servants he wrote, "these were all commended for their faith" (Heb. 11:34,39).

We already know everyone who appears in the chapter, although we are a bit surprised at Nebuchadnezzar's reversion to pagan idolatry and brutality after his "testimony" in 2:47. Daniel's name does not even appear in the chapter, and commentators have speculated numerous reasons for its absence. He may have been ill; his office may have excluded him from the demands of the king on this occasion; or he might simply have been out of town on business of state.

An **image** (most likely goldplated rather than solid gold) of this enormity could have been seen from at least fifteen miles away from any direction as it rose above the flat sun-baked Mesopotamian plain. Likely the height included the base, since a ten-to-one ratio of height and width would have presented a very slender king.

The word for "image" here is *tselm,* which appears in several Semitic languages and normally means "a likeness of some living thing." As we know from the Greeks and Romans, kingdoms of the ancient world were fond of statues, and this may well have been a reproduction of the likeness of Nebuchadnezzar himself. The very existence of this type of structure provokes a sense of awe such as many Americans feel when they stand before the Jefferson or Lincoln memorials.

3:2–3. We've noted earlier that Daniel is fond of lists, and this chapter illustrates that point (vv. 2–3,7,10,15,27). Seven types of governmental officials are specifically named, and the list is identical in verses 2 and 3. But to emphasize the widespread demand of the king's edict, Daniel adds, **and all the other provincial officials**. Some scholars have noted that the very titles used favor the early dating of Daniel in the sixth century. We cannot be sure of the specific duties of these various officials, nor would that knowledge enhance our understanding of the chapter. In wording this kind of edict today, we might say, "Everyone on the federal payroll must show up." There were no options; no one was excluded.

It seems hardly accidental that the gold-plated image (common in ancient times) took something of the character of Nebuchadnezzar's dream, thereby representing both the king and his empire. Some interpreters spin chapter 3 off 2:47 and suggest that this image actually honored the God of Israel. They cite Aaron's golden calf (Exod. 32) and Rehoboam's two golden calves (1 Kgs. 12) as examples of idolatrous objects theoretically dedicated to Jehovah. Such an argument seems far-fetched, however, and nothing in the chapter supports it. Indeed, the testimony of the lads in verse 18 seems to indicate that, despite his emotional outburst of 2:47, the king had not forsaken his pagan deities.

3:4–5. At the proclamation of the herald, everyone **must fall down and worship the image**. The six named instruments certainly did not exhaust all those available, and Daniel lets us know that by adding **and all kinds of music** to the list. Some interpreters have made much of the Greek terms appearing for three of the instruments (**zither**, **harp**, and **pipes**). Their argument targets the dating of Daniel in the second century when Greek words would have been readily available. The *NIV Study Bible* observes, however, "Greek musicians and instruments are mentioned and Assyrian inscriptions written before the time of Nebuchadnezzar" (p. 1303). Furthermore, these are the only three Greek words in Daniel. If written in the second century, the entire manuscript would surely have been peppered with Greek, perhaps large sections written in that language.

3:6. All of a sudden punishment for defying the king's edict became instant immolation. This contrasts with chapter 2 where the Chaldean faculty was threatened with having their bodies "cut into pieces" and their "houses turned into piles of rubble" (2:5). Furthermore, it would happen **immediately**. There seems to be little evidence that this was a standard form of execution in ancient Babylon and might well have been some hideous instant whim of the king or one of his lackeys.

3:7. The phrase **men of every language** repeated in verses 4 and 7 indicates that even foreign dignitaries who served in some way at the Babylonian court fell under this edict. We can imagine the entire assembled mass falling prostrate at the first note of the orchestra—except three young Jews who, to the shock of everyone and the anger of their fellow politicians, remained standing.

B Effect on the Three Jews (3:8–12)

SUPPORTING IDEA: *Christians are under biblical mandate to obey the laws of their land—except in situations where human laws defy divine law.*

3:8–11. The **astrologers** of our text again became the spokesmen for their fellow faculty members (2:4), of which the three Jewish young men were a part. They **denounced the Jews**, an Aramaic expression which indicates slander or accusation, and (somewhat repetitiously it would seem) review for the king the whole edict story. If Daniel wasn't there, how did he know exactly what they said? Several plausible answers may play a role in our understanding of the matter. These words may have been spoken in the presence of Shadrach, Meshach, and Abednego; the king may have reviewed the entire affair after it happened; and the Holy Spirit brought to Daniel's mind exactly the words which appear on the page of the original text.

3:12. In an early evidence of anti-Semitism, the Chaldeans leveled three accusations against the Jews:

- They held no regard for the king himself.
- They did not serve the king's gods.
- They failed to **worship the image of gold**.

Furthermore, the words **whom you have set up over the affairs of the province of Babylon** indicate some deep resentment and even open criticism of the king himself. Since in ancient cultures the worship of a variety of deities (religion) was so bound up with the affairs of state (politics), refusal to bow down became, in effect, an act of treason. The separation of the gods from the king may support the idea that this statue was designed for the direct worship of Nebuchadnezzar, not just the general worship of the gods of Babylon. Therefore, the three young heroes were simply obeying Old Testament law: "You shall have no other gods before me. You shall not make for yourself an idol in the form of anything in heaven above or on the earth beneath or in the waters below. You shall not bow down to them or worship them; for I, the LORD your God, am a jealous God, punishing the children for the sin of the fathers to the third and fourth generation of those who hate me" (Deut. 5:7–9).

 Examination by the Great King (3:13–18)

SUPPORTING IDEA: *Temptation to sin often carries with it not only a threat of death if one refuses, but a second chance to act on the temptation in order to save one's life.*

3:13–14. Doubtless the king held little esteem for the Chaldean nobles who jealously accused three of their own, but the offense was so great that he became **furious with rage**. Both the KJV and NIV translate the king's question as **is it true**. The king was incredulous that anyone, particularly three men as brilliant as those before him, could defy the edict and therefore commit suicide for what surely seemed to him like no good reason.

3:15. Just in case their refusal was occasioned by a misunderstanding of the rules, Nebuchadnezzar recited it all again, and Daniel offered the final enumeration of the instruments in the Babylonian jazz band.

Nebuchadnezzar's respect for Daniel's god had not elevated his elementary theology one whit. He challenged the accused with a rhetorical question: **what god will be able to rescue you from my hand**? Some 150 years earlier a man by the name of Sennacherib had challenged the God of Israel and in one night lost 185,000 fighting men to the death angel (2 Kgs. 19).

3:16. Rhetorical or not, these men made bold to answer the king. But rather than the familiar (and safe) "O king, live forever!" that the Chaldeans used in verse 9, they merely addressed the king by his name. We should hardly find disrespect in this answer, more likely a death row urge to cut to the chase. The KJV rendering of "we are not careful to answer thee in this matter" stems from the concept of need well captured in the NIV. They simply stated that, contrary to Nebuchadnezzar's own viewpoint, he was not in control of their lives.

3:17. The grammar and syntax of this verse raises some question. For one thing, there is no definite article before **blazing furnace**, indicating that God could deliver them from any blazing furnace, not just the one Nebuchadnezzar intended to use. Furthermore, the conditional phrase **if we are thrown** interacts with other words in the sentence to produce other potential translations. Archer, for example, suggests that "a more appropriate rendering in this context would be 'if our God exists . . . He is able to deliver us from the furnace of burning fire; and from your hand, O king, He shall deliver'" (Archer, 54). Theologically we must distinguish the difference between God's power and God's will in verses 17–18. Verse 17 proclaims God's complete capability to deliver these men in any way he chose to do so; verse 18 raises the question of whether or not he makes that choice.

3:18. Miracle or not; deliverance or captivity; life or death—none of these things factored into their decision. Whatever God did or did not do was up to him, and they would accept the outcome. For their part, they had made their stand to obey God's commands as best they knew them. So the king learned that two of the three accusations brought by the Chaldeans were true—these fellows **will not serve your gods or worship the image of gold you have set up**.

The ultimate display of godly courage is not to die with desperate expectations that God will somehow intervene at the last moment but rather to live or die in complete confidence that God will do what he will do. The Book of Daniel depicts the sovereignty of God in the lives of his people and in the affairs of the nations of the world. In the dynamic final chapter of Hebrews, that author cites the passage from Psalm 118 to summon Christian courage in his readers: "So we say with confidence, 'The Lord is my helper; I will not be afraid. What can man do to me?'" (Heb. 13:6).

D Experience in the Fiery Furnace (3:19–26)

SUPPORTING IDEA: *Christians must stand ready to serve their Lord whether by life or by death. Sometimes the blood of martyrs fulfills the plan of God; sometimes miraculous deliverance better suits his purpose.*

3:19. Now a king who was already furious became more furious, and a furnace that was already hot became **hotter than usual**! Nebuchadnezzar seems to have had a propensity for losing his cool and it happens again here. Walvoord says:

> He is as angry as he possibly could be under any circumstances, his face is distorted, his pride has been severely punctured, and he gives the foolish order to heat the furnace seven times hotter than usual, as if this would increase the torment. . . . There is no fool on earth like a man who has lost his temper. And Nebuchadnezzar did a stupid thing. He ought to have cooled the furnace seven times less if he had wanted to hurt them; but instead of that in his fury he heated it seven times more (Walvoord, *Daniel*, pp. 89–90).

3:20–21. Time to get serious. No more debate. No more opportunity to insult the king. Nebuchadnezzar **commanded some of the strongest soldiers in his army** to carry out the execution. Not only that, but the victims were fully dressed when thrown into the blazing pit. Why the point about **robes, trousers, turbans and other clothes**? Archer thinks this was part of Nebuchadnezzar's command "so as to make sure the flames would envelop them" (Archer, p. 56). More likely the text merely intends to tell us this happened immediately. They were grabbed exactly as they were dressed and tossed immediately into the fire. Contrast, for example, the removal of Jesus' clothing before the crucifixion. We shall see shortly why Daniel elaborates on what they were wearing.

Some interpreters will wonder about the fuel for such a fire (possibly charcoal or some early form of petroleum), and others will ponder how ancient politicians could possibly know when a furnace is **seven times hotter than usual**. Surely the latter expression is not to be taken literally any more than when we say to a child, "When you disobey next time, your punishment will be ten times worse."

3:22–23. There is no reason to consider anything short of a miracle here. The three would not have survived in a normal furnace, but in this case the flames were so hot that even the **soldiers** were killed just by being close to the edge of the pit into which they hurled the three Hebrews.

Unless one has seen another person go completely berserk with fits of fury, it is difficult to understand Nebuchadnezzar on this occasion. A brilliant architect and a great warrior, he could be a man of great compassion and tenderness. But as an absolute monarch, he could not and would not tolerate any defiance of his will. Later in this book Daniel will say to Belshazzar:

> O king, the Most High God gave your father Nebuchadnezzar sovereignty and greatness and glory and splendor. Because of the high position he gave him, all the peoples and nations and men of every language dreaded and feared him. Those the king wanted to put to death, he put to death; those he wanted to spare, he spared; those he wanted to promote, he promoted; and those he wanted to humble, he humbled (5:18–19).

As we attempt to picture this scene, our familiarity with furnaces which stand upright skews the picture improperly. Archer offers a most helpful descriptive paragraph.

> Apparently there was no door or screen to hide the inside of the furnace from view. Judging from bas-reliefs it would seem that Mesopotamian smelting furnaces tended to be like an old-fashioned glass milk-bottle in shape, with a large opening for the insertion of the ore to be smelted and a smaller aperture at ground level for the admission of wood and charcoal to furnish the heat. There must have been two or more smaller holes at this same level to permit the insertion of pipes connected with large bellows, when it was desired to raise the temperature beyond what the flue or chimney would produce. Undoubtedly the furnace itself was fashioned of very thick adobe, resistant to intense heat. The large upper door was probably raised above the level of the fire bed so that the metal smelted from the ore would spill on the ground in case the crucibles were upset (Archer, p. 56).

3:24–25. Instantly the king **leaped to his feet in amazement** because his mind could not compute what his eyes had just seen. Men who should be dead, alive and **walking around in the fire**. Men who were tied, now **unbound**. Although the soldiers who cast them to their death themselves died from the heat at the top of the furnace, the victims now stood in this same fire **unharmed**. Furthermore, their ranks had increased to four and **the fourth looks like a son of the gods**! The text does not justify the old KJV rendering "the Son of God."

Like the Roman centurion at the cross, Nebuchadnezzar merely acknowledged some form of deity. We cannot even imagine what Nebuchadnezzar saw in the fourth man that looked different from the other three. Many Christians (I among them) believe that this was probably a Christophany, an appearance of the preincarnate Christ, although that cannot be proven from the text.

Campbell put it this way:

> The fact that Nebuchadnezzar, a pagan, identified the fourth being as deity is remarkable, though it is extremely doubtful that he would have had the insight to understand that he was in the presence of the Son of God. Yet most Bible students do believe that this was a pre-incarnate appearance of Christ, who also appeared to Adam and Eve in the Garden of Eden, who walked with Enoch, who feasted with Abraham, who wrestled with Jacob, who spoke to Moses in the burning bush, who appeared to Joshua as Captain of the Lord's host, who spent the night with Daniel in the lion's den and who came to be born in a stable. God manifest in the flesh! (Campbell, p. 52).

3:26. This king, so given to mood swings, now wanted deliverance as badly as he wanted destruction seconds earlier. As usual, he barked his command, this time actually approaching the blazing furnace as close as he dared. Nebuchadnezzar, whose embryonic theology seems as capricious as his temperament, no longer asked, "What god will be able to rescue you from my hand?" (3:15). Now he rediscovered correct language to speak of Daniel's god and acknowledged the three victims of his anger must be **servants of the Most High God**. Shadrach, Meshach, and Abednego obeyed their king's command and emerged from the fire unscathed. The fourth man in the flames had disappeared, nor did the king's order have any effect on him.

E Elevation to the Royal Staff (3:27–30)

SUPPORTING IDEA: *Doctrinal and spiritual compromise are not necessary. God is able to deliver his people from any kind of oppression, even the fires of instant death.*

3:27. We have difficulty imagining how this crowd of dignitaries immediately formed around the rescued Hebrews. And now we learn why Daniel mentioned clothing in detail (3:21). This blazing furnace, stoked as hot as an angry king could make it, left not a single burn on their bodies, not **a hair of their heads singed; their robes were not scorched, and there was no smell of fire on them**. What was missing? Only the bonds on their hands and feet. The experience reminds us of Isaiah's prophecy about the nation of Israel: "When you pass through the waters, I will be with you; and when you pass through the rivers, they will not sweep over you. When you walk through the fire, you will not be burned; the flames will not set you ablaze (Isa. 43:2).

3:28. In a second "conversion" Nebuchadnezzar now wanted to worship the God of Shadrach, Meshach, and Abednego just as he once wanted to worship the God of Daniel. He still had no clue who or what that might be, but he certainly grasped the reality of the moment—**they trusted in him and defied the king's command and were willing to give up their lives rather than serve or worship any god except their own God**.

This time he reasoned that the fourth man in the fire must have been an **angel**, a different conclusion than he formed earlier. Certainly Nebuchadnezzar could be right here since God's use of angels in deliverance forms a major part of the fabric of both Testaments.

3:29–30. As absolute monarch of the only world he knew, Nebuchadnezzar could not restrain himself from issuing decrees. Notice that he did not turn away from his own gods but merely prohibited anyone in Babylon from saying **anything against the God** of the three Hebrews. There were still other gods in Nebuchadnezzar's pantheon; he was merely willing to say that **no other god can save in this way**.

In a poignant paragraph Walvoord captures the spiritual impact of the chapter:

The common excuses for moral and spiritual compromise, especially the blaming of contemporary influences, are contradicted by the faithfulness of these men. In spite of separation from parents and of the corrupting influences of Babylonian religion, political pressure, and immorality, they did not waver in their hour of testing. Critics are probably right that Daniel intended this chapter to remind Israel of the evils of idolatry and the necessity of obeying God rather than men. But the main thrust of the passage is not an invented moral story which actually never happened, as critics infer, but rather a display of a God who is faithful to his people even in captivity and is ever ready to deliver those who put their trust in him (Walvoord, p. 94).

MAIN IDEA REVIEW: *Verse 18 provides the key to an understanding of Daniel 3. The young men believed God would deliver them and testified, "Even if he does not, we want you to know, O king, that we will not serve your gods or worship the image of gold you have set up." Spiritual courage trusts and obeys God to the death.*

III. CONCLUSION

The Madness of King George

So goes the title of a movie released in 1995 depicting the latter days of George III, who began ruling Great Britain in 1760 and reigned until his death sixty years later. He saw the industrial revolution, overcame the power of the Whig aristocrats, and appointed the famous younger William Pitt as one of his ministers. Throughout much of his life, however, George was emotionally and mentally unbalanced and nine years before his death became hopelessly insane.

Since the history of the United States and Canada, indeed of the whole English-speaking world, springs from the roots of the British Empire, we all know the emotional instabilities of monarchy. Apparently, this was not a uniquely British problem since we see in Nebuchadnezzar both brilliance and buffoonery. Earthly kings who set themselves against the Most High God are doomed to fail, although God may at times use them for his purpose.

Despite the instability of their leaders, whether succeeding monarchs or elected politicians, Christians should be among the finest citizens in any country. Paul said, "Everyone must submit himself to the governing authorities, for there is no authority except that which God has established. The authorities that exist have been established by God" (Rom. 13:1). Since he wrote while the Mediterranean world was under the control of the despotic Roman emperors, we can hardly accuse Paul of describing an ideal situation.

Up to this point Nebuchadnezzar had clearly shown whimsical emotional imbalance, and in the next chapter he completely goes over the edge. Through it all, however, Daniel, Shadrach, Meshach, and Abednego stand firm and stable, resilient examples of trusting in a God far beyond and above the chaos of our troubled world.

PRINCIPLES

- God can and does use miracles to save the lives of his people.
- When God delivers us from harm, the purpose is as much for his glory as our safety.
- Don't trust the religious language of a pagan politician.
- God's public reputation is intimately connected with the obedient faith of his people, although not dependent upon it.
- Worship of any creature, even the figment of one's own religious imagination, is idolatry.

APPLICATIONS

- Be faithful to your commitments and leave the problems to God. Never doubt the power and purpose of the Heavenly Father.
- Trust God with your life at all times, especially in crisis or danger.
- Never underestimate the power of heaven for miracles of deliverance.
- Don't let success early in life blind you to possible failures and struggles at some later point.

IV. LIFE APPLICATION

Faith to Leap

On a visit to South Africa's famous Kruger National Park some years ago, I had the opportunity to see many native African animals in the wild. There the tourists are enclosed inside walled enclaves at night while the animals roam free. Actually the animals roam free all day as well, but officials let the tourists drive about in automobiles to observe the park's legitimate residents in their natural habitat. It is, to say the least, a dramatic experience.

One of the animals one sees quite commonly in Africa is the impala, that small deer-like creature often shown on the Discovery Channel as dinner for larger beasts of prey like lions and leopards. The impala can actually jump to a height of over ten feet and leap distances of more than thirty feet. Yet zoos often keep their impalas in enclosures with walls no more than three feet high. Such containment seems preposterous unless one knows the impala psyche—these magnificent creatures will not jump if they cannot see where their feet will land.

Jumping was hardly an option for our three Hebrews, but they certainly had no idea where their feet would land. Their courageous stand before a violent king serves to illustrate the wholehearted commitment God asks from all of us. One could well create a lesson for young people or young adults from this chapter, and doubtless that has been done thousands of times. Here is a possible outline for a message on victorious faith.

1. Complete Commitment—"we do not need to defend ourselves" (3:16)
2. Complete Confidence—"the God we serve is able to save us" (3:17)
3. Complete Courage—"even if he does not . . . we will not serve your gods or worship the image" (3:18)
4. Complete Conviction—"willing to give up their lives rather than serve or worship any god except their own" (3:28)

Without faith Satan can trap us in small enclosures with flimsy walls. With faith our service for God and usefulness in his kingdom know no bounds.

V. PRAYER

Father, thank you for the courage and faith of these three young men. May this passage inspire us to greater trust and dependence upon the same God they served. Amen.

VI. DEEPER DISCOVERIES

A. Golden Images in the Old Testament

The ancients had a fondness for images of wood overlaid with gold. We see it as early as Exodus 37 in the preparation of the golden altar (cf. Exod. 37:25–26). Isaiah also speaks about idols with gold exterior in Isaiah 40:19 and 41:7. And, Jeremiah writes:

> Hear what the LORD says to you, O house of Israel. This is what the LORD says: "Do not learn the ways of the nations or be terrified by signs in the sky, though the nations are terrified by them. For the customs of the peoples are worthless; they cut a tree out of the forest, and a craftsman shapes it with his chisel. They adorn it with silver and gold; they fasten it with hammer and nails so it will not totter. Like a scarecrow in a melon patch, their idols cannot speak; they must be carried because they cannot walk. Do not fear them; they can do no harm nor can they do any good" (Jer. 10:1–5).

B. Babylonian Idolatry

Both the image of Nebuchadnezzar's dream and the statue that he created for worship take the word *passim,* a word also used in Psalm 73:20: "As a dream when one awakes, so when you arise, O Lord, you will despise them as fantasies." The statue of this chapter represents the blatant idolatry of ancient Babylon. The Israelites played at idolatry now and again throughout most of their history after the release from Egypt; now God had placed them in two kingdoms (Assyria and Babylon) where idolatry was as common as breathing or eating.

Girdlestone says: "Idolatry in its first stage is a sort of symbolism. Some object is selected to represent the unseen Deity or to set forth one of his attributes. Little by little the material image takes the place of the spiritual reality for which it stands and idolatry ensues, bringing in its train that sensuality that is the sure attendant of every form of materialism" (Girdlestone, p. 328).

VII. TEACHING OUTLINE

A. INTRODUCTION

1. Lead Story: "Hail to the Chief!"
2. Context: We have no idea how many years elapsed between the end of chapter 2 and the beginning of chapter 3, but most scholars believe Daniel and his friends had been in their political posts for a few years. The chronology is not nearly as important as the theology that Daniel highlights by ending his record of the dream with Nebuchadnezzar's voiced allegiance to the God of gods and the Lord of kings and beginning chapter 3 with the notorious image of worship set up to himself. Nebuchadnezzar's behavior in chapter 3 also prepares us for his next dream of the great tree which appears in chapter 4.
3. Transition: Twice now Nebuchadnezzar has been confronted with the power of the God of heaven, but God still does not have his full attention. That will come in chapter 4 when the king finally comes to true awareness that "the Most High is sovereign over the kingdoms of men and gives them to anyone he wishes and sets over them the lowliest of men" (4:17).

B. COMMENTARY

1. Erection of the Golden Image (3:1–7)
2. Effect on the Three Jews (3:8–12)
3. Examination by the Great King (3:13–18)
4. Experience in the Fiery Furnace (3:19–26)
5. Elevation to the Royal Staff (3:27–30)

C. CONCLUSION: THE MADNESS OF KING GEORGE

VIII. ISSUES FOR DISCUSSION

1. What specific benefits did these three men receive from their strong faith?
2. In what ways does God call us to be faithful and courageous in our day?
3. What lessons can we draw from the way Daniel and his friends responded to the unreasonable demands of pagan government?
4. What spiritual lesson should we learn if Nebuchadnezzar did actually see Jesus in the furnace? What lesson if he saw an angel?

Daniel 4:1–18

The Green King

I. INTRODUCTION
Royal Tree Hugger

II. COMMENTARY
A verse-by-verse explanation of the chapter.

III. CONCLUSION
"A Masque of Reason"

An overview of the principles and applications from the chapter.

IV. LIFE APPLICATION
God's Sparrow

Melding the chapter to life.

V. PRAYER
Tying the chapter to life with God.

VI. DEEPER DISCOVERIES
Historical, geographical, and grammatical enrichment of the commentary.

VII. TEACHING OUTLINE
Suggested step-by-step group study of the chapter.

VIII. ISSUES FOR DISCUSSION
Zeroing the chapter in on daily life.

Quote

"Our personal relationship with God must be right,
or all else comes to naught.
It is like trying to add a lot of ciphers,
the sum of which is exactly nothing."

Christian Observer

Daniel 4:1–18

IN A NUTSHELL

God is in total control of his world and no human ruler, benevolent or evil, can resist or overturn his power.

The Green King

I. INTRODUCTION

Royal Tree Hugger

The chaotic ending to the 2000 presidential race ended up in multiple vote recounts for the state of Florida. Clearly prosperity topped the issues as Americans searched for the best candidate to provide them with more prescription drugs, better social security, more money for public education, some relief from skyrocketing college tuition costs, and, of course, a tax break of some type.

But charging around the country in the background was Ralph Nader, running as the candidate of the Green Party and drawing approximately 2 percent of the vote. Gathering favor mostly in the northwest, Nadar focused on environmental protection and attempted to draw the "tree hugger" vote away from Al Gore. Saving trees and growing more trees has become something of a focus for many Americans disturbed by pollution and the industrial savaging of the land.

Daniel 4 tells about an ancient tree hugger—Nebuchadnezzar. He not only dreamed about large trees; he also spent a lot of his time and money working with them. Ancient manuscripts tell us about his love for the cedar forests of Lebanon, his favorite place in the empire outside of Babylon itself. He imported beautiful cedar logs for the decoration of Babylonian buildings, and in the great metropolis of Babylon, he stored immense quantities of grain harvested from plants all across the empire. The city itself was decorated not only with magnificent buildings but also with great vegetation in a huge variety of sizes and shapes.

So in the dream of chapter 4, Nebuchadnezzar felt quite at home in the early stages and then quite disturbed when someone shouted, "Cut down the tree and trim off its branches" (4:14). He could hardly have known at the time of the dream, however, that he would not only be a lover and grower of trees but also a tree himself!

As we approach this chapter, we must prepare ourselves to see God working in tenderness and graciousness with a cruel and pagan monarch. All the kings in the Book of Daniel fall totally under God's control; Nebuchadnezzar is merely the first example. But in this chapter he becomes the universal and timeless prototype of someone allowed to run rampant over the people of God, then restrained by severe judgment, and finally redemptively corrected and restored to leadership.

That model is not out-of-date, even though the story may be over twenty-five hundred years old. In our day we see many holding places of leadership in the secular arena (or even in the church) whose behavior seems to deny any control by heavenly authority. Daniel 4:17 tells us of the futility of such a conclusion. This chapter was written "so the living may know that the Most High is sovereign over the kingdoms of men and gives them to anyone he wishes and sets over them the lowliest of men" (4:17).

II. COMMENTARY

The Green King

MAIN IDEA: *To deny the sovereignty of God in his world is to take sovereignty unto oneself, an attitude the great King of heaven will not tolerate. It is always better to humble oneself rather than wait for God's enforced disciplines of humility.*

A The Royal Explanation (4:1–8)

SUPPORTING IDEA: *When people are humbled by the hand of God, their attitudes and language change dramatically.*

4:1. Here we enter the only chapter in the Bible written by a pagan monarch. But that statement alone raises two questions: Did Nebuchadnezzar write it? And was he still a pagan at this time? Some scholars believe Daniel actually formed the wording of the chapter, though obviously the message comes directly from the king. He speaks throughout in the first person, and the document appears to be some kind of public paper circulated throughout **all the world**.

Some think this is just vintage Nebuchadnezzar, putting a personal spin on another one of his wild dreams and justifying his seven-year absence from the kingdom. Veldkamp says, "Apparently the poor man has returned to his senses and no longer lives like an animal, but he has not yet been cured of his insane pride and his desire for self-glorification!" (Veldkamp, 70). To the contrary Walvoord claims, "It may well be that this chapter brings Nebuchadnezzar to the place where he puts his trust in the God of Daniel. Even merely as a lesson in the spiritual progress of a man in the hands of God, this chapter is a literary gem" (Walvoord, *Daniel*, p. 95).

In either case the broad application of the passage as a part of Scripture cannot restrict it to this king alone. Here we learn that the Almighty God of the universe controls all kings, all nations, and all events in his world and does with them and through them whatever he wishes.

4:2–3. Quite remarkable in their direct praise of God, these two verses could form part of a worship service in any evangelical church. Veldkamp's emphasis on Nebuchadnezzar's ongoing pride and self-centeredness seems to fade a bit in light of this introduction to the dream event. Taken with verse 37, they make up the last will and testimony of the great king who will soon disappear from the pages of Daniel. From the text of this chapter, we cannot argue that Nebuchadnezzar experienced spiritual conversion, but at the very least he placed Daniel's God above the multitude of gods in the Babylonian pantheon, and what he did say he certainly got right.

God's power through Daniel in interpreting dreams and rescuing his three friends from the roaring furnaces of death provided dramatic evidence. But Nebuchadnezzar considered it inclusive until God dealt personally with him both in judgment and restoration. As Miller puts it: "At last Nebuchadnezzar had come to realize that Yahweh ('The Most High God'), not himself or the gods of Babylon, was sovereign. Through the experience recorded in this chapter, it was also graphically illustrated to him that his kingdom as well as his life could be taken away by the Lord at will" (Miller, p. 129).

4:4. One immediately gets the impression that the warrior king has begun to age, most of his enemies have been subdued, and things have calmed down in Babylon. Even the great construction projects and the overall greening of the city had perhaps been completed. Indeed, this ancient king sounds like a twenty-first-century American who just checked with his stockbroker and discovered that he has reason to be **contented and prosperous**. The KJV uses the words "flourishing in my palace," from a word used of plants and trees, quite an appropriate metaphor for this chapter.

Is there any way to determine when Nebuchadnezzar issued this decree? We know it was after he came back from the experience of insanity for seven years. We should probably conclude that it occurred toward the end of his reign. Leon Wood offers a helpful summary:

> Nebuchadnezzar ruled forty-three years (605–562 B.C.), and following his period of insanity, he was restored to his throne for at least a few months. This period of restoration does not appear to have been long, however, perhaps not more than a year. Twelve months elapsed following the dream until the beginning of the seven years of insanity (Dan. 4:29). Thus, one must add this year to the seven years of insanity, plus the approximate year of restoration to the throne, and subtract them from the total years of his reign to get the latest date in the reign for the dream. This works out to be the king's thirty-fourth year, which perhaps is the most likely date. If this is correct, then thirty-two years had elapsed since Nebuchadnezzar's first dream (which came in his second year), (Dan. 2:1), and Daniel was now about forty-nine years old (Wood, p. 57).

4:5. Despite the peace, prosperity, and contentment of Nebuchadnezzar's monarchial retirement, a new dream brought fear and terror. He was about to discover that the enemies outside, now subjugated by the might of his realm, were as nothing compared to the enemy inside (Prov. 16:32). It is difficult to tell from the grammar of the verse whether the dream came first, followed by the **images and visions** which he pondered after awakening. Perhaps the images and visions were a part of the overall dream. Such frivolous details should not distract us from the fact that once again the Most High God interrupted the life of a pagan monarch and communicated to him directly.

4:6–7. We learned this drill in chapter 2, so we are not surprised to see again the march of the wizards and the king's challenge laid before them. This time they were apparently not asked to recount the dream, so we wonder why they didn't offer some kind of interpretation. The text tells us that **they could not interpret it**, but that may be what they told the king. Most commentators suggest the symbolism of the dream was so negative that the wizards preferred not to tamper with it in any way lest the threat of extinction (which this time did not come with the initial challenge) might fall upon them if they predicted the king's violent demise.

But a larger question haunts us in this verse: Why didn't Daniel come in the first time with **all the wise men of Babylon**? We can only speculate here. Daniel was the dean of the faculty at this point, and he may have chosen to practice decentralized leadership and let the others try their hand first. Or he may have been deliberately detained by God and sent to the king at the appropriate moment of divine timing. Notice that in this case the king did not call for Daniel; he simply came later in response to the general summons.

4:8. Some interpreters have used Nebuchadnezzar's choice of the name **Belteshazzar** as indication that he still wanted to worship his own god. But that seems a rather flimsy argument. Daniel's official name at court, probably the one by which the king always addressed him, would surely be appropriate on a public document like this. Furthermore, the intent of the parenthesis seems to be a clear identification of the man extolled in this report. Belteshazzar would have been much more familiar to people "who live in all the world" (4:1) than Daniel would have been.

Of great importance in this verse is the phrase **the spirit of the holy gods is in him**. This phrase sets Daniel aside from the rest of the Chaldeans who worshiped multiple gods but whose gods were worthless. Even if we accept the idea that Nebuchadnezzar may have come to true worship of the one God at this point, we should not expect to see in him a fully developed theology of monotheism. Some argue that the word **gods** can be translated in the singular, but few scholars have chosen that option, and it seems hardly necessary in the context.

Indeed, if Nebuchadnezzar wanted to be his brazen, pagan old self, he likely would not have said, **Daniel came into my presence**, when he could have used Belteshazzar on that occasion. Clearly, this is a different attitude than we have seen in the king throughout earlier chapters.

B The Ruined Monarch (4:9–16)

SUPPORTING IDEA: *Sometimes God's judgment can be so severe that we wonder about his grace, but his intent is always ultimate redemption.*

4:9–11. Twenty-five centuries after Nebuchadnezzar, we still understand the great value and pleasure found in trees. They give us shade for cooling and fuel for warmth. They provide fruit for food and shelter from storms. Thousands of useful products, including the page you are now reading, come to us from wood.

Trees have great significance in the Bible. We are told in Genesis 2–3 about one tree that represented knowledge and another life. The first psalm tells us that blessed people are like trees planted in the right place. In Ezekiel 31 Assyria takes the form of the mighty cedar of Lebanon. Jesus told parables about trees; Paul compared Israel to an olive tree and the Gentiles to a grafted branch; the cross on which Jesus died had been a living tree (1 Pet. 2:24); and the final book of the Bible refers several times to the tree of life.

The striking thing about Nebuchadnezzar's tree was its height, which he described as **enormous** because **its top touched the sky**. We can hardly imagine what Nebuchadnezzar must have seen in order to say about this remarkable tree, **it was visible to the ends of the earth**.

Criswell reminds us how important this symbol had become in Nebuchadnezzar's culture: "Often the tree of paradise can be seen in Assyrian and Babylonian culture. The people carved it on gems, on ornaments, and on great buildings. It was seen everywhere and signified the power and regal authority of the monarch himself" (Criswell, 22).

4:12. The size of this tree hardly tells its entire story. The king tells us **its leaves were beautiful, its fruit abundant**. The tree provided **food for all** as well as **shelter** and **from it every creature was fed**. From our vantage point we understand from Daniel's interpretation that this verse describes Nebuchadnezzar himself and the benefits of his vast empire which spread far beyond its boundaries. To be sure, Nebuchadnezzar was not the king of all the earth, but he had certainly conquered all the provinces of the east. He can hardly be accused of overstating his control and influence, especially since he was merely describing a dream and probably did not yet know that God would apply the metaphor to him.

4:13. As Nebuchadnezzar tried to come to grips with the importance of this tree, he saw **a messenger, a holy one** approach the earth from heaven. The old King James text calls this figure a "watcher," also repeated in the RSV. We know from all of Scripture that angels are God's messengers; that is their primary task. No one doubts that is precisely what Nebuchadnezzar saw—one of God's *watchers* who was a holy messenger with a dramatic message.

Baldwin suggests that the watcher, like the tree, would have been a familiar figure to an ancient Babylonian king: "The idea of heavenly beings whose task it is to keep watch seems to have originated in Babylon (Ezk. 1:17,18; Zc. 1:10; 4:10). . . . This 'watcher,' like the Lord he serves, 'neither slumbers nor sleeps' (Ps. 121:4) and has power to make decrees and carry them out in order to bring home to men the fact that the Most High rules in human affairs. If the idea behind the term is pagan in origin, as commentators suggest, that is in keeping with the present context, though it is also true that Nebuchadnezzar equates them with 'holy ones' of heavenly origin, whatever he may have meant by these terms" (Baldwin, p. 112).

It is hardly any shock to Bible students that God can and does send angels to speak to whomever he wishes whenever he wishes a message sent.

4:14. This angel, however, lacks environmental sensitivity; every good thing about this tree would soon come to an end. Up to this point we have read little in the text that would threaten Nebuchadnezzar (4:5), but now this dream is getting dangerous. Remember Nebuchadnezzar had personally supervised the felling of hundreds of trees in Lebanon and transported them back to Babylon for use in his building projects. He had probably never heard a lumberjack shout "Timber!" But he had often heard that thunderous crash when one of God's giant plants hit the earth. At any rate, the great tree was history, and anyone or anything that found usefulness in it must now look somewhere else.

4:15–16. Only the stump and the roots remained, and whatever protruded above ground would be **bound with iron and bronze** just to sit there lifeless **in the grass of the field**. A metal band around tree stumps hardly preserves anything, so some scholars consider this (particularly in context of the words **grass** and **field**) to refer to the bondage of Nebuchadnezzar in his insanity.

Indeed, all of a sudden the neuter pronouns turn masculine, and the tree becomes a man! Of no dead stump would anyone ever say, **let his mind be changed from that of a man and let him be given the mind of an animal**, a statement surely calculated to increase the terror of this ancient king. The word for **mind** describes the inner self, often called *heart* throughout the Bible. It includes emotions and morality, the decisions of one's will, and the way one behaves. The intelligent and reasonable king, highly sophisticated for his time, would plunge into insanity and behave like an animal **among the plants of the earth**.

This judgment would be imposed **till seven times pass by for him**. The word for **times** is *iddanin,* which appears again in verses 23, 25, and 32 of this chapter. Virtually every serious commentator understands the meaning to be *years* rather than some indefinite amount of time. Seven is the Hebrew number of fulfillment or completion. To be sure, the word can refer to seasons, and we will have to deal with the designation again in our study.

Baldwin states curtly, "Its duration is uncertain, and this is intentional" (Baldwin, 112). Archer, on the other hand, speaks for most conservative commentators when he says that the word "in this instance undoubtedly refers to years" (Archer, p. 61). We need no dogmatism here; watch this phrase unfold throughout the Book of Daniel and come to your own conclusion.

C The Righteous Principle (4:17–18)

SUPPORTING IDEA: *When things look bleak and life seems hopeless, God is in control of his world.*

4:17. We have already observed that if we had to select a key verse for the Book of Daniel, we could probably do no better than 4:17. The central message of the book (apart from its distinctive prophecies) focuses right here, and it comes from the mouth of Nebuchadnezzar, relating the message of the angel who declared the destruction of the tree. But now we learn that this decision comes from multiple **messengers, the holy ones declare the verdict**.

Furthermore, we understand that this judgment upon the great tree which represents the great king has a distinct purpose: **so that the living may know that the Most High is sovereign over the kingdoms of men and gives them to anyone he wishes and sets over them the lowliest of men**. We see this theme often throughout Scripture (Ps. 24:1; Isa. 40:15; Acts 17:24,26; Rom. 13:1). Nebuchadnezzar had been selected to serve as God's vice regent on earth and had fouled his office by slaughtering thousands of people, including the Jews. Now it is time for punishment—another theme common to Scripture (Amos 1:3–13).

God controls human kingdoms, and he may choose to select humble rather than proud leaders. Nebuchadnezzar had propelled himself into the latter category. This was not a revolutionary thought in the seventh century B.C.; we find it as early as Job 5:11: "The lowly he sets on high, and those who mourn are lifted to safety." Have a look at this key verse through the creative heart and pen of Eugene Peterson: "The angels announce this decree, the holy watchman bring this sentence, so that everyone living will know that the High God rules human kingdoms. He arranges kingdom affairs however he wishes, and makes leaders out of losers" (*The Message*).

4:18. Nebuchadnezzar concluded his account of the dream by calling upon his chief advisor, now the dean of the faculty, to interpret it. This he could do, claimed the king, **because the spirit of the holy gods is in you**.

According to Veldkamp:

> In Psalm 72 we read that Christ will rule the poor in a just, wise and gentle way, and that he will give ear to their complaints. This gracious rule of Christ represents the norm for all human kings. The methods of violence, oppression and self-glorification used by the heathen dictator were *anti-Christian*. It was high time for him to repent of those sins and reflect something of the image of *Christ* by being gracious to the poor and wretched in his kingdom. The doctrine that rulers are God's servants applied to Nebuchadnezzar too. "By *me* kings reign and rulers decree what is just" (Prov. 8:15 NRSV) (Veldkamp, pp. 73–74).

MAIN IDEA REVIEW: *To deny the sovereignty of God in his world is to take sovereignty unto oneself, an attitude the great King of heaven will not tolerate. It is always better to humble oneself rather than wait for God's enforced disciplines of humility.*

III. CONCLUSION

"A Masque of Reason"

In his delightful and refreshing little devotional book on Job, Henry Gariepy offers a chapter entitled "Not Why, But Who," which he begins with a recitation of a stanza from Robert Frost's poem, "A Masque of Reason." The lengthy poem offers an imaginary dialogue in heaven after Job's arrival following his years of suffering and blessing on earth. God says to Job:

> Oh I remember you well: you're Job, My patient.
> I've had you on My mind a thousand years
> To thank you someday for the way you helped Me
> Establish once for all the principle that
> There is no connection man can reason out

> Between his just desserts and what he gets.
> Virtue may fail and wickedness succeed.
> 'Twas a great demonstration we put on (Gariepy, p. 205).

Such was Nebuchadnezzar's lesson as well. His life, suffering, and relationship to the Most High God were considerably different from those of the ancient saint, but he became the unwitting and unwilling teammate of the Lord in accomplishing heavenly purposes on earth. Perhaps we cannot emphasize too many times that Daniel 4:17 is the key to the book: "For this has been decreed by the Watchers, demanded by the Holy Ones. The purpose of this decree is that all the world may understand that the Most High dominates the kingdoms of the world, and gives them to anyone he wants to, even the lowliest of men!" (TLB).

PRINCIPLES

- Successful people, even Christians, can become like Nebuchadnezzar when they experience too much success and too much praise from others.
- Material prosperity is not always a mark of God's blessing on one's life.
- Expect earthly leaders to fail us and let their failures force us into the arms of the living God.
- Public praise and testimony are the proper responses when God has rescued us or in some other way shown his grace.

APPLICATIONS

- If a pagan king like Nebuchadnezzar can praise God publicly, we should certainly be able to do so.
- Let's live in such a way that God will not have to humiliate us in order to bring us to repentance and righteousness.
- How important it is to humble ourselves before God does so.

IV. LIFE APPLICATION

God's Sparrow

My friend Les Flynn tells great stories, and this one requires no editing or paraphrasing: it can speak to us just the way he wrote it.

> One night a man was speeding down a highway when he fell asleep at the wheel. Soon his glassy stare was fixed on the centerline. For a while he held the steering wheel like a robot racing through the June, moonlit night.
>
> Suddenly a sharp pain in his chest jolted him awake. It was just in time, for looming out of the darkness were two headlights, and he was on the wrong side of the road, heading right toward them. He jerked his steering wheel to the right. He almost lost control of his car. A huge truck zoomed by, missing him by inches. He pulled off the pavement, limp.
>
> After regaining his calm, he opened the door to get out. As he stood up, an object fell from his lap to the ground. He stooped to pick up the still form of a little bird! As he held the small brown form in his hand, he remembered the pain which had struck his chest and aroused him just in time to avoid the accident. A sparrow had somehow made a flight in the night, which sparrows seldom do, and had darted into the open window of the speeding automobile, striking him in the chest with sufficient force to awaken him. It was the split-second timing of Providence. It was God's sparrow and the man knew it. Just then the bird fluttered into consciousness and flew into the night (Flynn, p. 192).

Nebuchadnezzar the Great was cruising on a collision course with hell. With the exception of a few carelessly uttered religious aphorisms, his entire life had been devoted to pillaging, looting, murdering, punishing, kidnapping, and pride. But now he saw God's tree, and more importantly, God's angel sent to wake him up and, after suitable punishment, restore him to world leadership.

How rarely we see world leaders today acknowledging God's sparrows, God's trees, or God's angels as warnings along the way. We have no idea why God forced Hitler to commit suicide in his bunker while Mao Tse Tung lived to a despicable old age. We do know that though God sends warnings, he in no way compels positive response to those warnings. Nebuchadnezzar could have done his time in the field and come back as rebellious and hateful as he was in earlier days.

The great lesson of this chapter is God's control over his world, but the secondary lesson shows how important it is for us to acknowledge the Lord's dominion over our lives. Pastors should be careful about phrases like "my church" or "my congregation." Christian college and seminary presidents should not look out across campus and marvel at the wonderful buildings their great fund-raising schemes have erected. Missionaries should never assume their brilliant strategies of evangelism account for unusual numbers of believers in any given area of service. God is sovereign in all the works and happenings of his world.

V. PRAYER

Father, thank you for showing us through Nebuchadnezzar that all earthly rulers, even those whose behavior we may despise, exist under the permissive hand of your almighty power. Amen.

VI. DEEPER DISCOVERIES

A. Textual Variations

Some minor squabbling goes on about the early verses of this chapter, which the ancient Hebrew version of the Old Testament connects to the end of chapter 3 (thereby putting Nebuchadnezzar's praise at the end of the fiery furnace adventure rather than in the announcement of the tree dream). The Greek Old Testament (Septuagint) corrects this problem, however, and most conservative scholars follow the Septuagint in this choice. Verse 37 connects so tightly with verses 1–3 that they virtually serve as bookends for the chapter itself and compact its record quite nicely.

On a far more serious note, liberal critics who argue for a much later authorship date of this book cannot accept the record of the chapter, arguing that such an experience could never happen to an ancient monarch. Therefore, they conclude, this book must be a second-century forgery. Any minor problem with the text feeds their substandard view of Scripture, and the difference between the Septuagint and the Masoretic text becomes an issue.

We have already dealt with the date of the writing of this book and need not return there now. Suffice it to say that if one accepts the ability and authority of Almighty God to break into human history, the record of this chapter presents not the slightest problem.

B. The Eternal Kingdom

Nebuchadnezzar could never pass the entrance exam to a legitimate seminary, but he had finally achieved a solid hold on the difference between flimsy and fragile earthly kingdoms, however great their apparent power at the moment. He had also grasped the truth of the eternal and heavenly kingdom of God whose dominion endures from generation to generation. God's kingdom is timeless since he is eternal; it had no beginning, and it will have no end. In this we distinguish between the eternal kingdom and that portion of it which forms the millennial kingdom on earth.

Pentecost writes:

> What has made this troublesome for many is that throughout the Bible there seem to be numerous contradictions concerning the kingdom over which God rules. On one hand the kingdom is described in terms that are strictly eternal—but on the other hand it is described as temporal, with a definite historical beginning, progress, and termination. In the same way, in some passages it is depicted as universal, while in others it is clearly local. Further, the kingdom of God on many occasions is seen to be the direct administration of the sovereignty of God, while in other instances it is characterized as an indirect administration for appointed administrators (Pentecost, p. 15).

All this is true. God has rulership, a realm, and absolute authority. Nebuchadnezzar, of course, had no concept of the millennial kingdom on earth with its temporality and time limitations; he saw only the universal kingdom. McClain reminds us:

> Nothing lies outside its vast reach and scope. It includes all things in space and time; in earth, in heaven, and in hell. The nations of the earth may rebel, follow other gods, even deny the existence of the true God; but all to no avail; Jehovah is still the "King of nations" (Jer. 10:7 KJV). Nebuchadnezzar, made the golden head of an ancient world empire by divine appointment, forgets the heavenly source of his authority; and so he is cut down from his throne by the judgment of God (McClain, p. 24).

VII. TEACHING OUTLINE

A. INTRODUCTION

1. Lead Story: Royal Tree Hugger
2. Context: Unlike some Bible writers, Daniel rarely offers chronological helps, so with inference alone we sense the passage of time between the end of chapter 3 and the beginning of chapter 4. Daniel ends his treatment of Nebuchadnezzar with this chapter and moves on to his successor. In our study we have treated only half the chapter and now look forward to Daniel's interpretation of this great tree dream.
3. Transition: Every word of Daniel 4:1–18 is spoken by the king. Now it is Daniel's turn, and we shall see how God makes good on his announcement of Nebuchadnezzar's humiliation.

B. COMMENTARY

1. The Royal Explanation (4:1–8)
2. The Ruined Monarch (4:9–16)
3. The Righteous Principle (4:17–18)

C. CONCLUSION: "A MASQUE OF REASON"

VIII. ISSUES FOR DISCUSSION

1. What might Nebuchadnezzar have meant by his reference to "signs" and "wonders" in verse 3?
2. What world leaders can we identify in the past two thousand years with whom God has dealt in a way that is similar to his judgment on Nebuchadnezzar?
3. Apart from the sovereignty of God over all the affairs of his world, what other lessons for Christian living can we learn in this chapter?

Daniel 4:19–37

A Man Outstanding in His Field

I. INTRODUCTION
God's Tree

II. COMMENTARY
A verse-by-verse explanation of the chapter.

III. CONCLUSION
Bending a Soul
An overview of the principles and applications from the chapter.

IV. LIFE APPLICATION
The Ultimate Bad Day
Melding the chapter to life.

V. PRAYER
Tying the chapter to life with God.

VI. DEEPER DISCOVERIES
Historical, geographical, and grammatical enrichment of the commentary.

VII. TEACHING OUTLINE
Suggested step-by-step group study of the chapter.

VIII. ISSUES FOR DISCUSSION
Zeroing the chapter in on daily life.

Quote

"The worth of life is not to be measured by its results and achievement or success, but solely by the motives of one's heart and the effort of one's will."

George Seaver

Daniel 4:19–37

IN A NUTSHELL

This is our Father's world. Nothing and no one can thwart or alter his schedule of events. Nebuchadnezzar had it exactly right: God does as he pleases with the powers of heaven and the peoples of earth.

A Man Outstanding in His Field

I. INTRODUCTION

God's Tree

I learned the poem in grade school over fifty years ago, and it still remains lodged in my brain. Its beautiful simplicity directs one's attention to the literal "bottom line" in this much-loved and very American poem.

Alfred Joyce Kilmer was born in New Brunswick, New Jersey, in 1886. He served on the staff of the *New Standard Dictionary* as well as various other periodicals and was killed in France during World War I. He wrote many poems and published three different collections. *Trees* appeared in 1914, and its lyric flow won instant popularity.

> I think that I shall never see
> A poem lovely as a tree.
> A tree whose hungry mouth is pressed
> Against the earth's sweet flowing breast;
> A tree that looks at God all day,
> And lifts her leafy arms to pray.
>
> A tree that may in Summer wear
> A nest of robins in her hair;
> Upon whose bosom snow has lain;
> Who intimately lives with rain.
> Poems are made by fools like me,
> But only God can make a tree.

Daniel 4 tells us about Nebuchadnezzar, God's tree in Babylon. The great king had used thousands of trees, for construction and cosmetic decoration of his grand city, but now he would live like one—out in the field, intimately living with rain. Only God can make a tree, and only God can make a king. Nebuchadnezzar did not yet know this truth, but in seven years it would be clear to him.

II. COMMENTARY

A Man Outstanding in His Field

MAIN IDEA: *The theological message of this chapter centers in the truth of verse 25: "The Most High is sovereign over the kingdoms of men and gives them to anyone he wishes." The spiritual message resides in verse 27: "Renounce your sins by doing what is right, and your wickedness by being kind to the oppressed."*

A Identification of the Great Tree (4:19–22)

SUPPORTING IDEA: *When dealing with people in authority, respect and courtesy pave the way for understanding and agreement.*

4:19. Daniel immediately sensed trouble in River City, but translators have rendered his emotions in a variety of ways. The NIV chooses **perplexed** and **terrified**; the KJV "astonied" and "troubled"; the MLB says Daniel was "stunned" and "his thoughts appalling"; TLB chooses "stunned" and "silent"; and the RSV, "dismayed" and "alarmed." Furthermore, the KJV claims the experience lasted "for one hour" and the RSV "for a moment." The textual decision belongs to the reader, but a full hour seems unjustified as a translation for *saah*. This is not the same word as "times" in 4:16. Daniel did not offer a knee-jerk reaction to the king's dream but pondered the meaning for a while. At the least he found the implications for both king and kingdom quite frightening.

Any who wish to interpret some hostile motive for Nebuchadnezzar's use of "Belteshazzar" in 4:8–9 should notice that Daniel himself uses it here. This is no more complex than the variation on Saul and Paul in the New Testament where *Paul* commonly appears in Palestinian surroundings and *Saul* in the Gentile or Greek-speaking world. To be sure, Saul and Paul mean essentially the same thing, and he carried both of those names all his life. Daniel also had two names, and the one most commonly used in Babylon for decades had been **Belteshazzar**.

Politely, Daniel expressed his genuine desire that the dream would be fulfilled by someone other than the king he had come to respect. There seems to be no reason in the text for attributing political flattery to the prophet in what was commonly an appropriate way to address a reigning monarch.

4:20–22. Repeating the basic details of the dream, Daniel came rather quickly to the point—**you, O king, are that tree!** In 4:15–16 we clearly saw that the tree was something more than vegetation; a man's mind and life were involved in this prophecy. Possibly Nebuchadnezzar saw something of himself in the dream, but we can hardly argue that point from the text. Now, however, the key to interpretation is clear. Like the tree, this king had **become great and strong**, and his significance in the Asian world had **grown until it reaches the sky**. Coming up in this chapter is the famous statement of the king, "Is not this the great Babylon I have built . . . by my mighty power and for the glory of my majesty?" (4:30), hardly an exaggeration by the standards of the seventh century B.C.

We pause as we hear Daniel say to the king, **your dominion extends to distant parts of the earth**. The difficulty lies in the word **earth**, with which Archer helps us significantly:

> Here it seems to refer to the farthest reaches of the Semitic world as established by the earliest empires of Hammurabi's Babylon and the eight-century Assyrian rulers. Undoubtedly the region of Media to the northeast and of Elam, Persia, and India were well known to the Near East as totally distinct cultures from those of Mesopotamia and points west. But in designating the extent of empire in the Mesopotamian orbit, the custom of defining the limits of civilization as extending to the borders of Elam was at least as early as a Third Dynasty of Ur. Back in the Sumerian era, King Amar-Enzu referred to himself as *lugal dubdalimmubak* ("King of the Four Quarters" of the earth) in his dedicatory building inscriptions, even though his empire was far more circumscribed than Nebuchadnezzar's (Archer, p. 63).

In short, limitations on our understanding of Nebuchadnezzar's power and influence must be defined only in geographical terms, not in ways related to the completeness of his power and control.

B Interpretation of the Frightening Dream (4:23–27)

SUPPORTING IDEA: *True repentance that leads to restoration is demonstrated by both attitude and behavior, often to those who are less privileged.*

4:23–24. Again Daniel reviewed the details of the dream, but now we learn that the decree "announced by messengers" (4:17) actually originated with **the Most High**. We should remember that this expression means a good deal more in Daniel's use than in Nebuchadnezzar's. Again we encounter the words **seven times** and again we should understand them to be years. Wood says: "The word cannot be taken to mean a shorter period of time, such as days or even months, for neither would be long enough to be meaningful. A period of seven years, however, fits well with the idea behind the phrase, namely, the full cycle of seasons, with all their changes and types of weather, were made to *pass over* the king seven different times" (Wood, *Daniel,* p. 61).

One more thought is new to these verses: the decree has been **issued against my lord the king**. Nebuchadnezzar had ground to dust a variety of enemies beneath the wheels of his chariots, but now he had met a power whom he could not defeat, One who has never been defeated and will never know that experience.

4:25. Here comes the specific interpretation of the destroyed tree. Nebuchadnezzar would have his branches stripped, his fruit scattered, and all who had lived under his protection and rule dispersed. He would lose his mind so thoroughly that no mental institution of his time could care for him, and he would live like an animal for seven years. The goal of this punishment could not be more clear: **until you acknowledge that the Most High is sovereign over the kingdoms of men and gives them to anyone he wishes**. Nebuchadnezzar became the original prodigal son; making bad choices about himself in relation to others, he ended up with the animals.

We might call this *conditional punishment.* As harsh as the sentence may seem to us, God chose grace rather than vengeance. Before the insanity came, Nebuchadnezzar knew that it would end. Very close to this point in history another prophet predicted doom for another pagan monarch as Ezekiel explained God's dealing with the Pharaoh of Egypt (Ezek. 30:20–31:18). In the fascinating irony of God's plan, Nebuchadnezzar had been the instrument in his hands to punish Pharaoh. The similarity of the prophecies clearly emphasizes again the central theme of the Book of Daniel.

4:26. Then we see something about the strange retention of the stump. Normally a king who became insane would lose his kingdom. Rivals within or without his own family would seize power immediately in some kind of palace coup. But since God had promised Nebuchadnezzar he would return from the fields, he also told him that his kingdom would be **restored** to him. But the promise, like the punishment, was conditional; Babylon would come back under Nebuchadnezzar's control only when he would **acknowledge that Heaven rules**.

This verse fascinates Old Testament scholars because only here in the Old Testament does the word **Heaven** substitute for God. In Matthew we see *kingdom of heaven* and *kingdom of God* used interchangeably, but that is most unusual in the Old Testament. The conditional redemption of Daniel 4:36 offers a shade of background for the familiar Romans 10:9: "That if you confess with your mouth, 'Jesus is Lord,' and believe in your heart that God raised him from the dead, you will be saved."

4:27. The sermon has ended; now it's time for the invitation. The aging prophet-statesman had no wish to see his king living in dementia, so he offered a way out before it was too late: **Renounce your sins by doing what is right, and your wickedness by being kind to the oppressed**. The final phrase of this verse indicates that Daniel had no special revelation from God that this escape clause might be available. Indeed, everything we know about the dream up to this point indicates its full completion. Nevertheless, servants of God should always emphasize his grace even when explaining his judgment.

Some will argue that this verse teaches salvation by works. Indeed, the Latin Vulgate renders the offer, "Cancel thy sins by deeds of charities and thy inquiries by deeds of kindness to the poor." But the Vulgate reflects the thinking of its time, a theology which still prevails to the present hour in a variety of forms. The clear message of the Bible never offers God's grace in exchange for good deeds. Furthermore, Nebuchadnezzar's spiritual condition was not at stake here but rather the ongoing of his kingdom uninterrupted by the punishment of insanity.

Walvoord states it in one clear sentence: "Nebuchadnezzar is not promised forgiveness on the ground of good works or alms to the poor; but rather the issue is that, if he is a wise and benevolent king, he would alleviate the necessity of God's intervening with immediate judgment because of Nebuchadnezzar's pride" (Walvoord, *Daniel*, p. 106).

 Implementation of the Pending Judgment (4:28–33)

SUPPORTING IDEA: *God's commands allow no one to handle them carelessly, not the greatest ruling monarch of his day, and not the lowliest peasant of his realm.*

4:28–30. Like many before and many more after him, Nebuchadnezzar walked out of the meeting unconverted. He respected his prophet and listened politely to the interpretation, but he essentially said, "This gospel is not for me. I don't believe in a God who would punish people who don't follow his commands or listen to his word." So the Lord gave the king one more year which he probably spent admiring all the wonders of his reign, including the magnificent palace of Babylon with its high walkways, stone pillars, and hanging gardens. The green king had created an outdoor arboretum on the roof of his palace, and he was, to say the least, very pleased with himself.

But personal pride that locks God out of one's achievements leads to spiritual ruin. In Nebuchadnezzar's view everything he saw from his imperial balcony came about **by my mighty power and for the glory of my majesty**. Every extrabiblical source that deals with the history of Babylon confirms this attitude in the heart of the king. Humanly speaking, he had a great deal to admire and a good reason to be proud; Babylon was one of the great wonders of the world (see "Deeper Discoveries"). But God shares his glory with no one, especially not with one who had been warned a year earlier that his wicked pride would bring about certain punishment.

4:31–32. Daniel used a gripping phrase to tell us the instant judgment of God: **the words were still on his lips**. The king had refused to acknowledge "that Heaven rules" (4:26) so he heard a voice **from heaven** confirming the loss of the kingdom and the dreaded fate of uncontrollable insanity. He was not carefully whisked from the palace in an ambulance after his aides dialed 911; he was literally **driven away from people**. In the ancient pagan world, people often treated insane people like the person or object they claimed to be. If Nebuchadnezzar began acting like a wild animal, he may have been placed in some zoological park or just allowed to roam free wherever he wished to go.

The text does not tell us who assumed control of the kingdom for seven years, but certainly Daniel had to be a leading candidate for that choice. He was, in effect, the secretary of state or prime minister, and we know that

Nebuchadnezzar's son Evil-Merodach did not take command during that time. Some have speculated that Daniel's love and care for his monarch led to some carefully constructed and restricted area inside the palace grounds where the demented king could roam out of the sight of his subjects.

We can't leave verse 32 without noticing the third recitation of a phrase that carries this chapter and the entire book: **the Most High is sovereign over the kingdoms of men and gives them to anyone he wishes** (see 4:17,25).

4:33. Often people who lose their mental faculties slip slowly into that horrible state. Alzheimer's disease, for example, tends to eat away at one's mental capacity for years before it brings final destruction. Not so with Nebuchadnezzar. Daniel tells us that **immediately what had been said about Nebuchadnezzar was fulfilled**. He looked like an ox, and he ate like an ox; the grand and glorious king became a repulsive animal.

According to Archer:

> Physically he became like the brute beast he imagined himself to be, as his skin toughened into hide through constant exposure to outdoor weather at all seasons (the temperature in modern Iraq ranges from a high of 110 or 120 degrees Fahrenheit in summer—usually with high humidity—to a low of well below freezing in winter). Most particularly the hair of his head and his body, becoming matted and coarse, looked like eagle feathers; his fingernails and toenails, never cut, became like claws. So the boasting king, a victim of what is known as zoanthropy [see "Deeper Discoveries"], sank to a subhuman level (Archer, p. 66).

D Intervention of the Most High (4:34–37)

SUPPORTING IDEA: *When God punishes, the punishment is swift and sure; when God restores, the restoration is complete.*

4:34–35. How interesting that Daniel tells us Nebuchadnezzar raised his **eyes toward heaven**. As if on cue, the time of punishment ended, and this pitiful creature, stimulated by divine impulse, looked upward for deliverance. We notice also that the third-person narrative concludes and Nebuchadnezzar once again spoke for himself. God healed his mind, and, in good biblical form, he used it first for praise.

We have no strict confirmation that Nebuchadnezzar became a believer in any sense we would use that word. That is certainly possible but not verifiable. However, he certainly did meet God's requirement to acknowledge that the kingdom of heaven dominates all the kingdoms of earth. The king's brief benediction could be read or recited in any evangelical church, since it is completely in line with the biblical understanding of God. One could argue that this pagan monarch acted in accordance with whatever light he had.

This ancient king finally closed his hands around one of the most important doctrines of the Bible, a truth which permeates the Book of Daniel from beginning to end: God is sovereign in his world, and he **does as he pleases with the powers of heaven and the peoples of the earth**. Some people, even Christians, find this description of God's character somewhat uncomfortable. Others wonder how God allows the persecution of Christians around the world, the endless slaughter of the unborn and even infants, and the wicked cruelty that occurs everywhere we look. The answer lies in God's *permissiveness*, not his *determination*.

Boice points out:

> The explanation of the seeming contradiction is that human rebellion, while it is in opposition to God's expressed command, falls within His eternal or hidden purpose. That is, God permits sin for His own reasons, knowing in advance that He will bring sin to judgment in the day of His wrath and that in the meantime it will not go beyond the bounds that He has fixed for it. Many things work against the sovereignty of God—from our perspective. But from God's perspective, His decrees are always established. They are, in fact, as the Westminster Shorter Catechism describes them, "His eternal purpose, according to the council of His will, whereby, for His own glory, He has foreordained whatsoever comes to pass" (Boice, p. 152).

4:36–37. Gifts from the Most High continue to multiply—sanity, honor, splendor, and monarchial power **even greater than before**. One can imagine that Nebuchadnezzar, knowing what had happened to him and how it must have appeared to members of his court, returned to the throne with great concern. But God's full restoration pleased the king greatly and he tells us, **My advisors and nobles sought me out**.

Christian leaders need to look hard at this chapter for personal application as well as sound theology. How often we practice defensiveness and turf-guarding, trying to make sure we hold on to whatever authority and power we might have. Pastors boast about surviving votes of confidence, and politicians spend millions of dollars in order to be elected to office. But there is one Lord of the church, and there is one Most High God over all the earth. Every Christian in trouble, struggling to maintain or regain identity and purpose in life, can find hope in this chapter.

As Archer reminds us, this is precisely the position of the thousands of exiled Jews at the very time this event occurred:

> They might well have wondered whether the God of Abraham, Moses, and Elijah was truly alive and able to stand before the triumphant Gentile nations that had reduced his holy city, Jerusalem, to rubble and his holy temple to ashes. It would have been easy for them to conclude, as all the pagan observers assumed, that the Hebrew nation had been so completely crushed and uprooted from their native land because their God was too weak to defend them from the might of the gods of Babylon: Marduk, Nebo, and Bel. . . . The captive Jews needed to know that even the apparently limitless power of Nebuchadnezzar was under the control of the Lord God Almighty, who still cared for them and had a great future for them in their land. Therefore, each episode recorded in the first six chapters concludes with a triumphant demonstration of God's sovereignty and faithfulness and his ability to crush the pride of unconverted mankind (Archer, p. 68).

MAIN IDEA REVIEW: *The theological message of this chapter centers in the truth of verse 25: "The Most High is sovereign over the kingdoms of men and gives them to anyone he wishes." The spiritual message resides in verse 27: "Renounce your sins by doing what is right, and your wickedness by being kind to the oppressed."*

III. CONCLUSION

Bending a Soul

Born in 1812, Robert Browning became the benchmark poet for the dramatic monologue school, a literary composition in which the speaker reveals his or her own character. Browning had no formal education after the age of fourteen but published his first book of poetry at the age of twenty-one. His marriage to Elizabeth Barrett in 1846 necessitated a move from England to the more favorable climate of Florence, Italy, where they both continued to write until Elizabeth died sixteen years later. Today Robert Browning is considered one of the major poets of the Victorian era, admired not only for his careful style but also for his great psychological insight into human personality.

In his famous *Rabbi Ben Ezra,* Browning wrote thirty-two verses that attack the flesh and, quite frankly, youth. He elevates the importance of age when soul and flesh are no longer enemies and some sense of harmony can settle upon the human being. Age is not just the latter half of life, but the very best of life—hence the opening line, "Grow old along with me! The best is yet to be, the last of life, for which the first was made."

Nebuchadnezzar never read Robert Browning, but if he had, his reflection in Daniel 4 might have found him nodding amiably over stanzas XXVIII and XXXIII.

> He fixed thee 'mid this dance.
> Of plastic circumstance,
> This Present, thou, forsooth, would fain arrest:
> Machinery just meant
> To give thy soul its bent,
> Try thee and turn thee forth, sufficiently impressed.
>
> So, take and use thy work:
> Amend what flaws may lurk,
> What strain o' the stuff, what warpings past the aim!
> My times be in thy hand!
> Perfect the cup as planned!
> Let age approve of youth, and death complete the same!

"All's well that ends well," Shakespeare said. We have increasingly learned in Christian circles that one of the major challenges of serving Christ is to finish well, indeed to finish. If the last verse of Daniel 4 genuinely reflects Nebuchadnezzar's attitude in his declining years, we have every reason to believe his soul had been bent by the divine craftsman and he ended his life well.

PRINCIPLES

- The sad state of secular success drives a person from God and turns his focus inward rather than upward.
- God always prefers voluntary cooperation with his will rather than enforced discipline.
- Christians must always proclaim the message of redemption as a major part of the message of judgment against sin.
- True friends remain faithful even when those they advise do not take that advice.

APPLICATIONS

- Let every sense of personal accomplishment and achievement find its satisfaction in the knowledge that God has produced it.
- Proclaim the gospel as the reasonable solution to the madness and chaos of this world.
- Never allow the necessities of your service for God to distract you from common courtesy and civility.
- Remember that when God punishes with a gracious purpose, the end is better than the beginning.

IV. LIFE APPLICATION

The Ultimate Bad Day

Don't ask me to verify the story, but I read that fire authorities found a corpse in a burned-out section of forest while assessing the damage done by a forest fire. The deceased male was dressed in a full wet suit, complete with SCUBA tanks on his back, flipper, and a face mask. The pathology lab determined that the person died not from burns but from massive internal injuries. But what on earth would a fully clad diver be doing in the middle of a forest fire?

A check of dental records revealed that on the very day of the fire, the victim was diving off the coast of California about twenty miles away from the forest. Fire-fighting helicopters with their large dip buckets scooped water from the ocean, flew to the forest fire, and dumped it. One minute the diver was breaking the surface of the Pacific, and the next minute he found himself in a dip bucket three hundred feet in the air (adapted from the *California Examiner,* 3/20/98).

True, Nebuchadnezzar's bad day did not result in death by violence, but his life changed just as quickly. One minute he was parading on the palace roof admiring the brilliance of Babylon, and the next he had no control over his senses or his behavior. We have all seen death strike instantly and without warning. We have all seen a common headache diagnosed as brain cancer. We have all known people whose lives have been ransacked by tragedy at a moment when they least expected it.

This chapter teaches us readiness and repentance—readiness to give God the glory for everything in our lives and to praise him for all his blessings; repentance to judge our sin and wickedness and to do what is right.

The title of this chapter comes from an old joke commonly heard around the Midwest some years ago: "What is the definition of a farmer?" The answer—"A man out standing in his field." Many farmers are outstanding in their field in the best sense of that phrase. Nebuchadnezzar encountered the worst day of his life as he went from being a man outstanding in his field to a man out standing in his field.

Biblical Christians depend upon God for their very next breath and take nothing in the future for granted. James put it as well as anyone: "Now listen, you who say, 'Today or tomorrow we will go to this or that city, spend a year there, carry on business and make money.' Why, you do not even know what will happen tomorrow. What is your life? You are a mist that appears for a little while and then vanishes. Instead, you ought to say, 'If it is the Lord's will, we will live and do this or that'" (Jas. 4:13–15).

V. PRAYER

Father, in the words of the ancient king, we praise you, honor you, and glorify you as the one who lives forever. Your dominion is an eternal dominion; your kingdom endures from generation to generation. May we be constantly aware of your omnipotent control of our lives. Amen.

VI. DEEPER DISCOVERIES

A. The Royal Palace of Babylon (4:29)

We noted earlier that Nebuchadnezzar had, by human standards, every reason to be proud of his achievements. Extrabiblical sources provide volumes of information about the building projects of Babylon. Excavations of the area over the past century authenticate almost everything we had known earlier, especially the gigantic palace and the massive planting projects.

Josephus wrote of Nebuchadnezzar:

> So when he had thus fortified the city with walls, after an excellent manner, and had adorned the gates magnificently, he added a new palace to that which his father had dwelt in, and this close by it also, and that more eminent in its height, and in its great splendor. It would perhaps require too long of a narration, if anyone were to describe it. However, as prodigiously large and magnificent as it was, it was finished in 15 days. Now in this palace he erected very high walks, supported by stone pillars, and by planting what was called a *pensile paradise,* and replenishing it with all sorts of trees, he rendered to the prospect of an exact resemblance of a mountainous country (Josephus, p. 613).

The great Hanging Gardens of Babylon were identified by the Greeks as one of the seven wonders of the ancient world. From the roof of his palace, Nebuchadnezzar could look down on the main drag, a processional boulevard lined with brightly colored enameled brick adorned with images of bulls and dragons. According to Miller: "Many outstanding achievements may be attributed to Nebuchadnezzar, but sadly he failed to give God the glory for his blessings. His heart was filled with pride and self-importance and he began to boast of his own greatness and ability. . . . In his pride the king took for himself the glory that rightly belonged to God and invited divine judgment" (Miller, p. 141).

B. Zoanthropy (4:33)

Zoanthropy, sometimes identified as *insania zoanthropica,* describes the condition of insanity in which people think of themselves as animals, particularly an ox. What happened to Nebuchadnezzar was divinely caused but became in itself a known if uncommon disease. This would be similar to lycanthropy, the famous werewolf syndrome of which cheap Halloween movies are made. It describes the supposedly magical ability to assume the form and characteristics of a wolf. Zoanthropy and lycanthropy, though different, tend to be similar in the nature of the affliction. One could argue in modern terms that Nebuchadnezzar had come down with "mad cow disease."

C. Nebuchadnezzar's Conversion (4:37)

We have asked throughout the commentary on this chapter whether Nebuchadnezzar's final "confession of faith" indicates whether he actually became an Old Testament believer in Jehovah. Commentators are by no means agreed on this point, so let me offer a brief sample.

> The head of gold (2:38) had bowed in humble submission to the God of Daniel (Archer, p. 67).
>
> Inasmuch as in all ages some men are saved without gaining completely the perspective of faith or being entirely correct in the content of their beliefs, it is entirely possible that Nebuchadnezzar will be among the saints (Walvoord, *Daniel,* p. 112).
>
> This impersonal reference to God keeps Him at a distance and this last word of Nebuchadrezzar in the book, while formally acknowledging the power and justice of God, appears to fall short of penitence and true faith (Baldwin, p. 116).
>
> When all matters are taken together, it seems more probable that he did exercise personal faith than that he did not (Wood, *Daniel,* p. 65).
>
> Indeed the whole aim of this central section of the book of Daniel is to raise this issue of personal salvation. In this chapter one king is saved because he faces it squarely and answers with repentance and faith (Wallace, p. 85).

Clearly I agree with the majority. Salvation is a matter of the heart, and God apparently changed Nebuchadnezzar's heart so that words of accurate and honest praise could come from his mouth.

VII. TEACHING OUTLINE

A. INTRODUCTION

1. Lead Story: "God's Tree"
2. Context: Daniel 4 flows out of the context of the first three chapters. One lesson above all others has confronted us in all four of these chapters: We must worship "the King of heaven, because everything he does is right and all his ways are just."
3. Transition: Daniel offers no transition between chapter 4 and chapter 5. In 4:37 Nebuchadnezzar is alive, well, prosperous, and powerful. At the beginning of chapter 5, King Belshazzar gives a great banquet.

B. COMMENTARY

1. Identification of the Great Tree (4:19–22)
2. Interpretation of the Frightening Dream (4:23–27)
3. Implementation of the Pending Judgment (4:28–33)
4. Intervention of the Most High (4:34–37)

C. CONCLUSION: BENDING A SOUL

VIII. ISSUES FOR DISCUSSION

1. In light of the controversy over whether Nebuchadnezzar was converted, what similar cases can you recall from Old Testament times?
2. Why do you think prosperity is such a dominant concept in our modern world?
3. In addition to the ongoing lesson of God's sovereignty, what other applications to Christian life and service do you see in this chapter?

Daniel 5:1–16

Oddity at the Orgy

I. INTRODUCTION
The Night of Bad Calls

II. COMMENTARY
A verse-by-verse explanation of the chapter.

III. CONCLUSION
God Can Find You

An overview of the principles and applications from the chapter.

IV. LIFE APPLICATION
"Lest We Forget!"

Melding the chapter to life.

V. PRAYER
Tying the chapter to life with God.

VI. DEEPER DISCOVERIES
Historical, geographical, and grammatical enrichment of the commentary.

VII. TEACHING OUTLINE
Suggested step-by-step group study of the chapter.

VIII. ISSUES FOR DISCUSSION
Zeroing the chapter in on daily life.

Quote

"Prosperity is only an instrument to be used, not a deity to be worshiped."

Calvin Coolidge

GEOGRAPHICAL PROFILE: MEDIA

- A geographical region northeast of Babylon and the Tigris River
- Generally bounded by the Zagros Mountains, the Araxes and Cyrus rivers, Hyrcania, and Elam
- May have been named for Madai, the son of Japheth
- Famous for its horses

GEOGRAPHICAL PROFILE: PERSIA

- Roughly the area of modern Iraq
- Gained control of Media in 550 B.C.
- Ultimately extended its empire from Asia to the Mediterranean Sea and from the Baltics to the Persian Gulf
- Prominent in the biblical records of Daniel and Esther

PERSONAL PROFILE: BELSHAZZAR

- Son and coregent with Nabonidus, the seventh and last king of Babylon
- Much debated as a historical character but confirmed through a series of archeological studies
- Considered a weak and worthless king by both biblical and extra-biblical sources

PERSONAL PROFILE: DARIUS THE MEDE

- Darius is quite possibly a title (like Caesar) rather than a name
- High officer in the army of King Cyrus
- Probably governor of a Persian province near Babylon
- Son of Ahasuaerus of Esther 1:1

Daniel 5:1–16

IN A NUTSHELL

From Nebuchadnezzar to Nero, from Belshazzar to Mao, pagan rulers have defied God. But the Lord of heaven always wins.

Oddity at the Orgy

I. INTRODUCTION

The Night of Bad Calls

Weeks after the presidential election of 2000, the American people did not know the identity of their next president. A virtual circus of manual recounts, tabulating of absentee ballots from overseas, and endless wrangling in the courts had delayed the announcement in what turned out to be a dead heat. The media, incapable of patience, plunged ahead, and all the major networks called both George Bush and Al Gore the winner at various points during the early morning hours of November 8. The next day a variety of newspaper headlines blared their messages, in a desperate effort to be first with the big news. The fact that they were ultimately right does not mitigate their unwarranted haste.

- "It's Bush in a Tight One" (*Boston Globe*)
- "Bush Wins!" (*Boston Herald*)
- "Bush!" (*Austin American-Statesman*)
- "Bush Wins!" (*New York Post*)

Reviewing this mess in a *Newsweek* sidebar, Mark Hosenball entitled it "The Night of Bad Calls!" (*Newsweek*, 20 November 2000, 17).

Belshazzar had such a night, not in reference to his election but to his eviction. It was a bad call to throw the party in the first place with enemy armies surrounding Babylon. It was a bad call to send for the holy vessels of the Jewish temple in order to celebrate pagan deities. It was a bad call to summon the faulty faculty of weak wizards to determine the mysterious cryptogram. And it was a bad call not to fall on his face in repentance after God's prophet told him the meaning.

Our text lies theological miles away from the closing verses of Daniel 4. Nebuchadnezzar had died in 562 B.C., and twenty-three years had passed before the opening words of Daniel 5. The Babylonians had watched a series of worthless kings come and go: Evil-Merodach (562–560); Neriglissar (560–556); Labashi-marduk, who reigned less than a year; and Nabonidus, who took the throne in 556 and reigned until the very night described in this chapter, October 29, 539 B.C.

Daniel had not been playing golf between these chapters. He was occupied with receiving and writing prophecies that we shall read later in this book. Walvoord says: "In the quarter of a century which elapsed between chapter 4 and chapter 5, the further revelations given to Daniel in chapters 7 and 8 occurred. Chapter 7 was revealed to Daniel 'in the first year of Belshazzar, king of Babylon' (Dan 7:1) and the vision of the ram and he-goat in chapter 8 occurred 'in the third year of the reign of [King] Belshazzar' (Dan 8:1 KJV)" (Walvoord, *Daniel*, p. 116).

II. COMMENTARY

The Night of Bad Calls

MAIN IDEA: *In God's priority list, spirituality is more important than history. The casual Bible reader might consider this chapter valuable information about ancient empires, and the beginning and the end of the chapter certainly provide that. But the great bulk of the verses center on the foolishness and wickedness of a pagan king and how God's heavenly judgment ended his kingdom.*

Wickedness at the Great Feast (5:1–4)

SUPPORTING IDEA: *The true God always opposes pagan revelry, especially when it is connected with idolatry.*

5:1. Although this verse clearly sets Belshazzar apart from Nebuchadnezzar in his closing years, it does not surprise students of ancient history. The *NIV Study Bible* reminds us that "the orgy of revelry and blasphemy on such occasions is confirmed by the ancient Greek historians Herodotus and Xenophon" (p. 1668). Belshazzar (whose name means "Bel, protect the king") reigned in Babylon while his father Nabonidus was off fighting the Persians. However, he had already been captured, and the forces of the united Medes and Persians at that very moment surrounded the territory of Babylon and had already conquered the suburbs.

Why, on such a frightening evening, would a king decide to throw a party? Many reasons have been offered. Perhaps a reaffirmation of pagan gods to build the courage of his royal leaders seemed like a good idea at the time. Or maybe they genuinely believed that the gigantic walls of Babylon would protect them from any kind of invading force indefinitely. So we crash the party as the top brass of the kingdom decide to do a Babylonian impression of Isaiah's condemnation of Jerusalem: "But see, there is joy and revelry, slaughtering of cattle and killing of sheep, eating of meat and drinking of wine! 'Let us eat and drink,' you say, 'for tomorrow we die!'" (Isa. 22:13), a philosophy that Paul considered quite reasonable if there was no hope of resurrection (1 Cor. 15:32).

We should not consider this a proper banquet with china, silver, and candles. These people gorged themselves until the capacity to eat anything was exhausted. Then they drank until they could barely sit or stand. This kind of orgy, common in all the ancient kingdoms, was described in detail by no less a thoughtful man than Socrates.

The words **a thousand of his nobles** may just be a general term since we know nothing about a given number of officials which could be at the party. But the words **with them** offer more of a challenge. The KJV says that Belshazzar "drank wine before the thousand," indicating that the king set the example of drunkenness, quite possibly on a platform or dais with a head table in view of all the guests. This would seem quite common to us, but ancient kings more commonly ate and drank apart from others at a banquet like this.

Leon Wood observes: "Oriental custom called for the king to sit at a separate table at such feast; there he could give guidance for attitude, atmosphere, and tempo. The notice here that Belshazzar drank wine before the others is to say he was setting the atmosphere as one of carefree hilarity. All present, then, should not only feel free to follow his lead but make it a point to do so" (Wood, *Daniel*, p. 68).

5:2–3. To revelry and orgy Belshazzar now added blasphemy. At his worst, Nebuchadnezzar had never tampered with the sacred vessels of other gods, certainly not those from the God of Israel whose young men had become high officials in his government. Nor should we expect that Nebuchadnezzar would have raised Belshazzar (who was not his son but more likely his grandson; see "Deeper Discoveries"). Neither Hebrew nor Aramaic has a term for grandfather or grandson. When used in the plural the word *fathers* can refer all the way back to Abraham, Isaac, and Jacob as we see many times in Scripture. A single grandfather was never called "father's father" but always just **father**.

Some commentators believe that Belshazzar would not have tampered with these sacred vessels had he been sober, thereby taking the phrase **while**

Belshazzar was drinking as motive or impetus rather than time reference. That may be so, but the act could have betrayed the complete fear and failure of the moment or even the malignant character of the man as much as liquor-inspired motive.

Belshazzar's father Nabonidus, though hardly a sterling example of righteousness, comes across in secular history as something of a priest and scholar. But the weakness of the son he left behind to mind the store glares at us from the first four verses of Daniel 5. Veldkamp offers a modern metaphor: "We might compare it to a group of drunks stealing the church's communion set in order to drink from its glasses at their favorite bar. It's a wonder that Belshazzar and the other revelers didn't choke on the wine, that no one was struck dead" (Veldkamp, p. 92).

We would be wrong to think this an act of carelessness or mere stupidity. Certainly Belshazzar was both, but the record in Daniel seems to portray a distinct contrast between the gods being worshiped at the feast (there was no such thing as a secular Babylonian feast) and the use of the sacred temple objects of the living God to celebrate and worship false gods. In other words, this was not mere revelry but brazen idolatry and defiance of the God whom Nebuchadnezzar had called "the King of heaven" (4:37). Chapter 5 illustrates the last line of 4:37: "Those who walk in pride he is able to humble."

Had Belshazzar spent some time reading Jeremiah, he might have had some different thoughts about his behavior that fateful October day. Well before the Persians ruled the area, Jeremiah said that Babylon would be attacked by "a nation from the north" (Jer. 50:3). Not only does the prophet devote two full and lengthy chapters to the fall of Babylon (Jer. 50–51), but the prophecy includes some fascinating specificities. Have a look at *The Message:*

> "Then I, GOD, step in and say,
> 'I'm on your side, taking up your cause.
> I'm your Avenger. You'll get your revenge.
> I'll dry up her rivers, plug up her springs.
> Babylon will be a pile of rubble,
> scavenged by stray dogs and cats,
> A dumping ground for garbage,
> a godforsaken ghost town.'
>
> "The Babylonians will be like lions and their cubs,

ravenous, roaring for food.
I'll fix them a meal, all right—a banquet, in fact.
They'll drink themselves falling-down drunk.
Dead drunk, they'll sleep—and sleep and sleep . . .
and they'll never wake up." GOD'S Decree
(Jer. 51:36–39, *The Message*).

"I'll get them drunk, the whole lot of them—
princes, sages, governors, soldiers.
Dead drunk, they'll sleep—and sleep and sleep . . .
And never wake up." The King's Decree.
His name? GOD-of-the-Angel-Armies!

GOD-of-the-Angel-Armies speaks:

"The city walls of Babylon—those massive walls!—
will be flattened.
And those city gates—huge gates!—
will be set on fire.
The harder you work at this empty life,
the less you are.
Nothing comes of ambition like this
but ashes."
(Jer. 51:57–58, *The Message*).

5:4. We can hardly misunderstand the importance of the wine, since Daniel mentions wine or drinking in each of the first four verses. In this verse he links drinking with the pagan worship of **gods of gold and silver, of bronze, iron, wood and stone**. The curse of Deuteronomy 32:15 falls upon all those who practice idolatry. Jerome, following the hermeneutics of his time, applies the text figuratively to pagan thinking:

> We should have to say that it applies to all the heretics or to any doctrine which is contrary to truth which appropriates the words of the Biblical prophets and misuses the testimony of Scripture to suit its own inclination. It furnishes liquor to those whom it deceives and with whom it has committed fornication. It carries off the vessels of God's temple and waxes drunken by quaffing them; and it does not give the praise to the God whose vessels they are, but to gods of gold and silver, of bronze, of iron, of wood, and of stone (Jerome, pp. 56–57).

Obviously Daniel is not writing about secular philosophy in this text, but Jerome has a point. In our day, especially in Western civilization, "idea-olatry" has become the favorite form of idolatry. We are far too sophisticated to worship gods of wood and stone with vessels of gold and silver, but we worship the gods of our own minds, a dethroned earthly Jesus stripped of his deity and a mystical but emasculated God whose record of Old Testament history is nothing more than a collection of interesting stories. It may well be time for another round of handwriting on the wall.

B Writing on the Plaster Wall (5:5–9)

SUPPORTING IDEA: *Sometimes we ignore God's warnings too long, and all we have left is a notification of doom.*

5:5. The room in which Belshazzar probably sat was 56 feet wide and 173 feet long; at least archeologists have uncovered a throne room in the ruins of Nebuchadnezzar's palace with these dimensions. The center part of the long wall was covered with some kind of white plaster, surely the divine screen for this media event. The word for **lampstand** appears nowhere else, but most scholars consider it a reference to some kind of large chandelier containing many candles or torches. In other words, the handwriting appeared in a part of the room that was well illuminated. Once again the God of heaven offered a PowerPoint® presentation in public. With Nebuchadnezzar a quarter century earlier, judgment came while "the words were still on his lips" (4:31). Now the heavenly hand began to write **suddenly** and in full view of the king.

Though never experiencing it personally, I am told that shock produces sobriety. The language of this verse describes the part of a human hand below the wrist with the fingers in the actual act of writing. No more dreams and visions—now the message scrolled in view of everyone. Wood says: "This would fix its reality more firmly in mind, and, besides, no one could later say that someone only thought he saw something miraculous for a fleeting moment. The writing, further, provided an objective sign that the king could not change or manipulate to his advantage in any way" (Wood, *Daniel*, p. 70).

This is one of those Bible passages that have become part of modern conversation even among people who never read the Bible. When one sees "the handwriting on the wall," one knows that some dramatic event, usually sinister and negative, will soon occur. When people think they might lose their jobs, they often say later, "Well, it was inevitable; I saw the handwriting on the wall weeks ago." Or if a teenager is arrested for using drugs, parents will sometimes wring their hands and say, "We should have seen the handwriting on the wall."

5:6. Daniel gives us a vivid description of the king's emotional and physical fear. Suddenly the raucous laughter and drunken shouting stopped because God had invaded the feast. The message came not to the thousand nobles but rather to the king himself, and God made sure he could see it clearly. Pentecost details possible behavior of the threatened monarch: "The king had evidently arisen from the chair in which he had been seated to lead the festivities and stood to watch. He became **so frightened that . . . his legs gave way** and he fell to the floor" (Pentecost, p. 1345).

5:7. There had been many changes in Babylon in the past twenty-five years, but the faculty was still assembled at the king's command. Rather than the threats which we have seen in earlier chapters, Belshazzar now offered generous rewards. The challenge was twofold—read **this writing and** tell **me what it means**, the first two steps of inductive Bible study. The rewards included a purple robe (the symbol of royalty and power among Babylonians, Medes, Persians, and Greeks) and golden chains (a symbol of high office in government).

Much interpretative fuss has been made about the third offer: **he will be made the third highest ruler in the kingdom**. Some argue that the Aramaic word for **third** is in doubt, and perhaps Belshazzar only intended to put some high office on the table here. The word *shalish* is rendered "officer" in 2 Kings 7:2, so that argument offers a certain possibility. But specificity seems in order. Belshazzar was not the first ruler, so whomever he rewarded could not become the second ruler. That lineup would ignore Nabonidus, the real king of the Babylonian Empire. With the Persians at the door, Belshazzar was the de facto monarch; in the hour of crisis he offered the highest position available.

5:8–9. What a surprise! The faculty failed again. Faced with two tasks, they could perform neither. The question is not translation but code, and we will deal with that in our study of verses 26–28. We must analyze the nature of the cryptogram itself but give special focus to the meaning. Miller summarizes it well:

> One might wonder why these counselors, or for that matter the king and his nobles, could not read the writing. The message was written in Aramaic, as vv. 25–28 make clear, and that language was well-known in Babylon. According to Jewish tradition, the letters were not comprehensible because they were written vertically instead of horizontally. Wood suggests that these were unusually shaped characters. Of course, vowels were not written with the consonants in Aramaic so that even if the letters were understood the meaning of the terms could still have been ambiguous. Most likely the words were understood, but they simply did not convey any intelligible meaning (Miller, pp. 158–59).

However badly the king had felt a few minutes earlier, he was now **more terrified** and **more pale**. The vain and profane Belshazzar had become the latest victim of Psalm 2:4–5: "The One enthroned in heaven laughs; the Lord scoffs at them. Then he rebukes them in his anger and terrifies them in his wrath."

We need not ponder why Daniel has not yet appeared since we understand from the flow of the text and the history of the times that he had been placed in retirement. He was Nebuchadnezzar's man, the source of that great king's departure from Babylonian religion in his declining days, apparently in disfavor with the kings who occupied the throne of Babylon after Nebuchadnezzar's death. But, as we have already seen and will see very soon again, even in retirement Daniel served God and stood ready for whatever the Most High required of him.

C Wisdom of the Aging Prophet (5:10–16)

SUPPORTING IDEA: *A simple peasant with no formal education can, through the power of the Holy Spirit, know God's truth better than the most educated pagan who cares nothing for divine revelation. But the trained and experienced prophet, wise in years and rich in life, offers the greatest hope for explaining and applying God's Word.*

5:10. Enter **the queen**. In modern language we would immediately conclude that this was the wife of Belshazzar, but we know that his wives and his concubines (see 5:2) were already in the banquet hall. Three reasonable possibilities arise at this point. She might have been the daughter of

Nebuchadnezzar, the wife of Nebuchadnezzar, and/or the wife of Nabonidus. Archer assumes she was "the king's mother, who was in all probability a daughter of Nebuchadnezzar" (Archer, p. 72).

That strikes me as the best choice, and we might go a step further and identify her as Nitocris, known in secular history as an ambitious and resourceful queen. Clearly she had unusual authority and esteem at court because she **came into the banquet hall** on her own initiative. After the traditional greeting, she spoke like any mother might: **Don't be alarmed! Don't look so pale!**

5:11. So Daniel was not completely forgotten after all. Nitocris remembered that her husband considered Daniel a man **who has the spirit of the holy gods in him** (see 4:8–9,18). We have already dealt with the relationship between Nebuchadnezzar and Belshazzar, and we will come back to that in "Deeper Discoveries." Indeed, the tone we noticed in verse 10 continues in verse 11—a mother reminding a son of the good old days. She referred to **your father** three times, the last time telling Belshazzar that Nebuchadnezzar was **your father the king**, perhaps suggesting that Nebuchadnezzar acted like one and Belshazzar did not. The dean of the faculty may now be dean emeritus, but he still can outinterpret the rest of the profs.

5:12. How interesting that the queen should first use Daniel's Hebrew name and then recall his Chaldean name. She attributed to him quite a bag of tricks and had complete confidence that he could handle this matter of words on a wall that brought such terror to so many: **Call for Daniel, and he will tell you what the writing means**. Indeed. Having served as a dean of faculty twice in my own career, I can attest to the fact that deans invest a great deal of time untangling riddles and solving problems.

5:13–14. Daniel was not unknown to Belshazzar, although the young king had no opportunity to see what the aging prophet could really do. However, it seems less than complimentary to refer to the distinguished former prime minister as **one of the exiles my father the king brought from Judah**. Nevertheless, the king recognized that in this aging prophet (well into his eighties) God had placed **insight, intelligence and outstanding wisdom**.

5:15–16. Belshazzar recited for Daniel's benefit what we already know from the earlier part of the chapter and offered to him the same threefold reward proffered to the faculty earlier. Again, the task was twofold—**read this writing and tell me what it means**. According to Criswell:

> We find our rightful places only in the crisis of life. At the banquet table the people are busy with the hum of conversation and the ordinary things of the day. They are talking alike, laughing alike, carrying on alike, the great, the small, the famous, the infamous, the good, and the bad, all of them. But when a crisis comes, there is an unexpressed law by which men somehow take their rightful places. It is then that the man with the keys of the kingdom stands up and cries out (Criswell, p. 89).

MAIN IDEA REVIEW: *In God's priority list, spirituality is more important than history. The casual Bible reader might consider this chapter valuable information about ancient empires, and the beginning and the end of the chapter certainly provide that. But the great bulk of the verses center on the foolishness and wickedness of a pagan king and how God's heavenly judgment ended his kingdom.*

III. CONCLUSION

God Can Find You

During my forty years of ministry in Christian higher education, my time divided almost in half between Bible colleges and seminaries. During the earlier years, and even back into my student days in the 1950s, questions of geography invariably centered on where God wanted us to serve. We clearly understood that the *place* of service was unimportant except as it related to God's choice and God's will. Frequently we would ask one another and be asked by chapel speakers and faculty, "Are you really ready to serve wherever God wants you?"

Somehow through the years "God's choice" surrendered to "my choice" in too many students looking toward ministry opportunities. Perhaps I misread the intent, but it seems to me that students over the past couple of decades have been far more concerned with climate, culture, adjacency to relatives or perhaps their home states, and a number of other factors which center on personal preference.

But the Bible allows none of that. Obviously Daniel would rather have served God in Israel, but he was in Babylon. He would have preferred the king's recognition earlier, but he was the last called. One thing stands clear in the narrative, however: God knew where he was and (like Jonah) knew where to find him when he was needed. What a great lesson for us. We don't have to waste human effort trying to grasp a certain position, hold a certain title, or build up high visibility. Wherever we are, whenever he needs us, God can find us. In his poem "Your Place," John Oxenham offers a helpful reminder.

> Is your place a small place?
> Tend it with care;—
> He set you there.
>
> Is your place a large place?
> Guard it with care!—
> He set you there.
>
> What 'ere your place, it is
> Not yours alone, but His
> Who set you there.
> (quoted in Robertson, 163)

PRINCIPLES

- The life of Belshazzar shows us that parents can reap chaos in their adult children if they have done nothing earlier to prevent it.
- When unsaved people come to a time of crisis, they often turn to people who are in touch with God.
- Even when the political system crumbles around them, mature Christians can still trust God.
- Though older people often feel rejected by younger leaders, God will often call on them for service when he needs them.

APPLICATIONS

- The Bible repeatedly tells us to avoid idolatry in any form.
- Like Daniel we need to be ready for action wherever and whenever God calls us.

- If we as God's vessels are found in pagan surroundings, may it only be because we were forced there.
- Let's remember that God can put us into situations in which we have no alternative but to cast ourselves completely on him.

IV. LIFE APPLICATION

"Lest We Forget!"

Rudyard Kipling was born on December 30, 1865, in Bombay, India, and became very much a child of that country and of the British Empire of his time. He spent his schooling days in England but at seventeen returned to India to become a journalist. In 1894 he wrote his famous work *The Jungle Book* and in 1907 won the Nobel Prize for Literature.

During the sixtieth year of Queen Victoria's reign, he was commissioned to write a piece and produced *Recessional,* from which these lines were taken. It may be worth remembering that when Kipling put these words on paper, the British Empire had reached the pinnacle of its power in the world. I offer just two stanzas here.

Far-called our navies melt away—
On dune and headland sinks the fire—
Lo, all our pomp of yesterday
Is one with Nineveh and Tyre!
Judge of the Nations, spare us yet,
Lest we forget—lest we forget!

If, drunk with sight of power, we loose
Wild tongues that have not Thee in awe—
Such boasting as the Gentiles use
Or lesser breeds without the Law—
Lord God of Hosts, be with us yet,
Lest we forget—lest we forget!
(quoted in Robertson, pp. 128–29)

We should find the application of Daniel 5 to our present lives a rather easy task. We may boast in our advanced civilization, but a comparison of our age with any of the ancient empires—certainly Rome, but even in some ways Babylon—sets us up for the same kind of disaster Belshazzar experienced in 539 B.C. We may criticize Belshazzar's orgy and consider ourselves better by comparison, but I dare say never has a nation been as completely given over to economic prosperity as twenty-first-century America. Our friends in other countries know that "the American way of life" no longer stands as clearly for justice, freedom, and unity as it does for business, profits, and bank accounts. Two words describe the concerns of many Americans—Dow Jones.

So the spiritual lessons of Daniel are far more important for us than its history. One Belshazzar seems enough of a problem. A banquet hall full of one thousand or more people only complicates the danger. But a whole country given over to its own pleasure should frighten us all. We do well to pray Kipling's prayer, "Lest we forget—lest we forget!"

V. PRAYER

Father, give us the dignity, courage, and readiness of Daniel to serve you at any time despite the danger or threat to our own lives. Amen.

VI. DEEPER DISCOVERIES

A. The Babylonian Dynasty

We reviewed this briefly in the commentary portion of our study, but here we can add more detail. Nebuchadnezzar had died in 563 and his son Evil-Merodach (sometimes called Amel-Marduk) took the throne and released the Jewish king (Jehoiachin) from prison (2 Kgs. 25:27–30). Evil-Merodach was assassinated by his brother-in-law, General Neriglissar, who died four years later. Then after nine months of Labashi-marduk, Nabonidus took over. He apparently married into the kingdom, thereby attempting to legitimatize his claim to the throne. Archer describes him: "A devoted worshipper of the moon-god, Sin (Sumerian Nanna), he was the son of a high priestess belonging to his cult. Intensely interested in the history of Mesopotamia, he seems to have collected a museum of artifacts from earlier ages, consisting partly of dedicatory and building inscriptions of bygone dynasties and partly of early statues taken from various temples throughout his dominions" (Archer, p. 69).

Among the important documents which help us understand the historical background of Daniel is the *Nabonidus Chronicle,* which describes much of the military activity of Cyrus and the role of Nabonidus in the battles against Persia. That document also gives us some information about the attitude of the Babylonians the very night of the attack described in this chapter: "Mounting upon the battlements that crowned their walls, they insulted and jeered at Darius and his mighty host. One even shouted to them and said, 'Why do you sit there, Persians? Why don't you go back to your homes? Till mules foal you will not take our city'" (Archer, p. 69).

B. "Nebuchadnezzar His Father" (5:2,11)

For centuries scholars have pondered the relationship between Nebuchadnezzar and Belshazzar. Certainly it was not father and son; that we have seen. Some interpreters, however, reject the idea of grandfather/grandson (the view taken in this book) and argue that Belshazzar was only the son of Nebuchadnezzar in the legal sense, much in the way Jesus was said to be the Son of David. Clearly it was a matter of court etiquette to refer to Belshazzar quite commonly as the son of Nebuchadnezzar.

But a relationship to Nadonidus is also at issue here. Sir Robert Anderson writes, "On clay cylinders discovered by Sir H. Rawlingson at Mugheir and other Chaldean sites, Belshazzar (Belsaruzur) is named by Nadonidus as his eldest son. The inference is obvious, that during the latter years of his father's reign, Belshazzar was King-Regent in Babylon" (Anderson, p. 221).

Robert Dick Wilson gives a lengthy chapter to Belshazzar and offers yet other options which we have not mentioned: "Or Belshazzar may have been the adopted son of Nebuchadnezzar and the only son of Nabunaid. An adopted son might call his adopted father, 'father' or, Nebuchadnezzar may have been the grandfather and Nabunaid, also the grandfather of Belshazzar. Or, finally, it is possible that Nabunaid was a lineal descendant of Nebuchadnezzar" (Wilson, p. 121).

Options abound, but I prefer simplicity and reasonableness, which seem to suggest that Belshazzar was the son of Nadonidus connected to Nebuchadnezzar through his mother, the daughter of the great king.

C. Sacrilege (5:3–4)

Sacrilege is not a biblical term but a modern English word which comes to us through middle English. It derives from the Latin *sacrilegium,* a description of a person who steals sacred things. It has come to mean desecration, misuse, or gross irreverence toward what others consider sacred and holy. Belshazzar was certainly guilty of this sin; in public display he willfully and unnecessarily used holy things for sinful purposes. When Jesus drove moneychangers out of the temple, he said, "'My house will be called a house of prayer, 'but you are making it a 'den of robbers'" (Matt. 21:13), a text based on Isaiah 56:7 and Jeremiah 7:11.

Yet we commonly see sacrilegious acts in our day and throughout the history of the church. Using God-indwelt bodies for purposes of sin is sacrilegious. Wrapping oneself in church doctrines or affiliations to gain political advantage is sacrilegious. The propagation of heresy (teaching that contradicts the Bible) and false doctrine is sacrilegious.

Wallace puts it this way:

> The danger for most of us today is not so much that of committing Belshazzar's kind of sacrilege. Such coarse behaviour is today usually punished by law as a criminal offense. Our temptation is simply to the careless use and lighthearted neglect of these means of God's grace. We treat the church, its services and sacramental worship, as if it had no greater significance than the coffee house or the public bar—and we sometimes talk as if they had lost their significance even for God himself (Wallace, p. 97).

VII. TEACHING OUTLINE

A. INTRODUCTION

1. Lead Story: The Night of Bad Calls
2. Context: As we have seen, Daniel does not concern himself with the chronological flow of either his prophecies or his history. Nearly a quarter of a century passes between the end of chapter 4 and the beginning of chapter 5. But the historical context is much more

important here than the textual. As this chapter begins, the armies of Cyrus commanded by Darius have already surrounded the city, and God's time for the fall of Babylon has come.

3. Transition: In the next chapter of our book, we will consider the second half of Daniel 5. So far we have seen the astonishing events of the evening and heard Belshazzar's request of the aging prophet. Now Daniel will speak and explain the famous handwriting on the wall.

B. COMMENTARY

1. Wickedness at the Great Feast (5:1–4)
2. Writing on the Plaster Wall (5:5–9)
3. Wisdom of the Aging Prophet (5:10–16)

C. CONCLUSION: GOD CAN FIND YOU

VIII. ISSUES FOR DISCUSSION

1. What other kings and kingdoms might we consider since the fall of Rome which reflect the lessons we see in this chapter?
2. In what specific ways does Daniel model for us the spiritual leadership to which we should all aspire in declining years?
3. What is the central spiritual lesson of Daniel 5:1–16?

Daniel 5:17–31

Heavenly Hermeneutics

I. INTRODUCTION
End of the Evil Empire

II. COMMENTARY
A verse-by-verse explanation of the chapter.

III. CONCLUSION
"The Paleface"

An overview of the principles and applications from the chapter.

IV. LIFE APPLICATION
"This Is My Father's World"

Melding the chapter to life.

V. PRAYER
Tying the chapter to life with God.

VI. DEEPER DISCOVERIES
Historical, geographical, and grammatical enrichment of the commentary.

VII. TEACHING OUTLINE
Suggested step-by-step group study of the chapter.

VIII. ISSUES FOR DISCUSSION
Zeroing the chapter in on daily life.

Quote

"The terror of being judged sharpens the memory: it sends an inevitable glare over that long-unvisited past which has been habitually recalled only in general phrases."

George Eliot

Daniel 5:17–31

IN A NUTSHELL

Power corrupts, and absolute power corrupts absolutely. Every reigning monarch of the ancient world illustrates that, but perhaps none so clearly as Belshazzar.

Heavenly Hermeneutics

I. INTRODUCTION

End of the Evil Empire

In 1980, Governor Ronald Reagan of California was elected to the presidency of the United States. Although inheriting a recessional economy from former president Jimmy Carter, Reagan set about investing in industry, instituting tax cuts, and reducing social programs which had reached outlandish proportions under the administration of Lyndon Johnson some years earlier. As he promised in his election campaign, he increased spending for the military and built American forces around the world.

But Ronald Reagan will be remembered most in history for his vigilant fight against what he called "the evil empire"—the Union of Soviet Socialist Republics. He intended to reverse the tide of Marxist revolution throughout the Western Hemisphere but primarily to combat the influence of Russia and its empire throughout Europe and Asia. Reagan left office in 1988, but the evil empire had been weakened to the point of crumbling, and on November 9, 1989, citizens on both sides began to demolish entire sections of the Berlin Wall without interference from government troops or officials. Just one year later the two Germanys were united as one nation, the Federal Republic of Germany. And today the U.S.S.R. exists no longer, and the military might of Russia has been reduced to a shadow of its former self.

But as evangelical leaders and missionaries began pouring into Eastern Europe and Russia during the 1990s, they found thousands upon thousands of praying Christians who had never lost hope during the nearly fifty years of Communist control. To the present hour the gospel is alive and well throughout all of the former U.S.S.R., although Christians are still persecuted in many of those countries. The evil empire came tumbling down, attacked by a conservative world leader from the outside, but imploded by faithful believers on the inside.

In Daniel 5, God destroys another evil empire. Babylon had pillaged, raped, and murdered for nearly seventy years, and God had seen enough. Daniel 4:17, Nebuchadnezzar's great lesson in theology, now becomes history for the empire over which he once presided.

II. COMMENTARY

Heavenly Hermeneutics

MAIN IDEA: *God holds everyone responsible for sin, even powerful monarchs hiding behind seemingly impregnable fortresses. Babylon is finished, and King Belshazzar has already seen the handwriting on the wall.*

A Historical Review (5:17–21)

SUPPORTING IDEA: *A true prophet's services are not for sale; he deals only in the truth of God and makes it available to anyone who will listen.*

5:17. Some suggest that Daniel responded in contempt for Belshazzar's behavior since he did not use the formal introduction, "O king, live forever." But let's remember that he had already addressed Nebuchadnezzar twice without such an introduction (2:27; 4:19). It is also important to note that we probably have a summary of the conversation.

As for the renouncing of **gifts** and **rewards**, the prophet was simply keeping the atmosphere clear of any inappropriate motives for what he was about to say. This reminds us of Elisha's refusal of Naaman's gifts (2 Kgs. 5:15–16) and his punishment of Gehazi when he accepted them. Then too, since Daniel knew exactly what would happen to Babylon, the purple robe, gold chain, and number-three slot in the empire meant nothing at all. One hundred percent of zero is still zero, and that is exactly what Babylon would soon become. Keep in mind that Daniel had retired. Even if Belshazzar's empire had continued, it seems unlikely he would have accepted these gifts under any conditions.

5:18–19. Daniel wanted Belshazzar to know that he was intimately familiar with Nebuchadnezzar. One almost sees in this description an earlier reflection of words once spoken during a presidential campaign to candidate Dan Quayle after he had alluded to John Kennedy: "Sir, I knew John Kennedy, and you are no John Kennedy." That's a paraphrase, of course, but certainly Belshazzar was no Nebuchadnezzar.

But there is more here. Daniel would contrast the absolute earthly power of Belshazzar's grandfather with the absolute heavenly power of the Most High God, showing the former was as nothing when compared with the latter. This is, in effect, the introduction to the sermon and therefore explains the reason for the judgment Babylon would soon experience. I find it fascinating that a hall full of drunken leaders would now be forced to end their night (and likely their lives) with a sermon!

5:20–21. In preparation for identifying the sins of Belshazzar, Daniel reviewed the sins of Nebuchadnezzar—**his heart became arrogant and hardened with pride**. God's gifts to Nebuchadnezzar had made that great king responsible for handling them in a reasonable and righteous manner, and his failure to do so brought judgment. So in the final analysis the description of Nebuchadnezzar in Daniel 5:19 actually applies only to God. Daniel ended his first paragraph (his introduction) with the great theme of this book: **the Most High God is sovereign over the kingdoms of men and sets over them anyone he wishes**.

B Contemporary Repetition (5:22–24)

SUPPORTING IDEA: *Idolatry and sacrilege are terrible sins, worsened when flaunted in God's holy face.*

5:22. The sermon is about sin. My *Encarta Computer Encyclopedia* tells me that "in no other sacred book is the sense of sin so fully developed as in the Bible. Throughout the Scriptures sin is the element in humanity that puts human beings at enmity with God, requiring repentance and God's forgiveness." That is exactly correct and precisely what happens here. In ancient Israel the Jews quoted a proverb about their land: "The fathers have eaten sour grapes, and the children's teeth are set on edge" (Jer. 31:29).

But the prophets brought a different message detailed most particularly in Ezekiel 18:19–20: "Yet you ask,

> Why does the son not share the guilt of his father?' Since the son has done what is just and right and has been careful to keep all my decrees, he will surely live. The soul who sins is the one who will die. The son will not share the guilt of the father, nor will the father share the guilt of the son. The righteousness of the righteous man will be credited to him, and the wickedness of the wicked will be charged against him."

Belshazzar would not be punished for Nebuchadnezzar's sin; his grandfather ultimately "acknowledged that the Most High God is sovereign" (5:21).

No, Belshazzar would pay for his own sins, and all Babylon would pay with him. Furthermore, Belshazzar's sin was greater because he had had the example of God's dealings with Nebuchadnezzar and had failed to recognize how much the Most High hates the sins of pride and idolatry (Rom. 1:21,24).

5:23. The prophet accused Belshazzar of pride, intentional rejection, idolatry, desecration (sacrilege), and drunkenness. Archer says, "He was guilty of blasphemy in using the Lord's holy vessels as common dishes for his drunken orgy (v. 23). How could he hope to measure his puny human strength against the power of the Almighty, on whom his very life depended and who was completely sovereign over all his fortunes?" (Archer, p. 73).

The end of this verse offers a short but poignant sentence worthy of frequent reflection by all of us: **But you did not honor the God who holds in his hand your life and all your ways**. It is likely that this sermon was heard by everyone in the room; we can hardly imagine trivial conversation going on around the tables while the dean emeritus addressed the king. Nor was this an evangelistic appeal such as we saw Daniel present to Nebuchadnezzar (4:27). Wallace grasps the severity of the moment: "To Belshazzar [Daniel] preaches as one standing on the other side of the great chasm. . . . He preaches a sermon without the trace of any appeal. All he does is to relate the facts that justify the condemnation that has been pronounced in the writing on the wall. Belshazzar knew the truth that might have saved him, and did not obey it" (Wallace, p. 100).

5:24. The verse stands by itself without need for explanation, but let's remember that probably several hours had passed since the writing first appeared. We must allow time for the initial attempt to read it, the call of the wizards and the deliberations with the king, the entrance of the queen mother, the arrival of Daniel, and Belshazzar's explanation to God's prophet. And this was not a game in which the home team was ahead by thirty points with two minutes to play and the crowd headed for the parking lot. You can bet that no one had left the room since the mysterious hand had appeared.

C Divine Retribution (5:25–31)

SUPPORTING IDEA: *God is judge as well as savior, and one must choose which role one will experience from his almighty hand.*

5:25. Right at this point we must invest a good bit of space to grasp the uniqueness of this message and the context in which God sent it. First, let's deal with the language. Our Bibles have simply transliterated Aramaic into English, although some scholars have argued that the letters actually appeared in Cuneiform. The difference is crucial to understanding the evening since Aramaic script would not have provided any vowels (which would have been present in cuneiform). The absence of vowels in normal conversation presented no problem, but in a mystical cryptogram like this, most conservative scholars assume the words appeared in Aramaic. I have no reason to challenge that assumption.

Second, the letters appeared in the reverse order that we see them, since that is the way Semitic languages are read. In addition, the "u" at the beginning of **Parsin** simply means "and," an interpretive aid probably supplied by Daniel. With all that in mind, let's have a look at how Belshazzar might have seen the message, transliterated into English letters: SRP LQT NM NM.

We begin to understand the bewilderment of the faculty. Even if we add the vowels we still end up with **mene, mene, tekel, parsin**, a phrase capable of a variety of meanings.

This message could have been read in terms of weights or value, such as *mene, mene, shekel, half shekel* (*peres* simply means "divided"). Or someone might have leaped to the conclusion that the last word sounded a bit like Persia (*Paras* in Aramaic) and therefore could refer to the army surrounding the walls at that very moment. The point is that even the best evangelical Old Testament scholars of our day could not have interpreted the meaning of this cryptogram; it came only by divine revelation to God's anointed prophet.

5:26–28. In the strictest, literal form Daniel interpreted the strange words to mean "numbered, numbered, weighed, divided."

Mene, mentioned twice, can mean "numbered," "counted," or "measured." The KJV says, "God hath numbered thy kingdom," but the NIV improves upon that by saying, **God has numbered the days of your reign**. In either case, Belshazzar was history.

Daniel describes **tekel** as the passive participle of the word for "weighed." Belshazzar was not only numbered; he was **weighed**. On God's scales he was **found wanting**. This reminds us of 1 Samuel 2:3, "Do not keep talking so proudly or let your mouth speak such arrogance, for the LORD is a God who knows, and by him deeds are weighed." Occasionally we see an old movie in which a pharmacist or grocer puts a metal weight on one side of a balanced scale and the product being purchased on the other side. The point is to balance the scales, to make them even. But when God placed his righteous standard on one side of the scale and Belshazzar's behavior on the other, Belshazzar failed to lift the standard weight. He probably didn't even move the beam.

Peres means "divided" and, according to Archer, "Daniel read it as a passive participle . . . and interpreted it to mean that Belshazzar's kingdom, the Babylonian Empire, had been divided or separated from him and given over to the Medes and Persians besieging the city" (Archer, p. 73). As noted earlier, the *U* at the beginning of the word represents the word *and* and the *IN* at the end makes it a plural.

So the various parts of the Babylonian Empire would be divided again (Jer. 51:44). Since the numbering and weighing had already been done, the present tense verb in the lineup is the one that pronounces instant judgment. Walvoord sums it up: "The interpretation of Daniel is clear and much more satisfactory than the alternatives offered by some expositors. Belshazzar is made to understand that Babylon will be given to the Medes and Persians. Even while Daniel was interpreting the writing on the wall, the prophecy was being fulfilled as the Medes and the Persians poured into the city" (Walvoord, *Daniel*, pp. 128–29).

5:29. Stop the presses! What's going on here? After we noted Daniel's complete disdain for the king's gift program, now we read that he apparently accepted it. Why put up a fuss? Belshazzar and Babylon were as good as gone, and none of this made a bit of difference.

In addition to an earned doctorate, I have three honorary doctorates generously given by reputable accredited institutions of learning. They each say something like, "Entitled to all honors, rights, and privileges pertaining thereto," which probably means I could check out a book from one of those libraries providing I have an appropriate picture ID and carry the diploma in with me. I do not demean these great and gracious tokens; I merely suggest the limits of their value. Indeed, if one or all of these institutions were to go out of existence overnight, it might necessitate a change of location of the diploma(s) from the wall of my study to some archival drawer.

5:30–31. Daniel ends the chapter with a very important historical observation accompanied by a biographical note. We shall deal with Darius the Mede in "Deeper Discoveries," but, as we have already seen, the Babylonian empire ended **that very night** with the fall of Babylon. Paul tells us in 1 Corinthians 3:17 that God will destroy those who defile his temple, a reference in that context to the human body. Belshazzar and his guests had been doing just that for hours, and probably years. The inferior kingdom of Daniel 2:39 toppled the head of gold as the Medes and Persians replaced the Chaldeans as masters of the world.

Everyone quotes Herodotus on the historical account of how this occurred. While Nabonidus had been defeated and held prisoner at Borsippa, the armies of Medo-Persia had diverted the waters of the Euphrates away from the city of Babylon, lifted the sluice gates, and quietly entered the city without a hand being raised against them. Extrabiblical history provides ample evidence of the event, but biblical texts are much more important to us (Isa. 13:17–22; 21:1–10; Jer. 51:33–58).

We close this chapter recognizing not only the downfall of Babylon as a nation judged by a righteous God but also an example of how God handles defiant debauchery and intentional idolatry. Daniel lives on, however, and has a great deal more to say in the chapters still to come.

MAIN IDEA REVIEW: *God holds everyone responsible for sin, even powerful monarchs hiding behind seemingly impregnable fortresses. Babylon is finished, and King Belshazzar has already seen the handwriting on the wall.*

III. CONCLUSION

"The Paleface"

Twice in this chapter we learn that Belshazzar "turned pale" and, for some reason I was reminded of the old Bob Hope film, *The Paleface*. Hope stars as a rookie gunfighter who gets so much conflicting advice about how to draw and dodge in a shoot-out that he becomes completely confused about how to handle the situation. So it was with Belshazzar whose whole life had been characterized by chaos that comes now to destruction on this fateful night. God's justice falls on those who listen to bad advice and fail to heed his will. We dare not treat lightly the phrase in verse 22 where Daniel tells Belshazzar, "You knew all this." How many people have heard the gospel over and over but refuse to respond. How many people can listen to a sermon grounded in truth but let its impact slip away as they consider the worldly philosophies that dominate all forms of media in our day. Back in 1923 Homer Rodeheaver wrote a simple song used in earlier days by male quartets:

> Babylon's fallen, fallen, fallen,
> Babylon's fallen to rise no more.
> Down, down, down, down,
> Babylon's fallen to rise no more.

Indeed it did. And its final king, the paleface, died with it.

According to Campbell:

> Most people who sin do not write the record on a wall, but it is written just as plainly in the books of God and his divine will was written on another wall, "Thou art weighed in the balances, and art found wanting' (Dan. 5:27). They will meet their sins someday because they have written them where they will be brought to light. The only escape is to find forgiveness in Jesus Christ 'in whom we have redemption through his blood, the forgiveness of sins, according to the riches of his grace" (Eph. 1:7) (Campbell, p. 86).

PRINCIPLES

- Those who sow to the flesh will from the flesh reap corruption.
- Those who do not know God's Word may often see it in the experiences of another.
- God cannot and will not allow worship that belongs to him to go endlessly to idols.
- No sin goes unpunished, but when the sinner knows better, the punishment will be greater.

APPLICATIONS

- Never lose a biblical sense of destiny, the grasp of a mighty God working out his plan in the world.
- Recognize that prophecy is not only true and reliable; it is also useful for spiritual growth.

- Understand the difference between the way God deals with the sins of unbelievers and the sins of believers.

IV. LIFE APPLICATION

"This Is My Father's World"

Maltbie Davenport Babcock was born August 3, 1858, in Syracuse, New York, a member of a socially prominent family of that city. He graduated from Syracuse University and Auburn Theological Seminary, getting recognition as a good student, a fine athlete, and a competent musician. His first pastorate called him to the Presbyterian Church of Lockport, New York, and it was there he wrote the familiar hymn that many of us have sung scores of times.

Babcock would take early morning walks and tell his family he was going out "to see my Father's world." Babcock died while on a trip to the Holy Land in 1901, and the hymn was published in a book entitled *Thoughts for Everyday Living*. Here is the third verse of that moving hymn, which in its entirety is only a short portion of the complete poem composed by Babcock:

> This is my Father's world, O let me ne'er forget.
> That tho' the wrong seems oft so strong,
> God is the Ruler yet.
> This is my Father's world: why should my heart be sad?
> The Lord is king: let the heavens ring!
> God reigns: let earth be glad!

A dramatic way to sing about Daniel 5. With all his greatness and apparent absolute authority on earth, Nebuchadnezzar's empire was doomed to destruction. Yet at the end of his life, he came to the realization "that the Most High God is sovereign over the kingdoms of men and sets over them anyone he wishes." Sadly the rulers who followed him had no such spiritual insight, and Babylon perished in history, if not in end-time prophecy.

But we need face no such doom. When the culture around us crumbles into meaningless moral miasma, we can pray, we can sing, and we can even shout: "This is my Father's world; the battle is not done. Jesus who died shall be satisfied, and earth and heaven be one."

V. PRAYER

Father, thank you for controlling your world with such justice and righteousness. Help us to stand firmly on the side of Daniel, denouncing the evils of Belshazzar wherever and however we see them today. Amen.

VI. DEEPER DISCOVERIES

A. The Fall of Babylon

Cyrus the Great became king of Persia about 550 B.C. and held that post for twenty-one years. The son of Cambyses I, he came to military distinction by leading a rebellion against the Medes while ruler of the Persian district of Anshan. As king of Persia, he ruled the territory from the Halys River in Asia Minor to the Babylonian empire. Until 539 the combined powers of Babylon, Egypt, and Lydia and the rising city-state of Sparta in Greece held Cyrus somewhat in check, but Lydia fell in 546 and Babylon in 539.

Babylonian civilization had survived from the eighteenth until the sixth century, longer than the Sumerian and Akkadian societies which preceded it. The powerful Assyrian dynasty which controlled the world before Babylon had adopted Babylonian culture much in the way the Romans borrowed from the Greeks.

Babylon came to its close on October 16, 539, when Darius the Mede, acting under the authority of his king, Cyrus of Persia, brought down the city. Babylon was then annexed to Persia. Secular accounts of the collapse of Babylon do not include any record of Darius the Mede, and they attribute the victory to Cyrus of Persia. That is why the next section of "Deeper Discoveries" is so important.

B. Darius the Mede (5:31)

Most often confused with Darius I (Hystaspes), Darius the Mede has become a nonentity in secular history and a favorite target of Daniel's critics. Daniel specifically notes his age (quite unusual in the text of this book) as "sixty-two," quite impossible for Darius Hystaspes, who reigned thirty-six years and therefore would have lived ninety-eight years if he began his reign in 539 B.C.

Admittedly, my own opinions regarding Darius the Mede were formed in the classroom where I studied Daniel under the tutelage of Dr. John C. Whitcomb Jr., whose book *Darius the Mede* offers one of the best studies on the topic. He taught us what he later wrote: "The book of Daniel gives far more information concerning the personal background of Darius the Mede than of Belshazzar or even of Nebuchadnezzar. For he is the only monarch in the book whose age, parentage and nationality are recorded" (Whitcomb, p. 8).

Extrabiblical resources abound, however, and the logical conclusion connects Darius the Mede of Daniel with Gubaru, frequently mentioned as governor of Babylon (also called Gobryas). True, he was not king, so we wonder why he is called that no fewer than twenty-eight times in Daniel 6. Whitcomb claims that distinction has to do with the linguistic relationship between Aramaic and Persian languages.

Certainly Gubaru is not the only possible choice. Baldwin wonders in print whether the name might be a reference to Cyrus himself: "Cyrus is known to have been related to the Medes, to have been called 'King of the Medes' and to have been about 60 years old on becoming king of Babylon. This suggestion requires that 6:28 be translated, 'So this Daniel prospered during the reign of Darius, that is, in the reign of Cyrus the Persian'" (Baldwin, 26).

Baldwin does not argue this dogmatically, but I offer it as another possible suggestion. Robert Dick Wilson, whose name we have mentioned before, devotes an entire chapter to Darius the Mede and lends his considerable scholarship to the views espoused by Whitcomb; indeed, he was probably most influential in Whitcomb's thinking. After detailed discussions of historical and linguistic issues, Wilson says: "While such examples do not prove that Gobyras was also named Darius, they do afford a presumption in favor of the probability that he was; and in view of the other indications in its favor, they should deter anyone from asserting that Gobyras and Darius the Mede were not the same" (Wilson, vol. 1, p. 141).

Somewhat surprisingly, Walvoord supports the Cyrus argument developed in detail by D. J. Wiseman. He considers it the most obvious solution and notes, "The fact that monarchs had more than one name is common in ancient literature, and Wiseman's view offers another conservative explanation of this problem in Daniel" (Walvoord, *Daniel*, p. 134).

Normally, I would be drawn to the simplest solution to a historical or textual problem like this, but long hours of contemplating the question under Whitcomb's supervision place me in the Gubaru school. And, I might add, not in such shabby company, since Robert Anderson and Leon Wood espouse the same view. Archer, another proponent, details the point of difference between Gubaru and Ugbaru, an explanation worth reproducing here.

> Thus the passage just quoted makes it quite clear that while it was Ugbaru who engineered the capture of Babylon, he lost his life to a fatal illness less than a month later. . . . It was not Ugbaru, then, but Gubaru whom Cyrus appointed vice-regent of the Chaldean domains on 29 October. The Nabonidus Chronicle and other Cuneiform texts of that era indicate that he continued on as governor of Babylonia for at least fourteen years even though Cyrus may have taken over the royal title at a solemn public coronation service two years later. . . . Daniel 9:1 states that he "was made ruler (Heb. *homlak*) over the realm of the Chaldeans"—a term never applied to one who seizes the sovereignty by force of arms but rather to one who is appointed to kingship by a higher authority. All this fits Gubaru perfectly, and it is only reasonable to conclude that he was the one referred to in Daniel 5:31 as "Darius the Mede" (Archer, pp. 76–77).

VII. TEACHING OUTLINE

A. INTRODUCTION

1. Lead Story: End of the Evil Empire
2. Context: Daniel 5 with its record of the final night of Belshazzar and the collapse of Babylon forms an essential bridge in Daniel's story between the kingdom of Nebuchadnezzar and the kingdom of Cyrus. We have now left the head of gold and entered the era of the "belly and thighs of bronze," the joint powers of Media and Persia, presided over by the great King Cyrus.
3. Transition: Approximately seventy years have passed since the beginning of this book and twenty-three years since the end of chapter 4. The reign of Belshazzar was inconsequential, since the entire

quarter of a century between Nebuchadnezzar and Darius forms no significant part of either prophecy or history as far as Daniel is concerned. Now, however, Daniel comes out of retirement once again to assume a major position at court. In chapter 6 he will tell us all about it.

B. COMMENTARY

1. Historical Review (5:17–21)
2. Contemporary Repetition (5:22–24)
3. Divine Retribution (5:25–31)

C. CONCLUSION: "THE PALEFACE"

VIII. ISSUES FOR DISCUSSION

1. How do we know when to receive gifts from people more important than ourselves and when to refuse them?
2. Discuss the major differences between "absolute power" on earth and "absolute power" in heaven.
3. If God were to write on the walls of the Senate chamber in Washington, D.C., what might the message say?

Daniel 6:1–28

The Lions' Den

I. INTRODUCTION
The Bear and the Dragon

II. COMMENTARY
A verse-by-verse explanation of the chapter.

III. CONCLUSION
Waffling in Prayer
An overview of the principles and applications from the chapter.

IV. LIFE APPLICATION
Chorus No. 28
Melding the chapter to life.

V. PRAYER
Tying the chapter to life with God.

VI. DEEPER DISCOVERIES
Historical, geographical, and grammatical enrichment of the commentary.

VII. TEACHING OUTLINE
Suggested step-by-step group study of the chapter.

VIII. ISSUES FOR DISCUSSION
Zeroing the chapter in on daily life.

Quote

"Prayer lifts the heart above the battles of life and gives it a glimpse of God's resources which spell victory and hope."

C. Neil Strait

PERSONAL PROFILE: CYRUS THE PERSIAN

- Cyrus II (the Great), son of Cambyses I
- A competent and greatly admired ruler
- Built the capital of Persia at Pasargadae, north of Persepolis
- Gave the Jews permission to return to Israel (see "Deeper Discoveries")

Daniel 6:1–28

IN A NUTSHELL

Prayer stands at the entrance to every divine act of deliverance and sometimes causes the need for deliverance. In the words of John Bunyan, "In prayer it is better to have a heart without words than words without a heart."

The Lions' Den

I. INTRODUCTION

The Bear and the Dragon

In our comfortable homes with all the amenities of prosperity surrounding us, we find it difficult to grasp that hundreds of thousands of Christians are persecuted daily in today's world. In some countries Christian children are regularly kidnapped and sold as slaves, Christian women raped, the homes and lands of Christians stolen, and their owners thrown in prison.

The growing church in China thrives in spite of the best efforts of that repressive regime to throttle any open proclamation of the gospel. Some Chinese pastors have been arrested repeatedly, and others have spent most of their adult lives in prison. In North Africa entire countries still enforce laws against the practice of Christianity; any known adherents of that faith face constant harassment and even death.

This problem is so well-known that best-selling author Tom Clancy made it a major subtheme in his 2000 best seller, *The Bear and the Dragon.* He describes an incident of partial-birth abortion in which a young evangelical pastor and a Catholic priest are both shot for attempting to interfere. The particular story is fiction, of course, but the scene may very well be played out daily across the cities of several repressive countries.

This chapter is about persecution and prayer. The persecution was not widespread but aimed mainly at Daniel. The way Daniel faced the crisis comes back to us in the honor roll of faith in Hebrews: "And the prophets, who through faith conquered kingdoms, administered justice, and gained what was promised; who shut the mouths of lions, quenched the fury of the flames, and escaped the edge of the sword" (Heb. 11:32–34).

Indeed, the New Testament is full of reminders like this for God's people. It all began with Cain's murder of Abel and will not stop until Jesus comes again to take charge of the world. Jesus told the Pharisees, "Therefore I am sending you prophets and wise men and teachers. Some of them you will kill and crucify; others you will flog in your synagogues and pursue from town to town" (Matt. 23:34). True, the context here is different and Daniel was rescued from any personal suffering, but the theme is the same.

Many churches observe Persecuted Christians Sunday on the second Sunday of November each year. That's a good idea if we bolster it with year-long prayers for those who face the oppression of wickedness and constantly live in danger because of their faith in Christ.

II. COMMENTARY

The Lion's Den

MAIN IDEA: *When the crises of life threaten us, and our very lives are at stake, calm and quiet dependence upon God is our only recourse.*

Political Entry (6:1–9)

SUPPORTING IDEA: *Jesus said, "The children of this world are wiser in their generation than the children of light." Christians can never win the battle against evil by relying on political leaders.*

6:1–2. Some time has passed since the fall of Babylon, and Darius has organized the territory. These local officials serving throughout that portion of the Persian Kingdom that once formed Babylon functioned as governors or regional directors answering to three federal officials who seem equal in power. This reminds us of Esther 1:1 where we read about 127 provinces in Persia, and we must not confuse the two numbers. This is a reasonable system designed by a reasonable man. Darius stands in contrast to both Nebuchadnezzar and Belshazzar. He obviously had lesser power than the greatest king of Babylon but considerably more sensitivity than his grandson. The satraps had a mission in their work, and they also were held accountable **so that the king might not suffer loss**.

This well-known and fascinating chapter of Daniel contains no prophecy and relatively little history. Yet the hermeneutical principle of *proportion* requires us to acknowledge its importance not just because it's in the Bible but because God gives it the same length as the seventh chapter upon which students of prophecy have pounced with vigor for centuries. To put it simply, it would seem that living righteously in alien surroundings and depending upon God to deliver us from danger offers a biblical lesson no less important than an analysis of future events.

6:3. Our familiarity with Daniel prepares us to expect exactly what we read here. This good and godly prophet, now approximately eighty-three years of age, had **distinguished himself** throughout his career. Now Darius had a plan to restructure the organizational chart and make Daniel provost instead of just one of three vice presidents. At various points in this book we have seen how Daniel's life and career parallel those of Joseph, and this is another good example—second in command to the king.

The issue was financial management, so a system of accountability up and down the bureaucracy made a good deal of sense. But Daniel's life had not been under the control of human reason at any point, so we must see God's hand manipulating Darius to set up the system that he had designed for the Medo-Persian Empire. Wood says, "His appointment can only be explained on the basis of God's direct superintendence" (Wood, *Daniel,* p. 79).

6:4–5. Even in our much-touted democracy Christians are well aware of political corruption, so this conspiracy hardly takes us by surprise. The first point of attack would naturally be his professional competence. With Daniel's track record this was probably a losing proposition from the start, but envious people attempting to bring down a political rival will look for dirt wherever they think they might find it. But Daniel was a special kind of politician: **he was trustworthy and neither corrupt nor negligent**.

Still, he was not without vulnerability; in a land of polytheism, this man was a monotheist. Some, in line with the thinking of more modern times, will argue both racism and ageism from the early part of this chapter. True, Daniel was still a Jew in a foreign land, but his mastery of the language, culture, laws, and literature would make age and ethnic background non-issues. Even the attack later in the chapter where Daniel is called "one of the exiles from Judah" (6:13) does not mean that Daniel's ethnic background made him vulnerable. To the contrary, Daniel's enemies aimed directly at one issue—Daniel's relationship to **his God**.

But these fellows faced a theological barrier; Persia had no law prohibiting monotheistic worship. Nevertheless, as astute politicians, they knew the king could be flattered and his ego stroked until something useful came their way. It may be worth noting that in a contest of this type, the early advantage usually falls to those with malicious intent.

6:6–7. Throughout this entire event Daniel describes the conspirators as **the administrators and the satraps**, so this was not just a plot by the other two who had been passed over in the king's plans to elevate Daniel. On the other hand, I find it hard to imagine how politicians from all corners of the realm could have been a part of this, so I suspect it was something of a local event. Since Babylon was the Washington, D.C. of the Babylonian Empire, there would be more than enough political lackeys to form this infamous **group**.

Although much has been made in this chapter about the respect and courtesy Darius showed to Daniel, we should not take that as anything more than it was. Darius was no theological giant, and he could not figure out that this phony edict would immediately target his key guy. On the surface the whole thing looked harmless. Archer sums it up: "The suggested mood of compelling every subject in the former Babylonian domain to acknowledge the authority of Persia seemed a statesman-like measure that would contribute to the unification of the Middle and Near East. The time limit of one month seemed reasonable. After it the people could resume their customary worship" (Archer, p. 79).

6:8–9. The crooked caucus would not be content with some verbal announcement; they wanted this decree issued **in writing so that it cannot be altered—in accordance with the laws of the Medes and Persians, which cannot be repealed**. Here we find another one of those phrases which has made its way through the centuries to claim a place in common vocabulary. When we speak of something that cannot be changed, we still might refer to it as governed by **the laws of the Medes and Persians**. The same phrase appears in Esther 1:19 and 8:8. Once it had been written, a royal edict could not be revoked. So by the end of verse 9, Daniel's enemies were ready to spring the trap.

Let's not miss the lie that made all this possible. They told the king that his subordinate leaders "have all agreed" (6:7) on this plan, and he had no reason to think Daniel had been excluded. Nevertheless, pride, injustice, and monarchial arrogance all paved the way for what would follow.

B Theological Entrapment (6:10–16)

SUPPORTING IDEA: *When everyone in the world seems to have turned against you, and your colleagues at work have betrayed you, fall on your knees before God.*

6:10. Central to the message of this chapter, this verse establishes the inner spiritual strength of God's servant. Here we see a man of sterling spiritual quality of whom God said to another prophet: "Son of man, if a country sins against me by being unfaithful and I stretch out my hand against it to cut off its food supply and send famine upon it and kill its men and their animals, even if these three men—Noah, Daniel and Job—were in it, they could save only themselves by their righteousness, declares the Sovereign LORD" (Ezek. 14:13–14).

In the estimate of the God to whom he prayed, Daniel stood in the company of two of the greatest and most courageous saints of all time. And how specific his record of the event. He didn't just go home to pray; **he went home to his upstairs room where the windows opened toward Jerusalem.** Should Christians obey the law? Absolutely—except when human law directly contradicts divine law—as in the case of the Darius decree. So Daniel continued what **he had done before**, offering a prayer of thanksgiving **to his God** while facing west to his homeland, which he had not seen for nearly seventy-five years.

This custom of facing the temple while praying, apparently first adopted by Solomon (2 Chr. 6:34–39), dominated Jewish worship all through the monarchial period, the exile, and the restoration right up until the time of the New Testament. Nor was this some last-minute panic prayer like Peter's fear of drowning in the Sea of Galilee. Everything about this verse tells us that Daniel regularly knelt by his window and prayed, and everybody knew about it.

Let's not miss how easily Daniel could have compromised his worship to save his life. The decree covered only three months. Why not suspend this public prayer pattern for a few weeks and then renew it again? Certainly God would understand that. Or just close the window and pray in private. They could accuse him of praying, but they couldn't prove it. On the other hand, if Darius asked Daniel directly if he had violated the decree, there is no doubt Daniel would have answered truthfully.

According to Archer:

> Daniel was in the habit of praying toward Jerusalem, for it was there in Solomon's temple that the glorious presence of Yahweh had come to reside (1 Kings 8:10–11). Even though this Shekinah cloud had forsaken the temple prior to the Fall of Jerusalem in 587 (Ezek. 11:23), Daniel knew that the Lord had promised to return there (Ezek. 43:2) and to restore Jerusalem (Jer. 29:10,14), even as he was then doing, for Cyrus' decree of restoration had probably been already promulgated. To what other direction should Daniel turn than the Holy City, the place of his heart's desire, the focal point of his hopes and prayers for the progress of the kingdom of God? (Archer, p. 80).

6:11–12. We have no difficulty imagining this crowd of conspirators standing on the street and looking up to Daniel's window. They saw him clearly and knew exactly what he was doing **so they went to the king and spoke to him about his royal decree**. But this verse offers something new about the prayer. In verse 10 we learned this was a prayer of thanksgiving like those Daniel would offer three times a day. Now we see that Daniel was also **asking God for help**.

Multiple sermons with a variety of outlines can be preached on this text. But before we move on let me offer six elements of this prayer which surface in its biblical description:

1. Place of prayer
2. Persistence in prayer
3. Posture of prayer
4. Praise in prayer
5. Pattern of prayer
6. Petition in prayer

We'll come back to the question of posture in "Deeper Discoveries," but meanwhile, back to the crooked caucus.

6:13–14. Daniel's enemies had him. Time to spring the trap and bring down this high-and-mighty interloper. After all, he was just **one of the exiles from Judah**, reminding us of Belshazzar's question in 5:13. Obviously they had every right to this condemnation because this Daniel **pays no attention to you, O king**.

This sounds like déjà vu all over again. A similar crowd approached Nebuchadnezzar a couple of generations earlier and said exactly the same thing about Daniel's three friends (3:12). One thing seems absolutely clear throughout this book: the people of God will serve no god but God himself.

The king's reaction seems unexpected. He **was greatly distressed**, not because someone violated his edict, but because his trusted and respected provost had been caught in the trap. There was nothing he could do about the law, but he spent the entire day **determined to rescue Daniel and made every effort until sundown to save him**. This was a job for the lawyers. Surely they could find some legal loophole through which the king could slide out of this pernicious plan hatched by perverted politicians. If only he had been living in America! But in Persia, no chance.

As Baldwin points out:

> Absolute power could not achieve the release of Daniel because of the greater power of united public opinion. This is an all together different dilemma from those which faced Nebuchadrezzar or Belshazzar, and presents another aspect of the limitation of a human ruler. . . . There is also more than a side-glance at laws which become absolute and are rigidly enforced, with resulting injustice to individual citizens (Baldwin, p. 130).

6:15–16. Here they came again, just to remind the king one more time he had no choices in this matter, a fact of which he was already only too well aware. **So the king gave the order, and they brought Daniel and threw him into the lions' den**. We did not mention the lions when they first appeared in verse 7, but here we should ask, "Whatever happened to the fiery furnace?" We are accustomed to a variety of death penalty options in our own culture—lethal injection, electric chair, gas pellets—but the contrast between being burned alive or chewed up by wild beasts seems not only brutal but unusual.

Keep in mind that one evil empire had been replaced by another. The Persians worshiped fire as a part of their Zoroastrian beliefs and would never have used it as a means of punishment. A comparison of fire, lions, and crosses merely serves to remind us of the bitter cruelty sin has caused in the world. Although they may be vastly different in political structure, philosophy, and religion, evil empires generally follow a common path of brutality.

The king had to follow through with the execution, but he did not have to handle the matter impersonally. He apparently followed Daniel right to the lions' den, and his final words represented hopeful expectation: **May your God, whom you serve continually, rescue you!** Quite a compliment to Daniel's service since the verb appears in the present periphrastic tense, indicating that the king believed Daniel served God at all times. Darius had tried human deliverance and failed. Now he fully recognized that Daniel's fate was in the hands of his God. The tense changes here for the verb **rescue** and takes on an imperfect sense, almost implying an obligation, or at the very least, an expectation that the hoped-for event would occur.

C Heavenly Deliverance (6:17–24)

SUPPORTING IDEA: *Although the choice is his, God often delivers his people from sickness and death through a miracle of his own design.*

6:17. Our familiarity with zoos and circuses with their stone-walled pits or iron bars makes it difficult to imagine this scene. Certainly the pit was underground and quite possibly contained various chambers. The stone placed over the opening had hot wax poured over it and the signet ring cylinders of the king and his nobles all placed on it so that no one could move it. The language at the end of the verse seems quaint: **so that Daniel's situation might not be changed**.

My take on this verse suggests that the king was the only one they needed to worry about, and he allowed the conspirators to guarantee the safety of the stone so they knew he would not attempt any midnight rescue. Although probably fuming inside, Darius was a subject of Cyrus and completely bound by Persian law. Baldwin describes the den: "The text implies that the lion-pit had two entrances, a ramp down which the animals would enter, and a hole in the roof by which the food would normally be fed to them. Whether Daniel was thrown in from the top or the side, there would be only one way out unless someone let down a rope" (Baldwin, p. 130).

6:18. The long night began. Darius would normally have eaten a huge and opulent meal and enjoyed some kind of **entertainment** before retiring. The *Modern Language Bible* renders this verse nicely: "Then the king went to his palace, and spent the night in meditation and fasting, instead of enjoying his usual diversions, and his sleep fled from him" (MBL).

6:19–20. Nor did he have time for breakfast. For **at the first light of dawn**, Darius rushed to the execution pit and **called to Daniel** even before he got to the den, still with an air of expectation. To the crooked caucus Daniel may have been one of the exiles from Judah, but for this king he was a **servant of the living God**. More than just the rescue of a friend, this was a test of deity. Darius knew of no gods who could stop the mouths of lions. If Daniel's God could do that, then the king's theology needed some reconstruction. Nevertheless, his agony of soul had not departed because he called **in an anguished voice**. The word is *asib*, portraying poignant sadness.

6:21–22. What a mighty morning message came back from the bottom of the pit! **My God sent his angel, and he shut the mouths of the lions**. Is there a relationship between the fourth person in the fiery furnace and the angel in the lions' den? To put it another way, when Daniel referred to **his angel**, did he mean *an* angel or *the* angel? It is speculation at best, but we should certainly not consider it impossible that the pre-incarnate Christ made another appearance by the side of his servant.

Campbell thinks so: "It seems probable that the deliverer of the three Hebrew youth (3:25,28) and of Daniel (6:22) is the same person, the Angel of Jehovah. Daniel not only spent the night in the company of the lions, but infinitely better, in the company of the pre-incarnate Son of God! It is difficult not to be curious about the conversation through those night hours!" (Campbell, p. 98).

Daniel offers two reasons for his rescue: **I was found innocent in his sight** and **nor have I ever done any wrong before you, O king**.

6:23–24. The king's anguish turned to joy as they hoisted Daniel out of the pit unscathed **because he had trusted in his God**. When God yanked his friends out of Nebuchadnezzar's fire, there was no smell of smoke nor the slightest singe of clothing or hair. When God delivers, he does it completely. Then suddenly this pagan monarch, who could be so close to the edge of faith, showed again the fury of a wicked heart and threw Daniel's accusers into the den **along with their wives and children**. Although the barbarity of the ancient world stuns us, this kind of judgment was even seen among the Jews and sometimes given by God himself (Num. 16; Deut. 19). Let's notice that the lions were not fed 120 families of politicians but rather the accusers, the crooked caucus who had placed the king in this dreadful dilemma.

In any case, there was no suffering because **before they reached the floor of the den, the lions overpowered them and crushed all their bones**.

D Royal Testimony (6:25–28)

SUPPORTING IDEA: *The Great King of Heaven so dominates the kingdoms of this world that he can change the minds and wills of their sovereigns to fit his eternal plan.*

6:25–27. Now well practiced in the art of writing decrees, Darius once more took pen in hand and sent a message **to all the peoples, nations and men of every language throughout the land**. Similar to the words of Nebuchadnezzar at the end of chapter 4, Darius's testimony even expanded the doctrine of sovereignty and identified specifically, **he rescues and he saves; he performs signs and wonders in the heavens and on the earth**. Walvoord observes, "Verses 26–27 are in the form of a hymn in the original. Once again throughout the world of Daniel's day, the tidings were carried of the great God who is living, powerful, everlasting, and greater than the gods of the pagans" (Walvoord, *Daniel*, p. 144).

6:28. This chapter ends with a clear delineation between Darius and Cyrus which should put to rest any arguments that they were the same person with different names. As for Daniel, he **prospered during the reign of Darius and the reign of Cyrus** much in the way he had prospered during the reign of Nebuchadnezzar. He would live several more years to study the Scriptures and pray as well as revise his memoirs which, according to Archer (p. 84), were likely published about 532 B.C.

Wood points out:

> The further statement that this was also during the reign of Cyrus does not mean that Cyrus followed Darius. As has been noted, the two served contemporaneously. Daniel continued to prosper during the rule of both, as they served at the same time. The force of the statement is to say that, whereas Daniel's accusers all died in the lions' den, Daniel, who had remained true to God in spite of their efforts, continued to live and prosper. He probably, in fact, received the advanced position planned for him by Darius with new appointees made to serve under him. Surely this testifies once more to God's faithfulness to those who are faithful to Him (Wood, *Daniel*, p. 87).

MAIN IDEA REVIEW: *When the crises of life threaten us, and our very lives are at stake, calm and quiet dependence upon God is our only recourse.*

III. CONCLUSION

Waffling in Prayer

In my retirement I live several months each year on the campus of Toccoa Falls College in northeast Georgia, just ninety miles north of Atlanta. One of our rivals in almost every sport is Atlanta Christian College, whose teams I have seen play basketball and soccer on numerous occasions.

On the campus of that institution floats a wonderful story from ten or fifteen years ago. Apparently the Atlanta Christian College choir travels on concert tours by bus, a practice common to almost every institution of its kind. On one occasion the choir stopped at a restaurant whose fame was known to all the locals—pecan waffles. All the students at one table ordered the specialty of the house. As the waitress set the waffles in front of them, they bent over, heads bowed to give thanks. The waitress, hardly knowing how to react in this situation, leaned over and whispered to one of the students, "If you're looking for the pecans, they're on the bottom."

Public prayer becomes a testimony to our faith in the grace of God. In this chapter we see it demonstrating faith, thanks, worship, and rock-solid trust in God's power to protect and care for his children. Remember, we have not yet come to John 4 and the recognition that place and posture contain no value in God's eyes. Daniel knew that there was a Jerusalem out there somewhere, in ruins and decay perhaps, but still the city of God. His was an exclusive faith—Jehovah alone, Jerusalem alone. We share that exclusivity without the attached geography: "There is one body and one Spirit—just as you were called to one hope when you were called—one Lord, one faith, one baptism; one God and Father of all, who is over all and through all and in all" (Eph. 4:4–6).

Daniel offers us one of the greatest models of the Bible, a clear-cut demonstration of courage and commitment from youth until death. He stood for what he believed even though the stars might fall, and no king, however powerful on earth, could dissuade his focus on the King of heaven. He would have enjoyed a brief prayer composed by Lancelot Andrewes during the years the Reformation spread across Europe: "Oh direct my life toward Thy commandments, hallow my soul, purify my body, correct my thoughts, cleanse my desires, soul and body, mind and spirit, heart and reins. Renew me thoroughly, O Lord, for if Thou wilt, Thou canst."

PRINCIPLES

- Wisdom often accompanies age, especially among the people of God.
- Abilities in both leadership and administration come as gifts from God only enhanced and polished by human training.
- Too often the true motive for evil behavior among public officials never comes to light.
- When people offer genuine witness of their faith in God, in both words and life, both words and life are unassailable.

APPLICATIONS

- If we act in a spirit of love and faith, there should be no offense to reasonable people.
- Regular routines of prayer provide the kind of discipline necessary for godly living.
- Watch for Satan's work in the disguise of law and order as well as in chaos and evil.
- Don't take pains to defend yourself when attacked; place your life in God's hands.
- Let's make sure that if anyone should accuse us of faithfulness to God, we will be found guilty.

IV. LIFE APPLICATION

Chorus No. 28

George Frederick Handel nervously approached the first London performance of *Messiah* in 1743. Was the theater the right venue? Would concert-goers think his words too sacred for such secular music? They even changed the name for that night, advertising his work as *A New Sacred Oratorio*. The Scripture texts used in Handel's work were arranged by his friend Charles Jennens, who placed the text in the order which takes the story of our Lord from birth to resurrection and ultimate heavenly praise. When the final "Hallelujah Chorus" begins, audiences across the world rise, some hardly knowing why. The accounts of the first audience reaction seem somewhat mixed though they center on George II at that first performance in 1743.

Payne and Lenzo emphasize the significance of the practice today:

> However it started, the custom of standing was the fashion in Handel's lifetime and remains popular today. Those early audiences were impressed with more than just the music of *Messiah*. They understood the story it told of a Savior. They stood up to honor the Son of God. The story was so important to them that many did not want to go to a show about the *Messiah*. They thought that such music should be heard only in a church (Payne and Lenzo, p. 99).

But what about Chorus No. 28? The entire choral text of *Messiah* stretches to about 252 pages. Almost directly in the middle (page 122) the chorus sings "All We Like Sheep Have Gone Astray," followed by a recitative for tenor (No. 27), "All They That See Him, Laugh in Scorn." The tenor solo lasts for only one page, however, because he is merely introducing Chorus No. 28: "He trusted in God that he would deliver him," from Matthew 27:43.

For some reason that chorus, which I have often sung, rises in my heart as I read Daniel 6. Like Jesus, Daniel was besieged by evil people with political and religious power. Like Jesus, his accusers wanted him to die and scorned the possibility of any miraculous rescue. True, Daniel did not experience death and resurrection, but his attitude throughout the crisis mirrors the spirit of Jesus at the cross. Daniel trusted in God and God did deliver him.

According to Archer:

> Three emphases stand out in this passage: (1) Daniel's God is alive and shows that he lives by the way he acts in history, responding, like a real person, to the requirements of justice and the needs of his people; (2) God's rule is eternal and will never pass away (as do empires built by human power), even though the Hebrew monarchy did not survive its apostasy; (3) God miraculously delivers his true worshippers, performing wonders both in heaven and on earth. He has furnished objective proof of his eternal power and godhead, in contrast with all other deities, whose existence is at best conjectural and traditional (Archer, p. 83).

V. PRAYER

Father, thank you for the courage and faith of Daniel. May our lives reflect the same kind of devotion to you, both privately and publicly. Amen.

VI. DEEPER DISCOVERIES

A. Prayer Posture (6:10)

A quick glance at any thorough concordance shows that kneeling in prayer is not as common as we might think. Psalm 95:6 calls us to "come, let us bow down in worship, let us kneel before the LORD our Maker." Isaiah 45:23 (in the context of Babylonian captivity and deliverance) allows us to hear God say, "By myself I have sworn, my mouth has uttered in all integrity a word that will not be revoked: Before me every knee will bow; by me every tongue will swear." We also find Paul kneeling with the Ephesian elders to pray (Acts 20:36) and again with other believers in Acts 21:5.

Some churches practice kneeling regularly as part of the Lord's Supper or perhaps at weddings, ordinations, or missionary commissionings. Though hardly commanded and quite possibly difficult and painful for some, kneeling is a way of acknowledging our humility before God. My friend Paul Cedar sums it up in a warm paragraph:

> Kneeling is not the only posture for prayer. But it is a wonderful place to begin as we approach God in prayer. Kneeling when we pray is a habit worth developing. It is a posture that enhances our sense of coming into the presence of God, of humbling ourselves before Him. Kneeling can remind us vividly of who God is and who we are. Of course, some individuals cannot kneel because of physical limitations. However, all of us can adopt a kneeling attitude in the presence of God (Cedar, p. 60).

B. Zoroastrianism

Not to be confused with a religion worshiping a masked rider with a black cape, Zoroastrianism lived on the dividing line between ancient and modern religions. It rose in ancient times (about 660 B.C.) yet is still practiced in the twenty-first century by cults and sects. The early forms were distinctly Persian, rising from the plains of modern Iran and replacing the typical polytheism of ancient religions, much like those of Assyria and Babylonia. Virtually everything about Zoroaster (Zarathustra) seems mystical, certainly his birth and even substantial data regarding his existence. What we know comes to us through ancient poems in the Avesta, Zorastranian scriptures. Apparently he was a wandering prophet and contemporary of Buddha, Confucius, and Jeremiah.

Rejecting polytheism, Zoroaster called his followers to Ahura Mazda and declared the goodness of that god. He warned of a coming day of judgment on which everyone would be faced with his record on earth. Matter was seen as evil, and a corpse was seen as the most defiling of all earthly things. Funerals could only be held in dry weather because rain must not touch the defiled corpse, nor could it be burned since fire was sacred.

Since this is the heart of our concern about the religion in relation to Daniel 6, I offer a paragraph by religious historian Charles S. Braden:

> The principle feature of modern Zorastrianism is the fire cult. This is conducted secretly, and no outsider is ever permitted to witness it. It is performed in the midst of the Fire Temple by properly ordained and ritually prepared representatives of the priesthood, which is among the Parsis strictly hereditary. The ceremony requisite for the kindling of the temple fire is most elaborate. It is made by compounding 16 different fires, each purified by an exceedingly involved ritual. One of the fires, for example, must be secured by kindling one from the other successively ninety-one times to the accompaniment of prayers" (Braden, pp. 84–85).

We need pursue the subject no further, but I raise it here to explain how the death penalty in Daniel moved so quickly from fire to lions.

C. Forced Faith (6:26)

The nonsense that a ruler can compel heart change in his followers is neither new nor old; it persists to the present hour. While we recognize the importance of what Darius wrote, let us not imagine that the entire kingdom began to worship Jehovah of Jerusalem because the king said so. Outwardly they could not defy their king, but true faith is of the heart—not obedience to monarchial dictates.

Christians are not immune to this disease. The great emperor Constantine would march entire battalions through rivers, thereby "baptizing" them to make them Christians. During and after the Reformation entire nations would be identified as "Protestant" or "Catholic" because of the commitment of their rulers. We demean neither the text of Daniel nor the intentions of Darius when we acknowledge that there is no such thing as forced faith.

D. Cyrus the Persian (6:28)

Son of Cambyses, King of Anshan, Cyrus was the virtual founder of the Persian Empire that began some years before the fall of Babylon. The Persians rose from the former Sumerian and Akkadian cultures. Cyrus entered Babylon on October 29, 539 B.C., and took the throne as a liberator of the people. As we shall see in chapter 7, during the third year of Cyrus's reign in Babylon Daniel 10–12 was written.

Generally Cyrus was a magnanimous conqueror, supporting local deities and repatriating captive peoples. Eventually he encouraged the Jews to return to Israel in order to rebuild their temple and their city (2 Chr. 36; Ezra 1; Isa. 44). He reigned supreme throughout the Middle East until dethroned by Alexander the Great. Cyrus was followed by Darius I, who built the enormous palace at Persepolis in 518 B.C. Alexander burned it to the ground in 330, though many of the carvings and pictures remain. The Persian Empire began to deteriorate by about 500, and their armies were defeated by the Greeks at the Battle of Marathon in 490. Xerxes I, son of Darius, suffered the defeat at Salamis in 480, 150 years before Alexander burned the temple at Persepolis.

VII. TEACHING OUTLINE

A. INTRODUCTION

1. Lead Story: The Bear and the Dragon
2. Context: Daniel 6 bridges the gap between the end of the Babylonian Empire and the rule of Cyrus the Persian. It completes the historical

section of Daniel, who will now immediately flash back to his own dreams that began "in the first year of Belshazzar."

3. Transition: Daniel offers no transition between chapters. We have already seen nearly twenty-five years lost between chapters 4 and 5. Daniel ends chapter 5 by saying, "Darius the Mede took over the kingdom" and ends chapter 6 by saying that he prospered "during the reign of Darius and the reign of Cyrus the Persian."

B. COMMENTARY

1. Political Entry (6:1–9)
2. Theological Entrapment (6:10–16)
3. Heavenly Deliverance (6:17–24)
4. Royal Testimony (6:25–28)

C. CONCLUSION: WAFFLING IN PRAYER

VIII. ISSUES FOR DISCUSSION

1. What does this chapter teach us about respect for older Christians?
2. List three things you have learned about prayer from Daniel 6.
3. Assuming you'll never be thrown into a den of hungry lions, what "lions" might you face in your life as a Christian?

Daniel 7:1–14

The Ancient of Days

I. INTRODUCTION
Bombay Brit

II. COMMENTARY
A verse-by-verse explanation of the chapter.

III. CONCLUSION
Left Behind

An overview of the principles and applications from the chapter.

IV. LIFE APPLICATION
Letter from O'Hare

Melding the chapter to life.

V. PRAYER
Tying the chapter to life with God.

VI. DEEPER DISCOVERIES
Historical, geographical, and grammatical enrichment of the commentary.

VII. TEACHING OUTLINE
Suggested step-by-step group study of the chapter.

VIII. ISSUES FOR DISCUSSION
Zeroing the chapter in on daily life.

Quote

"His chariots of wrath the deep thunder clouds form, and dark is His path on the wings of the storm."

Robert Grant

Daniel 7:1–14

IN A NUTSHELL

A comparison of Daniel 7 with the previous six chapters shows us immediately more differences than commonalities. God changes the revelatory method, and Daniel now receives information through angelic mediation rather than through dreams, a process that continues throughout the second half of the book. His reporting scheme also switches from the third person to the first person as he becomes an eyewitness of what God will do in "future world history."

The Ancient of Days

I. INTRODUCTION

Bombay Brit

Born just three years after American patriarchs signed the Declaration of Independence, Robert Grant became a member of the Scottish Parliament and governor of Bombay. According to Osbeck, "Throughout his entire life, Grant was a devoutly evangelical Christian who strongly supported the missionary outreach of his church and endeared himself to the people of India by establishing a medical college in Bombay" (Osbeck, p. 275).

But we remember him most for his outstanding worship hymn, which has become a model of the way we think about God. He repeatedly extols the greatness of the Almighty, using descriptive phrases reminiscent of Daniel's encounter with the King of heaven.

> O worship the King, all-glorious above
> And gratefully sing His pow'r and His love;
> Our Shield and Defender, the Ancient of Days,
> Pavilioned in splendor and girded with praise.

One's interpretation of Scripture forms one's theology, but once a theological system is in place, it also plays a significant role in interpretation. In chapter 2 we saw the importance of acknowledging both the reality of the present spiritual kingdom of God among his people and the ultimate visible and physical kingdom in the millennium after the second coming of Christ. In both chapters 2 and 7 this commentary takes the viewpoint that the emphasis rests on Christ's second coming, not his first. And therefore, much of what we read is yet to be fulfilled. This is what is known as a *premillennial* interpretation of the text.

Let me continue just a bit further with comparisons between chapters 2 and 7 since they are not only essential but even unavoidable. Culver has summarized them succinctly:

> The differences between the dream prophecy of chapter 2 and the vision prophecy of chapter 7 are chiefly as follows: (1) The *dream*

> was not seen originally by a man of God but by a heathen monarch, hence it was something that would appeal to such a man and which might be readily explicable to his intellect. The *vision* was seen by a holy man of God, and hence in terms more readily explicable to his intellect. (2) The *first* presented the history of nations and the outward aspect—majestic, splendid; the *second* in their inward aspect—as ravening wild beasts. This might be elaborated to say that the first is a view of the history of nations as man sees them, the second as God sees them (Culver, p. 126).

Some have suggested that chapter 2 is the cosmological view, perhaps even the cosmetic view of the nations, whereas chapter 7 provides the spiritual view, demonstrating the onerous reality of the pagan cosmos. We take up our task with what has often been called a *literal-natural* approach to the text.

II. COMMENTARY

MAIN IDEA: *Human kingdoms come and go and more often than not demonstrate cruelty rather than kindness, injustice rather than justice. But above all the human chaos the Ancient of Days runs his world with power and grace.*

Vision of the Four Beasts (7:1–7)

SUPPORTING IDEA: *For six chapters Daniel has been telling us stories flavored by history and prophecy; now he will tell us about his visions. What was heretofore recorded as general information now becomes prophecy.*

7:1. This chapter opens with a flashback to **the first year of Belshazzar king of Babylon**, approximately 553 B.C., about nine years after the death of Nebuchadnezzar. This is the first recorded vision Daniel has received himself, and he chooses it to begin the second half of his book. In Walvoord's words, "Conservative scholars . . . have hailed chapter 7 as one of the great prophecies of the Bible and the key to the entire program of God from Babylon to the Second Coming of Christ" (Walvoord, *Daniel*, p. 151).

7:2. How are we to understand metaphoric phrases such **the four winds of heaven**? The image of wind in the Book of Daniel tends to be used of

God's sovereign power and therefore suggests a picture of heavenly forces. Some have suggested that the number symbolizes the completeness of the whole earth, and even today we use the expression "four corners of the earth."

Daniel also saw **the great sea**, an immediate reference to the Mediterranean, with much wider application to another phrase we commonly use today, "the sea of humanity" (Luke 21:25; Matt. 13:47; Rev. 13:1). The Bible is never complimentary in its reference to worldly nations. The picture here suggests unrest and confusion as the cosmos rages like a sea bubbling its furor when whipped by heavenly winds. There are dozens of "seas" all over the world, but the focus of headline news year after year centers in the Mediterranean. Archer interestingly points out that in the new earth there will be no more sea (*thalassa*) (Rev. 21:1) and that "the four winds represent God's judgments, hurling themselves on the ungodly nations from all four points of the compass. And the successive rise and fall of the four empires of Babylon, Medo-Persia, Greece, and Rome, these destructive forces will exert their power through the centuries to come, till the final triumph of the Son of Man" (Archer, p. 85). Wind is mentioned more than 120 times in the Bible. More than half of those point to the sovereignty and power of God. Indeed, that is the only way Daniel uses the word.

7:3. The oft-repeated metaphors of animals and birds of prey in this chapter should not catch us by surprise. On their shields and banners many of the ancient empires used insignia and logos of such creatures. Furthermore, the first three beasts (the lion, bear, and leopard) were certainly well known to residents of the Middle East. In verse 3 they rise **out of the sea**, but in Daniel's interpretation of 7:17, they "rise from the earth." This lessens the importance of the Mediterranean issue and increases the significance of the metaphors. Luke 21:25 brings them together: "There will be signs in the sun, moon and stars. On the earth, nations will be in anguish and perplexity at the roaring and tossing of the sea."

Whether the sea or the earth are metaphors, these are the nations of the *world*, a common concept in the New Testament, always associated with wicked human domains under the ultimate control of Satan. *World* is a key word throughout the Gospel of John and appears again in his first epistle where he warns believers not to love it (1 John 2:15–17).

7:4. The **lion** with the eagle's wings parallels the gold head of 2:37–38 and the focus seems to center on strength and swiftness. Its wings have been clipped, its speed eliminated, and now it stands **on two feet like a man**. The reference to **the heart of a man** most likely points to the very heart and soul of the Babylonian kingdom, Nebuchadnezzar himself (Jer. 49:19–22). Throughout this book God consistently shows the great Nebuchadnezzar the source of his authority and how Babylon and all other monarchies fade into nothingness when confronted with the absolute heavenly theocracy.

So the lion symbolizes Babylon (Jer. 4:6–7). Commentators wonder whether the verse speaks as much of Nebuchadnezzar the man as it does of his empire, so closely connected were the two. The Bible has not spoken of Babylon from the eleventh chapter of Genesis to the major prophets, but then it comes in for significant treatment. Isaiah describes its destruction in Isaiah 13, and Jeremiah refers to Babylonia frequently, most notably in Jeremiah 25 and again in three long chapters at the end of the book (Jer. 50–52). We also find prophecies about Babylon in Ezekiel (Ezek. 17; 29; 30; 32).

7:5. The second beast **looked like a bear**. Bears appear some thirteen times in the Bible. The use of the simile in this context seems to identify the silver breast of 2:39, the kingdom of Persia. The bulky size of the animal reminds us that some Persian armies contained as many as two and one-half million men (notably in the battles of Xerxes against Greece). The posture **raised up on one of its sides** may indicate a predatory stance, but more likely it represents the dominance of Persia in the Medo-Persian alliance. Wood suggests a third possibility: "They may show that the legs are lifted as if walking and moving ahead; this points to the great Medo-Persian desire for conquest, carried out especially by Cyrus" (Wood, *Daniel*, p. 93). Some critical scholars have identified the second kingdom as Media alone. We will deal with that in "Deeper Discoveries."

What are we to do with the **three ribs in its mouth**? The interpretation which finds them to be the three previously conquered empires goes all the way back to Jerome (A.D. 345–420) and is held by many, perhaps most, evangelical scholars today. There is, however, some disagreement as to what kingdoms those might be, although Archer seems confident.

According to Archer:

> This corresponds perfectly to the three major conquests of the Medes and Persians made under the leadership of King Cyrus and

> his son Cambyses: viz., the Lydian Kingdom in Asian Minor (which fell to Cyrus in 546), the Chaldean Empire (which he annexed in 539), and the Kingdom of Egypt (which Cambyses acquired in 525). Needless to say, nothing in the career of the Median Empire before Cyrus' time corresponds to the three ribs. In view of these things, it is hopeless to make out any plausible link between this bear and the earlier, separate Median Empire that preceded Cyrus' victory over Astyages (Archer, p. 86).

Leupold is not convinced and generalizes the number as a symbol of conquest:

> Three appears to be a number that signifies rather substantial conquests and is not be to taken literally. For the Medo-Persian Empire conquered more than Babylonia, Lydia, and Egypt. Such enumerations of three definite powers are more or less arbitrary. Three does sometimes signify nothing more than a fairly large number and has no reference to God or the Holy Trinity. That is especially true in a case like this. Someone has rightly remarked that "the three ribs constitute a large mouth full" (Leupold, p. 292).

I tend to side with Archer rather than Leupold, but the ribs are not nearly as important as the recognition of the empire and its unbalanced composition, coinciding as it does with the two arms of chapter 2.

7:6. The third beast **looked like a leopard**. Daniel tells us **it had four wings like those of a bird**. It also had **four heads, and it was given authority to rule**. Babylon had seized power from Assyria in 612 B.C., only to lose it to the Medo-Persians in 539. Then in 336, leopard-like from his lair in Greece, came Alexander with an army headed by four generals and known, not for its size like Persia (Alexander fought with only about 35,000 men), but for its speed. Tutored as a child by Aristotle, Alexander accomplished some of the greatest feats of military history in a very short time. From 334 to 322 B.C. his armies marched irresistibly eastward until he became the master of all lands between the Mediterranean and the modern borders of Afghanistan.

The **four heads** were at one time considered to refer to Ptolemy, Seleucus, Phillip, and Antigonus (Jerome, Calvin). More contemporary commentators prefer a reference to the configuration of the empire about 301 B.C.—

Lysimachus, Cassander, Seleucus, and Ptolemy. As I noted earlier, and will deal with again in "Deeper Discoveries," the prejudicial nature of some scholars denies the early date of Daniel and therefore its historic authorship, assuming the book to be nothing more than a diatribe against Antiochus Epipahanes.

In one fanciful handling of this verse, Hanhart develops the imaginative notion that it describes Rome and opts for contemporary rather than consecutive kingdoms:

> A clue, hidden in Rev. 13:2, namely that the leopard in Daniel 7:6 must represent the Romans and not the Parthians, strengthens an earlier observation that the four beasts in Daniel 7 represent four *contemporaneous* kingdoms existing along side each other. These two data upset the age-old axiom that in Dan. 2:31ff. and in 7:2ff. the same empires are intended, for in the order of succeeding kingdoms the Roman Empire cannot possibly appear ahead of that of the Hellenes. The introductory phrase, "The four winds of heaven were stirring up the great sea," leads me to conclude that the four kingdoms in Dan. 7 are situated around the Mediterranean Sea according to the four points of the compass, to wit: south—Egypt, the lion; east—Persia, the bear; west—Rome, the leopard; north—Syria, the anonymous beast. Probably an elephant" (Hanhart, pp. 580–81).

I insert this quote merely to show how ridiculous schemes can become when they rest upon the assumption that God's Word is not accurate and predictive prophecy impossible. Nevertheless, there is some room for discussion on this point. No less a scholar than Edward J. Young sees in the four heads simply "the four corners of the earth, [symbolizing] ecumenicity of the kingdoms" (Young, p. 146).

7:7. But there is yet another beast, **terrifying and frightening and very powerful**, vicious, cruel, strong, and merciless. It **trampled underfoot whatever was left**. We will treat this more specifically in the latter part of the chapter, but suffice it to say here that virtually every evangelical scholar links Daniel 7:7 with Daniel 2:40: "Finally, there will be a fourth kingdom, strong as iron—for iron breaks and smashes everything—and as iron breaks things to pieces, so it will crush and break all the others."

In Daniel's vision this terrible fourth beast was uniquely different because **it had ten horns**. The comparison of Daniel 2 and Daniel 7 requires us to link the ten horns with the ten toes, and Daniel could hardly have missed the connection. Rome ruled the world for over seven hundred years from about 250 B.C. to 407 A.D. and lived on after the sack of the city of Rome so that there were still Roman rulers in the Renaissance. Even in the twenty-first century we talk about "Romance languages."

The identification of the fourth beast could not be more dramatic in our understanding of Daniel. But it presents no complicated mystery. If one accepts the sixth-century dating of the book and acknowledges the reality of predictive prophecy, there is absolutely no problem in seeing Rome here, and most conservative scholars do. The *a priori* rejection of predictive prophecy, however, forces first the second-century date, and then finds it necessary to erase Rome from the mix since Daniel could not possibly have known about that evil empire.

Walvoord offers an interesting twist on the argument:

> Probably the most decisive argument in favor of interpreting the fourth empire as Roman is the fact . . . that the New Testament seems to follow this interpretation. Christ, in His reference to the "abomination of desolation" (Mt 24:15 KJV) clearly pictures the desecration of the temple, here prophesized as a future event. . . . The New Testament also seems to employ the symbolism of Daniel in the book of Revelation, presented as future even after the destruction of the temple. These New Testament allusions to Daniel which require the fourth empire to be Roman . . . make unnecessary the tangled explanation of Rowley and others attempting to find an explanation of the ten horns or at least seven of them in the Seleucid kings (Walvoord, *Daniel*, pp. 161–62).

B Vision of the Little Horn (7:8,11–12)

SUPPORTING IDEA: *The most cruel and oppressive regimes of a cruel and oppressive world are still held by the leash of God's power.*

7:8. Rarely do I divide verses in the pages of this commentary, but here these references to the ten horns and the little horn are interrupted by the vision of the Ancient of Days to which we must return in a moment. The deterioration of the Roman Empire as it falls from iron to clay provides opportunity for the rising of weaker leadership, not only in the immediate wake of Alexander but throughout the ages until the end of time. But what did Daniel actually see?

In addition to the "ten horns" of verse 7 which gave him some pause, he saw **another horn, a little one, which came up among them; and three of the first horns were uprooted before it**. Despite the specificity of this verse, verses 11–12, and the interpretation in verses 23–25, amillennial scholars find in these horns and the little horn only generalities of power or perhaps historic fulfillment in the past record of the Roman Empire. Furthermore, we dare not confuse the little horn of chapter 7 with the little horn of chapter 8 that (as we shall see when we arrive there) seems to point clearly to Antiochus Epiphanes.

Archer vehemently argues (and I agree) that the toes and horns are identical, and all ten also reign contemporaneously. So the vision stretches on into the future of our world well beyond the boundaries of the ancient Roman Empire. Regarding **eyes like the eyes of a man and a mouth that spoke boastfully**, he says:

> These features seem to imply that this little horn symbolizes an arrogant and vain-glorious ruler rather than an entire kingdom. . . . This introduces us for the first time to the ruthless world-dictator of the last days who is referred to in 2 Thessalonians 2:3,8 as the "the man of lawlessness [*anominas*]" or "the lawless one [*anomos*]" who "exalts himself over everything that is God or is worshipped and even sets himself up in God's temple, proclaiming himself to be God" (2 Thess. 2:4). It should be carefully noted that *this* little horn emerges from the fourth empire, in contrast to the little horn of chapter 8 . . . which arises from the third empire (Archer, p. 87).

7:11. In the flow of his narrative, Daniel sets up the conflict of the ages. Even as the "Ancient of Days took his seat" (7:9), the boastful little horn continues to yap about his own authority. Then as Daniel watches, he sees the beast **slain and its body destroyed and thrown into the blazing fire**. If we are not careful, we will be tripped up here in Daniel's switch from **horn** to **beast** right in the middle of this verse. Clearly the little horn was a **beast**, and its destruction is described with some lurid details in Revelation

19:19–21. Since the little horn as well as the ten other horns were part of the fourth beast, its destruction rids the earth of all of them. But the vision yet contains information regarding the lion, bear, and leopard.

7:12. All of the beasts had been **stripped of their authority**, but each was **allowed to live for a period of time**. Some suggest this phrase means that each lived out its God-ordained time. Certainly another possibility is that each lived on into the next in the way that Greek culture continued throughout the Roman era. In any case, they are finished when the Ancient of Days gets through with them.

Sir Robert Anderson compares Nebuchadnezzar's dream and Daniel's vision:

> As the four empires which were destined successively to wield sovereign power during "the times of the Gentiles" are represented in Nebuchadnezzar's dream by the four divisions of the great image, they are here typified by the four wild beasts. The ten toes of the image in the second chapter have their correlatives in the ten horns of the fourth beast in the seventh chapter. The character and course of the fourth empire are the prominent subject of the latter vision but both prophecies are equally explicit. Yet the empire in its ultimate phase will be brought to a signal and sudden end by a manifestation of Divine power on earth (Anderson, *Prince*, pp. 36–37).

Baldwin is right on target when, after pondering the meaning of survival of the first three beasts, she suggests that the passage clearly states that "history has not yet come to an end, despite the intervention of God's judgment, though *a season and a time* implies a limited future" (Baldwin, p. 142).

C Vision of the Ancient of Days (7:9–10)

SUPPORTING IDEA: *Kings and judges come and go, but ultimately in heaven there will be only one king and one righteous judge who will destroy all evil forever.*

7:9. If Daniel's vision were a play, this would be a major scene change. The stage lights have gone off, the curtain has closed and now reopened, and in the place of the boastful little horn is a scene of heaven at the end of time. The description reminds us of Revelation 4 and 5. Some claim the **Ancient of Days** is the Lord Jesus Christ, claiming to find support in Revelation

1:12–14. In 7:13, however, "one like a son of man" comes before **the Ancient of Days**, establishing their distinct separation. This is a picture of God the Heavenly Father, and the Bible uses the phrase "Ancient of Days" only in 7:9,13,22. Plural **thrones** may indicate the seating of the Son and the Holy Spirit as well, although I would certainly not press that point. The **flaming** throne of God certainly portrays righteousness and judgment (Ps. 97; Rev. 1:14–15).

Wood says, "No indication is given as to who occupied the other thrones, but these were probably angels, who do the bidding of God (Heb. 1:14). Perhaps they were not mentioned specifically because they were acting only as passive observers" (Wood, *Daniel*, p. 96).

This picture of Jehovah as seen by Daniel reminds us of the marvelous worship hymn, "Immortal, Invisible, God Only Wise." The imagery of the passage points to holiness, authority, power, and worship.

7:10. Judgment flows from a throne of Almighty God. Millions of people stand before him as **the court was seated, and the books were opened**.

One cannot ignore the relationship of this verse to Revelation 5:11: "Then I looked and heard the voice of many angels, numbering thousands upon thousands, and ten thousand times ten thousand. They encircled the throne and the living creatures and the elders." The open books of verse 10 surely link with the books of Revelation 20. Of this designation (the Ancient of Days) Laney writes, "This phrase, along with other depictions of great age in the context, communicates the impression of 'noble venerability.' The designation calls attention to the eternality of God, who said, 'I am the first and I am the last, and there is no God besides Me' (Is. 44:6 NASB)" (Laney, p. 39).

D Vision of the Son of Man (7:13–14)

SUPPORTING IDEA: *All the ugliness and debauchery of human kingdoms will one day be put aside when Jesus takes over his everlasting dominion that will never pass away.*

7:13. Here we have another scene change. Now in addition to **the Ancient of Days**, Daniel sees **one like a son of man**. Jesus used this phrase of himself (with the definite article) twenty-seven times in Luke alone. If we had only this phrase in Daniel, we might interpret this verse to mean that the one who approached the Ancient of Days looked like a human being. But in the light of the New Testament we know immediately it means much more. The image of **clouds** takes us back to Sinai (Exod. 16:10) and forward to prophecy yet unfulfilled (Matt. 24:30). Bock points out how the New Testament development of the term "Son of Man" completes the picture begun by Daniel. That elongated list appears in "Deeper Discoveries."

Clouds are common in Scripture and important in this verse. After the resurrection Jesus returned to heaven in a cloud (Acts 1:9), and the angels promised he would come again in the same manner (Acts 1:11). Clouds often refer Bible readers to God's revelation (Exod. 13; 1 Kgs. 8; Isa. 19; Jer. 4; Ezek. 10). The reference to Jesus here, still denied by some modern scholars who insist it is merely a reference to humanity, was argued by Jerome less than four hundred years after the resurrection. In his battle against the Arians, he claimed that if they "were willing to give heed to all this Scripture with a reverent mind, they would never direct against the Son of God the Calumny that He is not on an equality with God" (Jerome, 80).

7:14. The son of man not only stands in the presence of the Ancient of Days, but **he was given authority, glory and sovereign power; all peoples, nations and men of every language worshiped him**. The New Testament interpretation of the concept of *kingdom* begins here. The millennium forms only the beginning of the eternal kingdom; even here in the Old Testament the concept merges into the eternal state. God's tomorrow will bring together the saints of all the ages who will possess the everlasting kingdom of the Son of Man.

Before our very eyes Daniel describes human history up to the first coming of Christ and then jumps over centuries to the end of the age and the revival of the fourth empire. But the focus of all of this is hardly the little horn or any of the beastly kingdoms. Staring at us from the center of the chapter is the description of the Ancient of Days and the everlasting kingdom of Jesus.

Walvoord offers a very important hermeneutical principle connected with this chapter:

> If Daniel 7 had concluded with verse 14, it is probable, with the help of the book of Revelation and other Scripture passages, that a reasonable explanation could be made of the text. In view of the complexity and importance of the prophecy, the chapter continues, however, to give the reader a divinely inspired interpretation. It

should be borne in mind that when a symbol is interpreted, while the symbol is obviously parabolic and figurative, the interpretation should be taken literally. Accordingly, the explanation can be taken as a factual exegesis of the truth involved in the vision (Walvoord, *Daniel*, p. 170).

MAIN IDEA REVIEW: *Human kingdoms come and go and more often than not demonstrate cruelty rather than kindness, injustice rather than justice. But above all the human chaos the Ancient of Days runs his world with power and grace.*

III. CONCLUSION

Left Behind

Just a few days before writing this portion of the commentary, I viewed the movie *Left Behind*, released October 31, 2000. Well done from the viewpoint of production as well as evangelism, the movie is only the latest in a hugely successful effort of what will eventually be a series of ten novels written by Tim LaHaye and Jerry Jenkins. The eighth installment, *The Mark*, hit the shelves in November 2000. By the time the movie was released, twenty-three million copies of paperbacks, audio books, and children series had been sold.

All this yet awaits us, and believers will not be "left behind." The beastly kingdoms of the world are still in charge, and as far as we know, the little horn has not yet appeared. But we continue to pray, "Thy kingdom come." The ultimate goal of God's linear history targets the eternal kingdom of heaven ruled by Christ. We sing about it every year in *Messiah*, whose words are taken from the brilliant text of Revelation 11:15: "The kingdom of the world has become the kingdom of our Lord and of his Christ, and he will reign for ever and ever."

PRINCIPLES

- However bad the kingdoms of this world, Christians never lose sight of the fact that God's righteous kingdom is coming.
- Whatever other forms evil might take, we commonly see it characterized by cruelty and arrogance.

- Like Daniel we need to be quiet and listen and watch.

APPLICATIONS

- Passages like Daniel 7 should teach us to read our Bibles very carefully.
- Since we will be worshiping God with millions of saints throughout eternity, we might want to learn how to do it better now.
- The sales of the Left Behind series should encourage us to utilize our country's interest in end-time events to proclaim the truth of God's Word.

IV. LIFE APPLICATION

Letter from O'Hare

Over a period of some five years roughly corresponding to 1978–1983, I was a witness to a federal trial examining numerous documents pertaining to the defendant and other events of the case. One of the important documents was a letter which I dictated in Chicago's O'Hare Airport immediately after a telephone conversation. At various points during the trial, attorneys paid special emphasis to the fact that the letter was dictated with "the best possible human recollection of the events" it portrays, primarily because of the immediacy of the record. So it is with the writing of Daniel's seventh chapter, although in this case the human dimension is of much lesser impact than the guarded inspiration of the Holy Spirit.

Those of us who belong to the Ancient of Days because we have trusted in the saving power of his Son should think with great enthusiasm of what the future holds. How discouraged we become as we watch petty politicians squabbling, lying, cheating, and conditioning the world for the arrival of the little horn. How tempting to think that the world lies so completely in the control of the evil one that testimony for Christ and expectation of his return must surely be futile.

Yet a passage like this jerks us out of our spiritual lethargy and reminds us of what lies ahead. When studying Daniel 7, never get so attached to the identification of beasts and horns that you miss the impact of verse 14, "His dominion is an everlasting dominion that will not pass away, and his kingdom is one that will never be destroyed."

V. PRAYER

Father, we acknowledge you as the Ancient of Days, and we acknowledge your Son as the Son of man. We look forward to the eternal kingdom of heaven when we can join the millions before you when the books are opened. Amen.

VI. DEEPER DISCOVERIES

A. Critical View of the Four Kingdoms

Although we find some variation, generally critics of prophecy who advocate the late date for the writing of Daniel identify the four kingdoms of both chapters 2 and 7 as Babylon, Media, Persia, and Greece. To do so, they have to play with the text at various points such as the mention of Darius the Mede in 5:31 and throughout chapter 6. But there was no Median Empire with any world authority at the time of the fall of Babylon in 539 B.C. Furthermore, neither description in chapter 2 nor chapter 7 fits Greece as the fourth empire. In fact, though all the monarchies in question were vicious and cruel, the descriptions of Daniel 7 hardly fit Babylon, Media, Persia, and Greece as well as they do Babylon, Persia, Greece, and Rome. It is not the purpose of my work to speak to the authenticity of the Book of Daniel to any great extent. But we certainly need to grasp the idea that a denial of sixth-century authorship throws the prophecies into confusion, and the only possible result is error.

B. "Son of Man" in the New Testament

Earlier I alluded to Darrell Bock's treatment of this theme in which he identifies nine basic principles involved in the interpretation:

1. Jesus progressively revealed his messianic understanding of the term.
2. The messianic significance of the term for Jesus was eventually directly revealed by Jesus *to the disciples* after Peter's confession at Caesarea Philippi.

3. Jesus fused the term with other Old Testament descriptions of his mission, specifically the Servant, and thus was able to speak of the Son of Man's necessity to suffer in the suffering sayings that dominate the middle portions of the Gospels.
4. As Jesus faced the cross, he began to reveal to his disciples the background and the significance of the term *Son of man* in terms of Daniel 7 with the apocalyptic sayings.
5. This same background was revealed publicly at his trial before the Sanhedrin.
6. Thus the term was a convenient vehicle for revealing himself to those who believed, while avoiding *the immediate* political connotations of the term *Messiah.*
7. The usage in John's Gospel parallels that of the Synoptics while reflecting a development of themes implicit in both the Synoptics and Daniel 7.
8. The term in its Danielic usage in the New Testament has in view his ultimate victory and apoplectic return, a significant fact in view of his approaching Passion.
9. Therefore, the term is most appropriate for summarizing Christ's Christology, for in it one like a man who was more than a man exercises dominion and authority to such an extent that he can also be considered divine. As such, he will be the center of a new kingdom, king in a new age when all men will recognize his authority and worship his person. God's sovereign plan of history will culminate in the completion of the Son of man's mission in eternal victory. His future return and vindication makes this certain, even as he heads for the cross. In the promise of his victory, disciples can walk in hope and expectation, even though he went to the cross. His rule will cause all men to pause at the marvelous grace of God as it is observed that Jesus the Christ, the Son of man, is truly the greatest One who ever walked the earth (Bock, pp. 97–100).

VII. TEACHING OUTLINE

A. INTRODUCTION

1. Lead Story: Bombay Brit
2. Context: Daniel 7 begins the second section of the book, a set of four visions recorded in the same type of chronological order used in the first part of the book. A grasp of the overlook is crucial, since the events of Daniel 7 occur approximately fourteen years before chapter 5. Actually chapters 7 and 8, set as they are in the first and third years of the reign of Belshazzar, fit historically between chapters 4 and 5.
3. Transition: This chapter links with the first part of the book partly because it is in Aramaic and therefore seems to continue the narrative of 2:4–6:28 but also because of the parallelism in subject matter, particularly with chapter 2. Of Daniel 7 Baldwin writes: "Looked at in relation to the Aramaic section, this chapter constitutes the climax, and it is the high point in relation to the whole book; subsequent chapters treat only part of the picture and concentrate on some particular aspect of it" (Baldwin, p. 137).

B. COMMENTARY

1. Vision of the Four Beasts (7:1–7)
2. Vision of the Little Horn (7:8,11–12)
3. Vision of the Ancient of Days (7:9–10)
4. Vision of the Son of Man (7:13–14)

C. CONCLUSION: LEFT BEHIND

VIII. ISSUES FOR DISCUSSION

1. How important is it to establish that Daniel wrote in the sixth century rather than the second, and what difference does it make?

2. How can Daniel 7 help prepare us for the future?
3. How might we worship the Father and the Son differently in the light of verses 13 and 14?

Daniel 7:15–28

The Everlasting Kingdom

I. INTRODUCTION
"Animal Farm"

II. COMMENTARY
A verse-by-verse explanation of the chapter.

III. CONCLUSION
"The Tape Ran Out!"
An overview of the principles and applications from the chapter.

IV. LIFE APPLICATION
"Walking Off a Cliff"
Melding the chapter to life.

V. PRAYER
Tying the chapter to life with God.

VI. DEEPER DISCOVERIES
Historical, geographical, and grammatical enrichment of the commentary.

VII. TEACHING OUTLINE
Suggested step-by-step group study of the chapter.

VIII. ISSUES FOR DISCUSSION
Zeroing the chapter in on daily life.

Quote

"In a certain sense,

every branch of literature

may be regarded as auxiliary

to the study of the history of the Kingdom of God."

John Peter Lange

Daniel 7:15–28

IN A NUTSHELL

This section of Daniel is a power pack of prophecy—detailed, definitive, and determined.

The Everlasting Kingdom

I. INTRODUCTION

"Animal Farm"

Eric Arthur Blair was born in 1903 in Motihari, India, and at the age of nineteen began his service with the Imperial Police in Burma. Five years later he returned to England where he had been educated and lived in poverty trying to publish his first book. In 1933 he released *Down and Out in Paris and London,* describing the sad conditions of the homeless poor.

But in his mind he had resolved to speak out against oppression and evil which abounded during his years in Burma. So in 1945, under his pen name George Orwell, he wrote *Animal Farm,* a condemnation of that society expressed in a witty and sweeping indictment of totalitarianism, particularly the communism of the mid-twentieth century. It describes a farm in which the animals take over, agreeing to create the perfect society in which all will have an equal voice. Sadly their inner nature wins out (the pigs are the worst), and the whole project ends in chaos. Considering the strength of communism in 1945, Orwell was something of a prophet, especially when we include his satirical novel *1984* which he produced four years later to describe the terrifying life of people under the constant surveillance of "big brother."

But Orwell wasn't the first prophet to speak out against wicked animals taking over the world. In a very real sense, this chapter describes the animal farm of earth for at least twenty-six hundred years and counting. Daniel had seen kings come and go. Now the vision God gives him demonstrates how heaven will prepare the world for Messiah. The beasts appear to be running amok, but they are actually important to the divine plan. The Persians will send the people of God back to their own land. The Greeks will develop a culture and construct a language by which the gospel can be communicated all over the Mediterranean world. And the Romans will build roads and write laws so that Christ's messengers may carry his word wherever he sends them.

As this part of the chapter begins, Daniel is still "troubled in spirit" and still stands in the presence of the Ancient of Days, the angels around the throne, and the one who was given "an everlasting dominion that will not pass away."

II. COMMENTARY

The Everlasting Kingdom

MAIN IDEA: *Not only does God control the world now, but he will set up his absolute reign in the future; all his people, the saints of both old and new covenants, will share in it.*

A Angelic Assistance (7:15–18)

SUPPORTING IDEA: *Throughout time God has used angels to communicate his message to his people, and one day he will gather them all together in his kingdom.*

7:15–16. We understand why Daniel was **troubled in spirit** and **disturbed**. Although the last six verses have been most hopeful and promising, he has yet to put them in context and grasp the relationship among the beasts, the horns, and the Ancient of Days. But the aging prophet, now wise enough to know that he did not know everything, broke one of the great rules of masculinity—he asked for directions. The text says he **approached one of those standing there**. Although angels have not yet been mentioned in the passage, virtually every interpreter of this verse assumes Daniel's informant was an angel. You and I are probably unaccustomed to speaking with people we see in dreams, but let's remember this was a vision. I expect it looked much more like a Star Trek hologram in which all the characters appeared completely real, and it seemed quite normal to interact with one of them.

Verse 16 reminds us of something throughout this book that we should never forget. Daniel was not some kind of mystical wizard with paranormal powers of perception and communication. His understanding of dreams and visions came from God himself and not from his own skill or learning. The angel (some speculate it may again have been Gabriel) seems quite willing to provide a heavenly hermeneutic for the inquisitive prophet.

7:17. Although we have been identifying the beasts as they rise through the early part of the chapter, Daniel has not yet specifically told us that **the four great beasts are four kingdoms**. Yes, the words **are four** do not appear in the Septuagint, but that should not trouble readers at this point in the chapter. Nor let us be disturbed by versions which say that four kings rather than kingdoms arose.

We must address in detail the question of the meaning of *kingdom*, but here Baldwin's comment will suffice:

> It is noteworthy that the concepts of king and kingdom are indissolubly bound the one to the other, for there is no kingdom without a king and vice versa no king without a kingdom. The interpreter is made aware of the fluidity of thought which can move easily between an individual and a collective idea, and will take note that rigidity of interpretation is out of place here. Nor should we stumble over their rising from the earth rather than the sea since we clearly understand by this point that these kingdoms will come out of the sea of nations which live upon the earth (Baldwin, p. 144).

7:18. Before we look at the fascinating introduction of **the saints of the Most High**, let's contrast 5:31 where Darius "took over the kingdom" with 7:18 where these saints **will receive the kingdom**. Embryonic ecclesiology resides in that brief phrase. Throughout the Old Testament kingdoms were seized by violence, a behavior which continued well into the centuries after the life of Christ on earth and can be found in various parts of the world today. Indeed, one could argue that the American presidential election of 2000 was seized by power in the courts, an attempt made by both sides. But new covenant saints do not grasp kingdoms or take them over by their own power. Theirs is not worldly strength or political clout. When the kingdom comes to them, it comes as a gift of God's grace, but once they have received it, they **will possess it forever—yes, for ever and ever**.

But who are these **saints**? The law of double interpretation must apply here. Daniel knew nothing of the church or the new covenant and therefore could not use the word the way Christians use it today. For him **the saints of the Most High** could be nothing more nor less than the chosen people of Israel from whom he had been snatched so many decades before. But this promise extends far beyond Israel and reaches to all God's people of all ages, emphasizing the particularity of the kingdom.

In Archer's words, "The reason for emphasizing the participation of God's people in the final kingdom seems to be that it is a literal, earthly kingdom, replacing the previous empires of men, rather than a spiritual domain, a sort of ideal kingdom of God consisting only of the Lord himself" (Archer, p. 93).

Let me quickly say that not everyone is disposed toward this interpretation. Some would see the **saints** (holy ones) as angels, but a reading of the rest of the chapter (particularly v. 27) seems to negate that. McClain, my own theological mentor whose work I will be using liberally throughout the remainder of this book, offers a helpful paragraph:

> Following his vision of the sequence of world empires, which is consummated by the coming of the King "like unto a son of man" to establish an everlasting kingdom on earth, Daniel observes that "the saints of the Highest one will receive the kingdom and possess the kingdom forever, for all ages to come" (7:13,18 NASB). This important fact is asserted three times within the space of a single chapter (vv. 18,22,27). As to the identification of these saints, it will be sufficient to say that they are the saved of God, doubtless glorified, for there is a resurrection set at this time of consummations (Dan. 12:1–3) (McClain, p. 210).

B Continuing Confusion (7:19–22)

SUPPORTING IDEA: *When you have questions about spiritual matters or doctrinal issues, ask someone who really knows.*

7:19. So far so good, but Daniel could not get this ferocious fourth beast out of his mind. He described it again for the angel and this time added **bronze claws** to the picture, although he repeated exactly the phrase **trampled underfoot whatever was left** (see 7:7). Clearly Daniel was being guided by the Lord to focus on the most important kingdom in end-time events. He more or less ignored the first three and targeted the fourth and its details such as the horns and the little horn.

We have already linked this beast with the legs and feet of the image in chapter 2, identifying it with the Roman Empire. Perhaps I have not specified sufficiently, however, that evangelical scholars of prophecy generally agree that the fourth kingdom will be revived in some form at the end time. We dare not overlook the obvious link with Revelation 17:12 or minimize the wider connection between Daniel 7 and Revelation 17. The intense cruelty demonstrated by the fourth beast serves as its primary distinctive. In wanton destruction it crushes the world.

7:20. Recalling the fourth beast prompted Daniel to review 7:8 and particularly **the horn that looked more imposing than the others**. Culver reminds us, "Nearly all Post-millennialists, A-millennialists, Pre-millennialists unite in affirming that the Man of Sin of Paul and the Antichrist and the first Beast of John are the same as this 'little horn' of Daniel seven" (Culver, 131). Apparently there will be dissension within the revived Roman Empire. Of paramount importance is the dominance of the eleventh king (**the other horn**) who will subdue three lesser kings.

Once again, those who insist Daniel is not writing prophetically find this victory somewhere in ancient history. But Anderson denies that possibility saying, "The Roman earth shall one day be parceled out in ten separate kingdoms, and out of one there shall arise that terrible enemy of God and His people, whose destruction is to be one of the events of the Second Advent of Christ" (Anderson, *Prince,* p. 40).

7:21–22. The angelic informant added a new wrinkle. Up to this point conflict had occurred only between the Ancient of Days and the fourth beast; now the horn not only attacked the saints; he defeated them. Clearly this passage describes the persecution of the people of God by the Antichrist until he is stopped by **the Ancient of Days**. He is defeated, the warfare stops, and the saints **possessed the kingdom**. According to Wood, "The saints in view here are undoubtedly those depicted in Revelation 7:9–17, commonly called tribulation saints, and saved Jews of Israel, mentioned in Revelation 7:1–8 and 14:1–5" (Wood, *Daniel,* p. 98). That may be more than we want to affirm at this point in the text; nevertheless, Wood has certainly grasped the correct idea. "Deeper Discoveries" will treat more thoroughly this question of **the kingdom**.

C Expert Explanation (7:23–25)

SUPPORTING IDEA: *When prophecy seems confusing, a comparison of texts is always useful, particularly between Daniel and Revelation.*

7:23. Nothing new here except that now we have divine confirmation for our considerations. We learned in chapter 2 that the fourth kingdom would be in existence in some form until violently destroyed by Christ at his coming, so it is clearly a future extension of the Roman Empire in some form. Furthermore, the beasts of both John and Daniel come out of the sea of nations before they **appear on earth**. Both have ten horns; both are blasphemous; and both follow a lion, bear, and leopard (although John indicates them in reverse order—Rev. 13:1–4).

Of this passage Ladd writes:

> The beasts may well be represented in the Roman Empire, but we have already noted that early Christian Christology expected the appearance of Antichrist at the end of the age, and there are features about this beast and his colleague—the second beast—which were in no way consonant with Rome's rule. The beast then is the eschatological Antichrist who was foreshadowed in certain aspects of Rome and other totalitarian states as well (Ladd, p. 177).

7:24. The language of the text can hardly be seen as cloudy. The only remaining question is whether this kind of activity has already occurred or is yet future. I am of the opinion that here in Daniel 7 God unfolds the first description in Scripture of the Antichrist. Antiochus Epiphanes may well fulfill Daniel 8 (we will deal with that when we get there), but only Antichrist meets the qualifications of Daniel 7, Revelation 13, and Revelation 19. How does God answer Daniel's question? At the beginning this little horn will be just another human king (7:8). But then he will rise to be greater than the **horns** before him, different, unique, and running the most absolute dictatorship the world has ever known (7:20,24). Through his keen intelligence he conquers three kings and boastfully represents himself as the ultimate lawless one (2 Thess. 2:9–10).

So the Antichrist surfaces out of some form of the remaining tenfold units of the Roman Empire, or perhaps a uniquely revived form of that fourth kingdom. Furthermore, he doesn't *create* the confederacy but *absorbs* it after conquering three of its kings. Daniel 7:24 speaks of the beginning of Antichrist's world conquest, an event instigated by God himself: "The ten horns you saw are ten kings who have not yet received a kingdom, but who for one hour will receive authority as kings along with the beast. They have one purpose and will give their power and authority to the beast. . . . For God has put it into their hearts to accomplish his purpose by agreeing to give the beast their power to rule, until God's words are fulfilled" (Rev. 17:12–13,17).

In dealing with this chapter Seiss writes:

> Thus, then, by the clearest, most direct, and most natural signification of the words of the record, we are brought to the identification of these seven mountain kings as the seven great world-powers, which stretch from the beginning of our present world to the end of it. . . . That which is first in Daniel is the third here, and that which is the sixth here is the fourth in Daniel. Only in the commencing point is there any difference. The visions of Daniel and the visions of John are from the same Divine Mind, and they perfectly harmonize, only that the latest are the amplest (Seiss, p. 393).

7:25. But the little horn is hardly satisfied with conquering the world; **he will speak against the Most High and oppress his saints**. Enemies of Antichrist are not just three of the ten kings who preceded him but ultimately the people of God and God himself. Even though the saints of God will be given into his hand, his time is limited, as we shall see in a moment. The relationship of Daniel's dreams and visions to the time of the tribulation is more properly a subject for the ninth chapter or even the twelfth, so we reserve the details for later. Daniel 7:25 allows us to see the language of this record switching back to Hebrew as chapters 8–12 treat Israel in its relationship to the Gentiles.

But what does the text mean when it says the Antichrist will **try to change the set times and the laws**? Payne suggests that in his world domination the Antichrist will rearrange "not simply the sacred calendar of Scripture or the laws of Moses (as was attempted by Antiochus Epiphanes), but also the seasons and the fundamental conditions ordained by God" (Payne, p. 379). He will use his absolute power to oppress the saints for **a time, times and half a time**. The NIV marginal note offers an alternative translation, "for a year, two years and half a year."

Walvoord summarizes the unfolding of this terror:

> After this ruler conquers three and then all ten nations, he will impose a peace treaty on Israel for seven years (9:27). Then he will break this covenant after three and a half years and will become a

persecutor of Israel. This period of time is called the Great Tribulation, a time of unparallel trouble (Dan. 12:1; Matt. 24:21; Rev. 7:14). When the Antichrist becomes ruler over the entire world, his rule will be Satan's attempt to imitate the worldwide millennial reign of Christ (Walvoord, *End Times*, p. 121).

Wood offers a terse and clear explanation:

> This formula for a specific period means three-and-a-half years. This follows from the fact that the use of a singular (time), a plural (times), and a "dividing" (half) of times makes sense only if used in reference to a total of three and a half of some unit of time; in other contexts, the equivalent of this formula is identified as three-and-a-half years (Dan. 12:7; Rev. 12:14; cf. 12:6). Further, the idea of three-and-a-half years fits the duration of the last half of the seven-year tribulation period, which, as will be seen in chapter 9, is the exact time when the Antichrist will enjoy the height of his power (Wood, *Daniel*, p. 98–99).

D Secure Saints (7:26–28)

SUPPORTING IDEA: *The saints of God have been persecuted for centuries, and there is more ahead; but in the end God rescues them for eternal life.*

7:26. The interpreting angel now picks up the narrative of the end of verse 10 where Daniel saw that "the court was seated, and the books were opened" (7:10). This is not some mystical or spiritual reference to general judgment, because now we see that it relates to the Antichrist. When **the court will sit**, he loses his power and control which will be **completely destroyed forever**. How the Antichrist has stunned the world with his brilliance. The ultimate spinmeister, he has charmed entire nations with his flawless oratory, quite possibly through radio, television, the Internet, and probably other technological devices still ahead of us. But now his time is finished.

7:27. Surely Daniel must have been astounded to learn that **the sovereignty, power and greatness of the kingdoms under the whole heaven will be handed over to the saints, the people of the Most High**. So before this chapter ends, we are not only done with the little horn, but the whole animal farm is under the control of the Creator and cultivator of the earth. God sets up his ultimate and eternal kingdom **and all rulers will worship and obey him**.

According to Criswell:

> In the blessedness of the kingdom of Christ, even though nations differ from each other, they shall not lift up sword against each other, neither shall they learn war any more. These swords shall be used for plowshares and these spears for pruning hooks. . . . They will need no candle, for the Lord God gives light in their helplessness, hopelessness, and darkness. And they will live and reign with God forever and ever. There will be no more sorrow and no more crying, for these things are all passed away (Criswell, pp. 57–58).

7:28. Daniel was upset at the beginning of this vision, and now after the explanation he was still **deeply troubled**. Using a trick he learned from Belshazzar, he tells us, **my face turned pale**. Many questions have been raised over the phrase, **this is the end of the matter**. Certainly it could mean that having seen the vision and heard the explanation, the issue of the four beasts and little horn is now concluded. Certainly it is not the end of the book or the end of Daniel's prophecies. At the time he received the vision, he tells us, **I kept the matter to myself**. Some suggest that the phrase is Daniel's way of saying, "This is the way the world ends," but that seems a bit of a reach when examined in context.

What a book! What a chapter! Campbell tells us that

> among the scribes, Daniel 7 was considered the greatest chapter in the Old Testament. Without question, it teaches some basic and understandable things regarding God, man, and human history. . . . God clearly sees human history as a chronicle of immorality, brutality, and depravity. Governments and governmental leaders may mask their true character from people for a time, but they are always

unmasked before God. He always knows what man really is (Campbell, p. 115).

MAIN IDEA REVIEW: *Not only does God control the world now, but he will set up his absolute reign in the future; all his people, the saints of both old and new covenants, will share in it.*

III. CONCLUSION

"The Tape Ran Out!"

My inept handling of videotape recording brings endless exasperation to my wife. With VCR plus and other technology at my fingertips, I still manage to record only 90 percent of some broadcasts due to a variety of human errors such as not rewinding completely or failing to make allowance for later program starts because a football game went into overtime. The result is that we watch with great interest a program which builds the suspense and prepares for a dramatic ending, and suddenly the screen goes blank and one of us proclaims, "The tape ran out!"

It doesn't work with novels, but when we handle prophecy, it's great to know the conclusion of the story, especially when the ending is happy. This watershed chapter of Daniel begins with a terrifying vision and ends with a vision of the kingdom of God. Yes, Daniel is still troubled, but he has been given a glimpse of the end of the story.

Throughout history from the days of Daniel's dream to the very day you read these pages, God has used nations for his own purposes. We have already seen how the Persians returned Israel to its land and temple; how Greece provided linguistic and cultural foundations for the modern world in which we live; and how Rome made possible the kind of travel and government most Western nations still use in some form. History is not cyclical; it is linear. We are moving toward the final showdown between the kingdoms of this world and the everlasting kingdom of heaven.

PRINCIPLES

- God gives amazing latitude to the most brutal and godless leaders on earth.

- No form of human rule will survive the final destruction of the Antichrist and his minions.
- God has specified a clear-cut timetable for the end of the world with dates known only to him.

APPLICATIONS

- We should always remember that suffering is a part of our life on earth, allowed by God to prepare us for glorious eternal destiny.
- Prophecy, far from being mystical mumbo-jumbo that no one can understand, correlates with historic events already past and points us to God's design for the future.
- Our understanding of end-time events should sober us but at the same time provide optimistic expectation for the coming of Christ and the rule of his eternal kingdom.

IV. LIFE APPLICATION

"Walking Off a Cliff"

As I prepare this commentary on Daniel 7, the much-vaunted Mid-East peace process is in shambles. All the efforts of international diplomacy applied to create harmony between Israel and the Arabs once again appear hopeless. In its exclusive coverage *Newsweek* used the headline "Walking Off a Cliff" and asked: "How did Israelis and Palestinians go from the cusp of a historic peace deal to the worst violence between them in two decades? Interviews with many of the key negotiators suggest the answers lie in the twists and turns of one dramatic day at Camp David. In the 24-hour period between July 17 and 18 [2000], Israelis and Palestinians finally confronted the sacred core of their 100-year conflict—Jerusalem. But the very attempt to resolve the dispute exposed the unbridgeable divide between Israelis and Palestinians" (*Newsweek*, 11/27/00, 54).

The Middle East continues at the center of world news and also at the center of prophecy. Yet those who study and teach prophecy are often accused of having no concern for the practical realities of the present. Before we leave this chapter, let us notice that along with its eschatological significance it contains a fine collection of lessons for the present hour. For example, it teaches that *the world today bears the mark of the beast* (notably lawlessness). Christians should not be deceived by any temporary appearance of peace and tranquility.

Through the rebellion of children at home and the flagrant and regular violation of traffic and other laws, contemporary Christians wittingly or unwittingly help prepare the world for the arrival of the little horn. The pensive prophet was more deeply disturbed by prospects of the future than we are. Perhaps our response to the deterioration of righteousness in our society ought to be a part of what we see in Daniel.

This vision reminds us that *the control of the world belongs to God.* This is a lesson Nebuchadnezzar had to learn in history, and we also have to learn it again. The world may deny him, curse him, laugh at him, or ignore him during the reign of the beast. But when the throne of the Ancient of Days is set in place, every knee shall bow. The link between the saints and the Son of Man, established in this chapter, will be developed in greater detail in the New Testament.

Boutflower points out that "'the saints' belong to the vision, and not merely to its interpretation. They have already appeared in the vision as a persecuted people. It is, therefore, most unlikely that in its further development they should be represented in symbol by a single individual. But in as much as the kingdom given to 'one like unto a son of man' is seen to be given also to 'the saints,' we are forced to conclude that the mysterious person thus described is the God-appointed head of the saints" (Boutflower, p. 59).

Yet another lesson reminds us that *the nations belong to Satan,* but such an awareness should not drive us toward monasticism. Daniel exemplifies godly leadership in a perilous pit of paganism. He helps us remember that we too are pilgrims and strangers in the world and we too can serve God without total withdrawal from the culture.

Finally, let's remember that *our lives should reflect our eschatology.* Peter makes the point succinctly when he asks, "Since everything will be destroyed in this way, what kind of people ought you to be?" (2 Pet. 3:11a). Then he answers his own question by saying, "You ought to live holy and godly lives as you look forward to the day of God and speed its coming"

(2 Pet. 3:11b–12a). With bowed hearts all of God's people recognize that the ultimate glory belongs only to him.

Careless seems the great Avenger, history's pages but record
One death-grapple in the darkness 'twix old systems and Thy Word.
Truth forever on the scaffold; wrong forever on the throne!
Yet that scaffold sways the future, and beyond the dim unknown
Standeth God within the shadows, keeping watch above His own.
(James Russell Lowell, "Once to Every Man and Nation")

V. PRAYER

Father, thank you for your eternal kingdom in which we will have such a peaceful and joyous part. May we look reverently for the coming of the Lord Jesus and his conquest of evil in the world. Amen.

VI. DEEPER DISCOVERIES

A. Antichrist (7:8,11,20,24)

The greatest and most powerful leader in end-time events, Antichrist consolidates ten portions of the Mediterranean world to assume what appears to be global domination. He signs a seven-year treaty with Israel and in the middle of that period of time, after three and a half years, becomes the ultimate power in human civilization. At the Battle of Armageddon he loses to King Jesus and is cast into the lake of fire (Rev. 19:20).

According to Ryrie:

> The beast's program will include the blasphemy and war (Rev. 13:5–7). He will speak insolently against God (Dan. 7:25). Objects of his blasphemy will include the name of God, the dwelling place of God and those who dwell in heaven. He will be allowed (notice that God is still in control) to make war with the saints (Rev. 12:17), and to kill them. But his power will be limited by God to forty-two months. Here is an example of the interweaving of the many forces behind events: God will control all, but Satan will empower the beast who will in turn act on his own in blaspheming God. Men who join his army and fight for him will do so voluntarily, and they in turn

will make martyrs of God's people who, though they are killed, will still be within God's protecting care! (Ryrie, p. 472).

B. Blasphemy (7:11,25)

Although this chapter offers reference to the "mouth that spoke boastfully" in verses 8, 11, and 20, in verse 25, the Antichrist actually speaks "against the Most High." Indeed, Revelation 13:5–6 says, "The beast was given a mouth to utter proud words and blasphemies and exercise his authority for forty-two months. He opened his mouth to blaspheme God, and to slander his name and his dwelling place and those who live in heaven."

What is blasphemy? Biblically understood, it does not refer to the careless oath of ignorant people who in the coarse and crude conversation of our day use the Lord's name in vain. That is profanity but not blasphemy. *Blasphemy is deliberately speaking untruth about God.* The word is actually a transliteration of a Greek word which appears some fifty-five times in the New Testament. The Law of Moses reminded the Jews that anyone who blasphemed the name Jehovah would be stoned (Lev. 24:10–16). And this law actually applied to foreigners as well as the Israelites themselves.

Although blasphemy may be committed against other people and even inanimate things, the primary target is usually God. And it doesn't require doctrinal details. Paul talked about women who blasphemed God's Word through their behavior (Titus 2:5) and people who disturbed the life of the early church (1 Tim. 1:20).

But the ultimate blasphemy is reserved for the Antichrist, who uses it as a major tool of his trade. In our day we have heard blasphemy in popular music from the Beatles to contemporary rap. We see it in art, often supported by the National Foundation for the Arts and funded by tax money, a portion of which is provided by Christians.

While we like to attribute this sin to pagan people, and nod our heads knowingly when we see it in the Antichrist, we should be more careful in our own attitudes and language.

C. Mediatorial Kingdom (7:14,18,22,27)

Our understanding of the phrase "kingdom of God" in any passage where the same identity is discussed in slightly different wording rests upon our whole understanding of Scripture. Invariably when the Bible uses this terminology, it designates a *ruler* with appropriate authority and status, a *realm* of people who are under control of the ruler, and *rulership* as a function. Many well-meaning people leap to passages like Luke 17:21 or Matthew 16:19 to argue that the kingdom is ethereal—a state of heart, not an actual physical reality. Yet the Hebrew word *makuth* and the Greek word *basileia* seem always to declare reality, and never more so than in Daniel and Revelation.

Furthermore, it seems futile to distinguish between the *kingdom of God* and the *kingdom of heaven*, although there seems to be some usefulness in identifying God's kingdom *over* the earth (as presently) and God's kingdom *on* the earth (yet future). McClain therefore chose to distinguish them in a slightly different way, pouring over five hundred pages into what is probably the greatest book in the English language dealing with the matter of the kingdom. Here I offer but one brief paragraph:

> In one sense it would not be wholly wrong to speak of *two kingdoms* revealed in the Bible. But we must at the same time guard carefully against the notion that these two kingdoms are absolutely distinct, one from the other. There is value and instruction in thinking of them as *two aspects* or phases of the one rule of our sovereign God. In seeking for terms which might best designate these two things, I can find nothing better than the adjectives "universal" and "mediatorial." These are not commensurate terms, of course, but describe different qualities; the first referring to the *extent* of rule, the latter to the *method* of rule. Nevertheless, in each case the designated quality seems to be the most important for purposes of identification (McClain, p. 21).

VII. TEACHING OUTLINE

A. INTRODUCTION

1. Lead Story: *Animal Farm*
2. Context: The second half of Daniel 7 explains the vision of the first half and prepares us to some extent for the vision of chapter 8.

However, it must be said that Daniel 7 stands alone, unconnected historically to the chapters which precede and follow it.

3. Transition: Several years pass between the visions of chapter 7 and those of chapter 8, and Daniel begins each chapter by identifying precisely when God spoke to him and then giving their respective messages.

B. COMMENTARY

1. Angelic Assistance (7:15–18)
2. Continuing Confusion (7:19–22)
3. Expert Explanation (7:23–25)
4. Secure Saints (7:26–28)

C. CONCLUSION: "THE TAPE RAN OUT!"

VIII. ISSUES FOR DISCUSSION

1. How would you describe the premillennial, postmillennial, and amillennial interpretations of end-time events?
2. Name some ways the content of Daniel 7 helps us in Christian living today.
3. How would you define *saint* according to biblical parameters?

Daniel 8:1–27

How the West Won

I. INTRODUCTION
Macedonian Menace

II. COMMENTARY
A verse-by-verse explanation of the chapter.

III. CONCLUSION
The Four Hundred Silent Years

An overview of the principles and applications from the chapter.

IV. LIFE APPLICATION
A Biblical Darth Vader

Melding the chapter to life.

V. PRAYER
Tying the chapter to life with God.

VI. DEEPER DISCOVERIES
Historical, geographical, and grammatical enrichment of the commentary.

VII. TEACHING OUTLINE
Suggested step-by-step group study of the chapter.

VIII. ISSUES FOR DISCUSSION
Zeroing the chapter in on daily life.

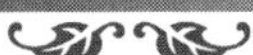

Quote

"The lesson of history tells us that no state or government devised by man can flourish forever."

Billy Graham

GEOGRAPHICAL PROFILE: SUSA

- A Babylonian city which became one of the capitals of the Persian Empire
- Also mentioned in Nehemiah 1:1 and Esther 1:2
- Susa is the Greek name and Shushan the Persian name

GEOGRAPHICAL PROFILE: ELAM

- A country located on the east side of the Tigris River, one of most ancient civilizations of all time
- By the time of Daniel, it had become a portion of the Babylonian empire
- Susa was its most important city
- One of the pagan nations judged by God (Jer. 25:25; 49:34–39)
- Acts 2:9 includes Elamite as one of the languages spoken at Pentecost

GEOGRAPHICAL PROFILE: ULAI CANAL

- A man-made canal connecting the Choaspes and Coprates Rivers
- Flowed beside the city of Susa
- Possibly as wide as nine hundred feet at points

Daniel 8:1–27

IN A NUTSHELL

The past history of the Persian and Greek empires foreshadows the future prophecy of the appearance, reign, and destruction of the Antichrist.

How the West Won

I. INTRODUCTION

Macedonian Menace

At first glance it appears that the title of this chapter may be missing a word. Wasn't the great old television series called *How the West Was Won*? Yes, but in Daniel 8 we find a recitation of how the West won power from the East in a period of time that changed the course of the world. During the historical period covered in this chapter, the center of global power moved from the Middle and Near East to what we still call the West. The central figure in the drama was a young king by the name of Alexander, just twenty years old when he succeeded to the throne of his father Philip of Macedon in 336 B.C. Philip had restored peace after the Peloponnesian War and Macedonia controlled Greece. He had already announced his intention of going to war against Persia. After his assassination his son Alexander put those plans into action.

Educated at the feet of Aristotle, Alexander became a tough and brilliant soldier who began by capturing Persian naval bases across the Mediterranean and defeating the Persian army at Issus in 333 B.C. When in control of Asia Minor, he pushed on east through Syria, attacking the Phoenician capital of Tyre with catapults mounted on boats. Then he moved south to Egypt, an easy battle since Egypt had always resented Persian rule and was far from the seat of Persian power. At the oasis of Siwa, Alexander was hailed as the son of the god Amman. All that remained was an eastward drive through the corridor between the Caspian Sea and the Persian Gulf, taking everything along the way. He fought Darius a second time in 331 B.C. and then pushed his army into India after routing Persepolis.

But as the Russian winter stopped Hitler's armies during World War II, India's heat and disease did what the Persian army could not, and Alexander was thwarted. He died of a fever in 323 B.C. at the age of thirty-three. His body was taken to Alexandria, that great Greek city on the coast of Egypt. At the time of his death, the Greek Empire stretched from the western coast of Macedonia to a portion of India east of the Indus River. It reached far northeast to another Alexandria in Bactria of southern Turkistan.

Delusions of deity grew with each conquest, carefully nurtured by Alexander himself who once said, "Would that the people of India may believe me to be a god, for wars depend upon reputation, and often even what has been falsely believed has gained the place of truth."

Never again would a power east of the Mediterranean rule the world. Even in medieval times when the seat of government centered in Constantinople of the Byzantine Empire, that city was located well westward of the ancient kingdoms of the Old Testament, indeed right across the Peloponnesus from Alexander's Macedonia.

But the Macedonian menace was only a tool in the hands of a mighty Monarch. God used the speed and skill of his armies to spread Greek culture and language across the Mediterranean world in preparation for the writing of the New Testament and the translation of the Old Testament into Greek. Daniel 8 tells the story of how Persia and Greece conquered the worlds of their time and how out of that latter nation rose a wicked ruler who became a prototype of the Antichrist, still ahead of us in human history.

II. COMMENTARY

How the West Won

MAIN IDEA: *Throughout the history of humanity, evil has often triumphed, and at times it seems unrestrained. But ultimately the people of God will persevere, and the Bible repeatedly assures their victory.*

A The Two-Horned Ram (8:1–4)

SUPPORTING IDEA: *All human history shows how God prepares the world for the comings of Jesus Christ.*

8:1–2. The history of the Old Testament appears actually twice in that set of books—Genesis through 2 Kings and in 1 and 2 Chronicles. The four Gospel writers, though including different details, essentially tell us about the birth, life, death, and resurrection of Jesus Christ. This kind of repetition is common in Scripture and popular in good education even today. Parents say to their children, "How many times do I have to tell you this?" The question is really rhetorical—as many times as it will take to learn it. So a portion of the message of Daniel 2 and 7 replays now again in chapter 8.

This vision appeared two years after the one recorded in chapter 7, and the Book of Daniel also now switches from Aramaic to Hebrew.

Since this vision deals with Persia and Greece, Daniel was transported in spirit to **the citadel of Susa in the province of Elam**. Some have argued this was actually a physical trip, part of government business. But support for that view seems difficult to garner. Daniel was at least partially retired at this time, and the language of the text certainly implies a spiritual rather than physical transport. To be precise Daniel wasn't actually in the city but just outside **beside the Ulai Canal**.

The deliverance of Daniel's people is more than ten years away with Babylonia still very much in control, although battles with the Persians are already underway. Yet God wanted Daniel to see not only what would happen in order to get his people back home but also how the flow of history will change. Susa lay about 250 miles east of Babylon, and the **citadel** that Daniel saw served as both palace and fortress for the Persian center of government.

8:3–4. When in Persia, think like the Persians. Since the head of gold/lion of Daniel 2 and 7 would soon expire as a world power, God now directed Daniel's attention to the chest and arms of silver/bear which now became **a ram with two horns**. Actually, as 8:20 clearly tells us, "The two-horned ram that you saw represents the kings of Media and Persia." As in chapter 7, horns are people; in this case one **was longer than the other but grew up later**.

In the early years of Medo-Persian dominion, the Medes were the stronger power. They joined with the Babylonians and Nabopolasser in 612 B.C. to destroy the Assyrian Empire at Nineveh. But that was before Cyrus, under whose leadership the Persians became masters of the dual empire. The **later** horn became the **longer** horn in 550 B.C. when the Medes betrayed their king into his hands. He conquered Ekbatana, the Median capital, and became Cyrus the Great, king of Persia.

This empire charged in three directions—**toward the west and the north and the south**. Persia did not move eastward into India but concentrated its attention on civilizations in the three other directions. **No animal could stand against him** (such as a lion for example), so **he did as he pleased and became great**. Archer thinks this latter phrase "carries with it the sinister suggestion that his over weaning pride was ripe for a fall" (Archer, p. 97).

By the time Daniel received this vision, the Persian Empire had already conquered Lydia, Asia Minor, Syria, Palestine, portions of Africa (including Egypt), and a variety of regions around the Caspian Sea. Babylon would be next, and then their armies would meet little resistance until Darius the Great was defeated in central Greece in 490 B.C. Ten years later Xerxes lost both an army and a navy at the sea battle of Salamis. Today, a shadow of its former self, the nation of Iran still represents enormous wealth in the world and significant power and influence in its own geographical arena.

B The One-Horned Goat (8:5–8)

SUPPORTING IDEA: *Just when the evil empires of this world think themselves to be at the pinnacle of power, God brings them down.*

8:5. All Hebrew words for directions are interesting. **West** is a combination of words for "evening" and "enter." The sun enters the night in the west. And from that direction **suddenly a goat with a prominent horn between his eyes came . . . without touching the ground**. Rams and goats are not like bears, lions, and leopards. They tend to be much more domesticated. Why this switch in animal types? Many believe that God described these nations in relationship to Israel, whereas in chapters 2 and 7 they were described in relationship to each other. Whether or not that can stand up to scrutiny, history does show us that Alexander behaved respectfully to the Jews, and Cyrus was the instrument God used to return them to their own land.

We saw this buck goat earlier as the belly and thighs of bronze/leopard, pointing to the nation of Greece. Indeed, 8:21 tells us "the shaggy goat is the king of Greece." But this empire does not *ram* its way into its opposition; it moves so swiftly that its feet do not even touch the ground, a characterization of the way Greek armies operated.

8:6–7. No surprise here. The goat attacked the ram **in great rage . . . furiously . . . shattering his two horns**. The one-horned goat (Greece under Alexander) trampled the two-horned ram and both kingdoms (Media and Persia) were destroyed. Notice the anger in this warfare. The Greeks had been battered around by the Persians long enough, and now they retaliated in fury.

According to Walvoord:

> There is no discrepancy between history, which records a series of battles and Daniel's representation that the Persian Empire fell with one blow. Daniel is obviously describing the result rather than the details. That the prophecy is accurate, insofar as it goes, most expositors concede. Here again, the correspondence of the prophecy to later history is so accurate that liberal critics attempt to make it history instead of prophecy (Walvoord, *Daniel,* p. 183).

Alexander developed a different kind of warfare, which caught the Persians completely by surprise. They had convinced themselves that size and strength were the only important elements in world conquest. Cyrus moved slowly across territories with special uniforms for each kind of warrior and ponderous cavalries of horses and elephants. Alexander's armies, by contrast, largely trained and developed by Philip, used infantry closely tied together with shields and spears forming a knife-like force called a *phalanx*. This type of warfare was still being used 1,500 years later by the Byzantine armies that controlled Constantinople.

It was not uncommon in the victories of Alexander to defeat forces ten times the size of his own. Josephus claims that as Alexander passed through Palestine the Jews showed him the Book of Daniel, which he immediately applied to himself. He also says Alexander was so impressed with the city of Jerusalem that he actually offered sacrifice in a manner described for him by the priests.

8:8. In 323 B.C., during the thirteenth year of his reign and the thirty-third year of his life, the goat began to crumble when **his large horn was broken off**. There followed twenty years of quarreling among Alexander's generals and Greek politicians until the final division of the Greek Empire was settled. In the place of the former horn, **four prominent horns grew up toward the four winds of heaven**. Wood says: "The thought here parallels the four heads of Daniel 7:6. Alexander's empire was divided among four of his generals: Cassander receiving Macedonia and Greece; Lysimachus, Thrace and much of Asia Minor; Seleucus, Assyria and a vast region to the east; and Ptolemy, Egypt" (Wood, *Daniel,* 102).

C The Powerful Horn (8:9–12)

SUPPORTING IDEA: *When evil empires of the world war among themselves, the people of the Lord are often hurt, and truth is often sacrificed.*

8:9. We must use great caution here. We meet **another horn** which arises not from the ten horns of the fourth kingdom (7:8) but from one of the four horns of the third kingdom. In other words, this is a ruler who eventually gained control of one of the four sections of Alexander's Empire. After humble beginnings, this horn **grew in power to the south and to the east and toward the Beautiful Land**. Geographically pinpointed in history, that leads us to Syria. Virtually all serious commentators consider this a prophecy of Antiochus IV called Epiphanes, the eighth king in the Syrian dynasty who held power from 175 to 164 B.C.

The phrase **Beautiful Land** appears again in Daniel 11:16 in a prophetic rather than a historical setting. Few have any doubt that it could be anything other than Israel of which the Sons of Korah once wrote, "It is beautiful in its loftiness, the joy of the whole earth" (Ps. 48:2). Throughout the Old Testament the city and the land are often connected; an attack against Israel ultimately becomes an attack against Jerusalem, precisely as we see it today.

8:10. We have no problem recalling Antiochus's historic attack against Israel, but what could Daniel mean when he says this horn **reached the host of the heavens, and it threw some of the starry host down to the earth and trampled on them**? Obviously Antiochus never literally threw out any stars. Almost every commentator assumes a reference here to the people of God, perhaps particularly the priests. We remember Joseph's dream about stars and leadership (Gen. 37:9–10) and how God promised Abraham that his people would be as great in number as the stars (Gen. 15:5; 22:17).

Some think the reference to **starry host** should be interpreted as angels, but Antiochus had no control whatsoever over God's messengers; such a connection is more poetic than realistic. Historians estimate that Antiochus killed about one hundred thousand Jews during his viscious onslaught to the south. This record appears in detail in 1 and 2 Maccabees, which, though we do not consider them inspired Scripture, are worthy sources for accurate history.

8:11. Here again we have an interesting phrase—**the Prince of the host**. Whether one finds in **the starry host** angels, stars, or holy people, the prince in every case is God himself. And when Antiochus extinguished the daily sacrifice at the temple in Jerusalem, he didn't just take it away from the people; he stole it from God himself. First Maccabees 1 tells us that Antiochus

> entered the sanctuary, and took away the golden altar, and the candlestick and all the vessels thereof; and the temple show-bread, the pouring vessels . . . and stripped the temple of the ornaments of gold. . . . For the king had sent letters by messengers unto Jerusalem and the cities of Judah, that they should . . . forbid burnt offerings, and sacrifices, and drink offerings in the temple; and that they should profane the Sabbaths and festival days; and pollute the sanctuary and holy people; set up altars, and groves, and chapels of idols, and sacrifice swine's flesh, and unclean beasts; that they should also leave their children uncircumcised, and make their souls abominable with all manner of uncleanness and profanation; to the end that they might forget the laws and change the ordinances (1 Macc. 1:21–49).

8:12. Once again God delivered **the host of the saints** into the hands of a wicked country **because of rebellion**. The very descendants of the courageous exiles led by Zerubbabel, Ezra, and Nehemiah had turned away from God again as this wicked horn **prospered in everything it did, and truth was thrown to the ground**. When biblical theology is overcome by power politics, truth is always a victim.

D The Crucial Question (8:13–14)

SUPPORTING IDEA: *Throughout history, whenever God's people are persecuted, he has always put a time limit on their suffering.*

8:13. By this time Daniel had learned to recognize the sound of "a holy one" (4:23) and knew that he was a participant in angelic conversation. One asked another the length of this time of suffering. The question was offered in great detail, specifically including **the daily sacrifice, the rebellion that causes desolation, and the surrender of the sanctuary and of the host that will be trampled underfoot**. But brush aside the question; all spotlights shine on the answer.

8:14. At first glance the answering angel's response seems clear: **It will take 2,300 evenings and mornings; then the sanctuary will be reconse-**

crated. But Walvoord reminds us that "the answer given in verse 14 has touched off almost endless exegetical controversy" (Walvoord, *Daniel,* p. 188). One view, held traditionally by Seventh-Day Adventists, understands the days as years which were culminated in 1884 with the second coming of Christ. Since that did not happen, a detailed examination of that view is hardly useful here. A more reasonable view takes the text to mean *days* and looks for some event twenty-three hundred days after the beginning of the Antiochan persecution.

The *NIV Study Bible* offers a succinct explanation:

> There were two daily sacrifices for the continual burnt offering (9:21; Ex. 29:38–42), representing the atonement required for Israel as a whole. The 2,300 evenings and mornings probably refer to the number of sacrifices consecutively offered on 1,150 days, the interval between the desecration of the Lord's altar and its reconsecration by Judas Maccabeus on Kislev 25, 165 B.C. The pagan altar set up by Antiochus on Kislev 25, 168, was apparently installed almost two months after the Lord's altar was removed, accounting for the difference between 1,095 days (an exact three years) and the 1,150 specified here (p. 1312).

The twenty-three hundred literal days view is supported by Wood, who argues the case as follows: "The verse indicates that the period would close with the cleansing or restoration of the Temple. This occurred in December 165 B.C. under the leadership of Judas Maccabeus. If we figure back from this date, the twenty-three hundred days bring us to September 171 B.C., which should be, then, the month when an event of sufficient significance occurred to mark it as the beginning of Antiochus' anti-Jewish activities. Though the identity of that particular event is not known (for lack of adequate history of the time), it is clear that the year 171 B.C. did see the beginning of these atrocities, and such an event could well have occurred in September of that year" (Wood, *Daniel,* pp. 104–5).

Walvoord supports this view, placing the conclusion of the persecution and the death of Antiochus Epiphanes in 164 B.C. He argues that

> using the figure of eleven hundred and fifty days only creates more problems as it does not fit precisely any scheme of events and has a

> dubious basis. By far the most simple and most honoring to the Scriptures is the solution that the twenty-three hundred days date from 171 B.C. to 164 B.C. This prophecy may safely be said now to have been fulfilled and does not have any further eschatological significance in the sense of anticipating a future fulfillment (Walvoord, *Daniel*, p. 190).

Baldwin supports the 1,150 view and Archer as well; she says, "There is not the slightest historical ground for a *terminus a quo* beginning in 171 B.C." (Baldwin, 103).

In view of scholarly differences like these, we do well to avoid dogmatism and emphasize that God clearly appointed a time frame for the persecution and designated its end with specificity. We must also recognize, as Walvoord has reminded us, that this entire first half of the chapter is located in history and has no lingering eschatological significance.

E The Heavenly Interpreter (8:15–18)

SUPPORTING IDEA: *God wants us to understand and apply prophecy, not relegate it to the realm of mysterious and unknowable information.*

8:15–16. This media experience by a river gets more complicated every minute. Daniel does exactly what you and I would have done in similar circumstances, **watching the vision and trying to understand it**. Then all of a sudden he sees someone **who looked like a man**. This man spoke **from the Ulai** and commanded Gabriel to **tell this man the meaning of the vision**. Such interactive participation in a vision seems rather high tech for an aging prophet in an ancient kingdom. He experiences a virtual reality situation.

Who is this one who looked and sounded like a man? Possibly another angel or some other heavenly being, although we wonder why Daniel did not call him a holy one. Some have speculated it could have been Michael, the only other angel named in the Bible. However, there is no reason to assume that the **one who looked like a man** in verse 15 is also the one who spoke with **a man's voice** in verse 16. Certainly that connection is possible, just not necessary. One would think a command to Gabriel would have come from God himself.

Gabriel only appears here, in 9:21, and in the message to Mary of Luke 1:19,26. The way we banter about the name, you would think he is mentioned fifty or sixty times throughout the Bible, but that is not the case. Whatever fuzziness surrounds these verses does not include the mission; Gabriel's task is clearly defined.

8:17–18. Now the one about to speak moved closer to Daniel so it would appear that Gabriel himself may have been the being Daniel saw in verse 15. We should not stumble over the similes of the vision, since they are completely secondary to the main message. Daniel reacted to angelic presence much the way John did on the Isle of Patmos (Rev. 22:8). Indeed, this is something of a biblical pattern (Dan. 10:9,15,17; Exod. 3:6; Isa. 6:5; Ezek. 1:28; Acts 9:3–4; Rev. 1:17). Daniel remembered himself in the dream/vision as prostrate on the ground **in a deep sleep**. But the angel touched the prophet and raised him to his feet.

However, if we believe that the message, not the medium, should concern us here, we must pause on Gabriel's words: **understand that the vision concerns the time of the end.** Clearly the immediate reference is to the end of the reign of Antiochus, but since all conservative scholars acknowledge Antiochus Epiphanes as a type of Antichrist, might there be a greater and yet future scope intended by this phrase? We must deal with this in our study of verse 19 where a similar phrase occurs.

We have already discussed the term **Son of man** in connection with 7:13. In Daniel it appears in only these two places, although we find it no fewer than ninety-three times in Ezekiel. In both cases it emphasizes the prophet's humanity, and Jesus used it frequently to describe himself in the same manner.

F The Exhausting Explanation (8:19–27)

SUPPORTING IDEA: *However difficult Bible study and prayer might be, however tired and ill we might feel, as soon as possible we must get up and get busy with the King's business.*

8:19. This may be the pivotal verse of the chapter. Again Gabriel used the phrase **time of the end**, this time accompanied by **the time of wrath**. Baldwin says specifically, "It does not necessarily mean the end of all things, but may refer to the question asked in verse 13; verse 19 supports this interpretation. . . . As in the annunciation to Mary (Lk. 1:28–30), Gabriel was bringing good news" (Baldwin, p. 159).

Wood doesn't think so. He picks up on the phrase "time of wrath," connects it to "time of the end," and says: "It refers certainly to God's time of judgment on Israel at the time of Antiochus Epiphanes; but it refers also to God's future time of judgment during the great tribulation, in the last half of which the little horn of Daniel's first vision will bring even worse affliction" (Wood, *Daniel,* p. 106).

Campbell adds:

> It should also be noted that the expression "time of the end" occurs in Daniel 12:4 where it clearly means the time approaching Christ's Second Coming. The conclusion, then, is that we are to see an Antiochus Epiphanes a dread picture and symbol of Antichrist to come in the end time, or Tribulation" (Campbell, 126).

Kelly, West, Seiss, Pentecost, and Walvoord all support this dual reference approach to our passage. Walvoord says, "The entire chapter is historically filled in Antiochus, but to varying degrees foreshadowing typically the future world ruler who would dominate the situation at the end of the times of the Gentiles (Walvoord, *Daniel,* p. 196).

Archer, though hesitant, throws his considerable weight with this position as well:

> This interpretation has much to commend it, for Daniel makes clear through the assignment of the symbol of the "little horn" both to Antiochus of Kingdom III and to Antichrist of the latter-day phase of Kingdom IV that they bear to each other the relationship of type-antitype. Insofar as Epiphanes prefigured the determined effort to be made by the Beast to destroy the biblical faith, that prophecy that described the career of Antiochus also pertained to "the time of the end." Every type has great relevance for its antitype. But the future dealings of Antichrist can only be conjectured or surmised. Therefore, our discussion will be confined to the established deeds of Antiochus Epiphanes (Archer, p. 106).

Fair enough. Historical fulfillment with typical prophetic significance.

8:20–22. We have discussed this interpretation in some detail in connection with verses 3–8. Suffice it here to say that though Alexander was not technically **the first king** of Greece, he clearly was the greatest king and the only one to whom the attributes of **the large horn** can be attributed.

8:23–25. One's interpretation of verse 19 will determine one's interpretation of verses 23–26. Certainly Antiochus Epiphanes was **a stern-faced king, a master of intrigue** who fits almost all the descriptions of this paragraph. Was Antiochus Epiphanes **destroyed, but not by human power**? According to 1 Maccabees 6, that is true. Rather than being slain in battle, Antiochus received word in Babylon that the Maccabees had defeated his armies and almost miraculously won control of Israel once again. The text says, "He was astonished and sore moved: where upon he laid him down upon his bed, and fell sick for grief . . . then calling his friends to tell them he knew he was to die, he said, 'I remember the evils that I did at Jerusalem . . . I perceive therefore for this cause I perish'" (1 Macc. 6:8–13).

It seems likely that we see in Antiochus a strong historical type of the wicked ruler yet to come whom the Bible calls Antichrist. Historical interpretation and prophetic typology form the *law of double reference*, a commonality throughout Old Testament prophecy.

8:26–27. Gabriel affirmed that the vision and its interpretation were exactly as Daniel had received them. But the prophet was ordered to **seal up the vision, for it concerns the distant future**. The words for **seal up** carry the idea of protection and safeguarding, suggesting that Daniel had no authority to release the vision at this point. Hence he tells us about it considerably later—but not after the events themselves took place. We see the same reminder again in 12:9 where the sealing is linked to the interesting phrase "the time of the end." But we should place less than complete authority in the word **distant**. Certainly the destruction of Antiochus Epiphanes and his final judgment at the hand of God were **distant** at the time Daniel received the vision.

All these interactive vision experiences left Daniel **exhausted** and **ill for several days**. Furthermore, even after he rested and recovered, now back on the job full time, he was still **appalled by the vision; it was beyond understanding**. Prophets would often hear, see, and write things which they could not grasp in their context. The only reason we make any sense out of it now is the precious perspective of hindsight. With Belshazzar still on the throne and Babylon very much in business, Daniel could hardly imagine how Persia, much less Greece, could ever take over his world, and how they could possibly stop sacrifices in Jerusalem when at the moment Daniel received the vision that city remained in utter ruin.

MAIN IDEA REVIEW: *Throughout the history of humanity, evil has often triumphed, and at times it seems unrestrained. But ultimately the people of God will persevere, and the Bible repeatedly assures their victory.*

III. CONCLUSION

The Four Hundred Silent Years

The West won control of the world during a block of four hundred years separating the Testaments. Those centuries from the time of Nehemiah to the birth of Christ are known as the intertestamental period, covering approximately 432 to 5 B.C. We often hear them called "the silent years," but they were anything but silent. Great events, including some of those predicted in this chapter, occurred during that time.

We have already briefly reviewed the histories of Persia and Greece and mentioned the two dominant Greek kingdoms which followed Alexander, namely Ptolemy (323–198 B.C.) and Seleucid (198–143 B.C.). The Ptolemies were tolerant of the Jews, but after 198 the Seleucids began to look south with increasing hostility. With the rise of Antiochus IV (Epiphanes) who ruled from 175 to 164 B.C., open hostilities began. This stern-faced king determined to rid the earth of Judaism once and for all and outraged the entire nation by erecting a statue of Zeus and sacrificing a pig in the temple at Jerusalem.

Enter Mattathias, an aged priest from the village of Modein who refused to offer heathen sacrifice, tore down the altar, killed the agent of Antiochus, and called for supporters to follow him. Mattathias and his five sons (John, Simon, Judas, Eleazar, and Jonathan) along with many other followers headed for the hills, and the Maccabean Revolt had begun. The result was a twenty-four-year-long war (166–142 B.C.), resulting in the independence of Judea until the iron kingdom of Rome took control in 63 B.C.

These were turbulent and bloody years in the history of Israel, but Judea gained religious freedom and the sons of Mattathias, particularly Judas, controlled their part of the country by sheer force and determination. The years from 142 to 63 B.C. are known as the Hasmonean rule when Simon, second oldest son of Mattathias, succeeded his younger brother Jonathan. Simon was killed by his son-in-law in 135, and his son John Hyrcanus took over for the next thirty-one years.

A general political aristocracy arose among the Hasmoneans. The religious fervor of the Maccabees vaporized into business as usual with Aristobulus I, Alexander Janneus, Alexandra, Aristobulus II, all maintaining some semblance of control. The era ultimately culminated with the appointment of Herod the Great in 37 B.C., the man on the throne at the time of Jesus' birth.

Hoehner offers a description of the four hundred years in one paragraph.

> When the Persians defeated Babylon, the Jews went back to their homeland with no desire to worship idols, but unable to restore the temple to its former glory. With the importance of the synagogue increasing, Jewish life centered around the Torah rather than the temple. With the increasing influence of Hellenism, they saw the need to have their Scriptures translated into Greek; persecuted by the Seleucids, they became more engrossed with the hope of a messianic deliverance. Rome's capture of much of the Mediterranean world brought peace, although its power brought tyranny. At this point, Jesus Christ entered human history to bring man into an eternal communication with God, to bring peace to individuals as well as to the world, and to deliver people from the bondage of sin. He was rejected and crucified both by his people and by the pagan world, but the message of Christ's death and resurrection went out in Greek, the *lingua franca* of the day, into a world that was under the Pax Romana, bringing the hope of messianic deliverance both for the present and for the future, when Messiah will rule the world (Hoehner, p. 193).

PRINCIPLES

- The faithful care of the heavenly Father over his people is a major component of faith in any age.
- The Bible presents the story of the world's preparation for the coming of Jesus Christ, including a strange cast of characters.
- Sometimes God removes his restraint on evil, and the world gets very ugly.

APPLICATIONS

- Don't be surprised at the violence and injustice in the world; sin holds the upper hand now, but God will soon overturn that.
- Be aware that even in a linear history leading to an ultimate goal, there are sometimes cycles of sin, punishment, and repentance for entire nations.
- Thank God for the peace that North America has enjoyed, and pray for those parts of the world which seem to live in constant violence.

IV. LIFE APPLICATION

A Biblical Darth Vader

How children scream in theaters when this sinister figure in the epic Star Wars series appears on screen. And how they cheer when he is outwitted or outmaneuvered by the people of "The Force." This chapter describes something of that same kind of conflict of the ages—the people of God versus the people of Satan, righteousness versus evil, morality versus immorality. And though they speak in the most mystical generalities, Christians really know what the Star Wars heroes should mean when they say to one another, "May the Force be with you."

When Antiochus Epiphanes took the Seleucid throne in 175 B.C., "Darth Vader" was about to attack. He was the instrument of affliction sent by God in response to the apostasy of the Jewish people. They had been down this road many times before throughout their history, including the seventy-year banishment to the pagan kingdoms of Assyria, Babylonia, and Persia. But now the attack comes right to their beautiful land and to the holy city of Jerusalem.

We note from history that one of the evils into which they had fallen was the secularization of their faith and service to God (1 Macc. 1:14–15). In an attempt to ingratiate themselves with the hellenistic monarchs of the Mediterranean world, the Jews imitated Greek behavior in almost every area, neglecting the study of the Hebrew language and the Holy Scriptures. They denied their faith, refused circumcision, changed Hebrew names to Greek names, and ostracized the conservative minority loyal to the faith.

As happens in modern times as well, the most offensive apostasy came from official clergy, people under covenant to support and advance the faith. Support for truth came from common people, the humble Mattathias and his family. In the early part of the twentieth century, this liberal spirit spread across Protestantism. Its impact decimated many mainline denominations and resulted in those hulking icons of apostasy, the National Council of Churches and the World Council of Churches. In our day it reflects itself as well in liberal politics which advances every worldly cause (pornography, homosexuality, witch group memberships, rebellion against parents, anarchy in the streets for the slightest provocation) and insists on tolerance toward every group except those conservative in religion or politics.

A comparison of Daniel, 1 Thessalonians, and Revelation with *U.S.A. Today* surely suggests that the world may be ready for another Darth Vader like Antiochus Epiphanes. Veldkamp warns:

> We need not look for spectacular sins as evidence of the secularization of the church, for in the church you find nice people who will have nothing to do with debauchery. You certainly can't accuse them on that score. What you *can* accuse them of, however, is the insidious sin of conforming more and more to the world. Not the law of the Lord but the world's way of thinking becomes normative for life. Everyone looks out for himself, and no one puts the welfare of others ahead of his own. What is this individualism but conforming to the world? Egoism flourishes, and the Savior's prophecy that the love of many will grow cold is borne out. Even if the ecclesiastical forms are preserved intact, the insides have become so rotten that the Antichrist will succeed in his very first attack (Veldkamp, p. 182).

V. PRAYER

Father, keep us faithful now in the times of prosperity and in any times of persecution that might lie ahead. Amen.

VI. DEEPER DISCOVERIES

A. Citadel of Susa (8:2)

The city of Susa was located on the Karkheh River in southwest Persia, about 150 miles north of the Persian Gulf. The nation of Elam had made it a capital of that government in earlier years. Darius I built a fine palace which covered two acres, a building in which Esther apparently lived during the times of Xerxes (Ahasuerus).

The phrase "citadel of Susa" appears in Nehemiah 1:1 and Esther 1:2,5; 2:3,5. This building is a fortified fortress and palace complex separate from the surrounding city which served as the king's residence, particularly during the winter.

B. Sheep in the Bible

We have already discussed the difference between the wild animals of chapter 7 and the domesticated animals of chapter 8, but we find ourselves surprised that God would choose a member of the sheep family (the ram) to represent Persia. Throughout the Old Testament Israel is frequently called God's flock (both sheep and goats appear that way) and their leaders, rams and bucks. Ezekiel 34 pushes this metaphor throughout the entire chapter and says in verse 17, "As for you, my flock, this is what the Sovereign LORD says: I will judge between one sheep and another, and between rams and goats." Zechariah 10:3 depicts sheep oppressed by goats. The English word *leaders* in the NIV text of Isaiah 14:9 is the Hebrew word for male goats. Apparently the Jews would have been accustomed to this kind of metaphor to describe strength and power.

C. Gabriel (8:16)

The name means "hero of God," and Gabriel apparently was God's major messenger (Dan. 8:16; 9:21; Luke 1:19,26). He does not hold the rank of Michael (archangel) but obviously stands high in the overall angel hierarchy. The Aramaic Targum attributes to him the burial of Moses and the defeat of the armies of Sennacherib. In extrabiblical sources Gabriel appears in the book of Enoch as an archangel, but we have no textual confirmation of that in either the Old or New Testament.

VII. TEACHING OUTLINE

A. INTRODUCTION

1. Lead Story: Macedonian Menace
2. Context: The textual context of this chapter is not consequential, but the historical context takes its place. The ram and the goat describe the empires of Medo-Persia and Greece which dominated the worlds of the Mediterranean and Middle East from 539 B.C. to 63 B.C.
3. Transition: Daniel identifies the year of each of his visions (chaps. 7–11) by telling us which king was on the throne and the year of his reign. Chapter 8 begins about 551 ("in the third year of King Belshazzar's reign"), and chapter 9 sets us into the Persian Kingdom ("in the first year of Darius son of Xerxes"), about 539 B.C.

B. COMMENTARY

1. The Two-Horned Ram (8:1–4)
2. The One-Horned Goat (8:5–8)
3. The Powerful Horn (8:9–12)
4. The Crucial Question (8:13–14)
5. The Heavenly Interpreter (8:15–18)
6. The Exhausting Explanation (8:19–27)

C. CONCLUSION: THE FOUR HUNDRED SILENT YEARS

VIII. ISSUES FOR DISCUSSION

1. What is your opinion on the question of whether this chapter deals only with history or also projects prophecies of the Antichrist?
2. What do the prophecies of this chapter tell us about God?
3. In light of what this chapter tells us, how should we conduct ourselves as Christians?

Daniel 9:1–19

Daniel's Prayer

I. INTRODUCTION
Prophet Profit

II. COMMENTARY
A verse-by-verse explanation of the chapter.

III. CONCLUSION
God Have Mercy!

An overview of the principles and applications from the chapter.

IV. LIFE APPLICATION
Raising the Bell

Melding the chapter to life.

V. PRAYER
Tying the chapter to life with God.

VI. DEEPER DISCOVERIES
Historical, geographical, and grammatical enrichment of the commentary.

VII. TEACHING OUTLINE
Suggested step-by-step group study of the chapter.

VIII. ISSUES FOR DISCUSSION
Zeroing the chapter in on daily life.

Quote

"Prayer lifts the heart above the battles of life and gives it a glimpse of God's resources, which spell victory and hope."

C. Neil Strait

GEOGRAPHICAL PROFILE: JUDEA

- Occupied Israeli territory from the Dead Sea to the Mediterranean and from north to south on a line just south of Jerusalem and Jericho to the beginning of the Negev
- Became the center of the Southern Kingdom during the divided monarchy
- Scene of the great revival under Josiah about 621 B.C.
- Fell to the Babylonians in 597 B.C.

GEOGRAPHICAL PROFILE: JERUSALEM

- Ancient capital of Jewish religion and culture
- First mentioned in Joshua 10:5
- Capital city of the Southern Kingdom of Judea
- Captured by Nebuchadnezzar in 597 B.C.

GEOGRAPHICAL PROFILE: EGYPT

- Ancient kingdom along the Nile River in North Africa
- Its history dates back to at least 3000 B.C.
- Appears in the Bible as early as Genesis 12:10
- A strong influence in Israeli politics during the days of the major prophets

- Will yet be blessed by God in the future (Isa. 19:24–25)

PERSONAL PROFILE: XERXES

- King of the Persian Empire beginning 539 B.C.
- In Hebrew the name is Ahasuerus
- This is not the Xerxes of Esther and Ezra

PERSONAL PROFILE: JEREMIAH

- Son of Hilkiah called to prophesy in 626 B.C.
- Lived through the sack of Jerusalem by Nebuchadnezzar
- Prophesied under the wicked Zedekiah and imprisoned by that king
- Described events in Judea after the destruction of Jerusalem (Jer. 40–45)

BIOGRAPHICAL PROFILE: MOSES

- Israel's greatest national hero who led the exodus from Egyptian slavery
- Born about 1520 B.C. and brought up in Pharaoh's court
- Spent forty years in seclusion as a desert shepherd
- Led Israel through the wilderness to the boundaries of the promised land
- Served as the intermediary between God and Israel in the giving of the Old Testament Law

Daniel 9:1–19

IN A NUTSHELL

When the agonies of life and the turmoil of the world depress your spirit, it's time to pray.

Daniel's Prayer

I. INTRODUCTION

Prophet Profit

As I struggle to work through the richness of the text of Daniel, I am reminded again that I am not a prophet or the son of a prophet; in fact, I spent forty years working for nonprofit organizations. But everyone who plumbs the depths of the latter part of the Old Testament can enjoy prophet profit. Interestingly, Daniel was no exception. One of the first things he tells us in chapter 9 is that he was stimulated to think about God's hand in his world because of Bible study in the Book of Jeremiah. We will explore the specific text to which Daniel refers just a bit later in the chapter, but here let's notice that both Jeremiah and Daniel were praying prophets. Jeremiah served as both a model of prediction and a model of prayer emulated by Daniel.

My favorite Jeremaic prayer occurs in chapter 32 of his book where we find him a prisoner in the dungeons of the wicked king Zedekiah in approximately 587 B.C. God asked him to purchase land from his cousin Hanamel and to "take these documents, both the sealed and unsealed copies of the deed of purchase, and put them in a clay jar so they will last a long time" (Jer. 32:14). From our perspective we understand that this gesture formed a dramatic prophecy that Israel would be restored to the land, something we also learn in Daniel.

But in the context of that crisis hour when Nebuchadnezzar's army was already pounding the walls of Jerusalem, Jeremiah apparently struggled greatly with what appeared to be an insignificant gesture in the face of national extinction. His brief prayer (which seems to have no ending except the expression of confusion in v. 25) begins by reminding God that he (Jeremiah) knows the greatness of the God to whom he prays: "Ah, Sovereign LORD, you have made the heavens and the earth by your great power and outstretched arm. Nothing is too hard for you" (Jer. 32:17).

Both Jeremiah and Daniel offer a wonderful demonstration of Bible study and prayer. When things look dark all around, when confusion reigns regarding what God might be doing in his world, study the Word and pray. Now let us plunge into chapter 9 and see if we can gain some prophet profit.

II. COMMENTARY

Daniel's Prayer

MAIN IDEA: *When God's people are mystified by the wonders of his word or his work in the world, the best recourse is always prayer—and sometimes the answer will astound you.*

A Confession in Prayer (9:1–6)

SUPPORTING IDEA: *When we come to God in prayer, especially in times of great need, our spiritual attitude is of primary importance.*

9:1. Again Daniel sets the scene chronologically, and we find ourselves somewhere in 539–538 B.C. Daniel had been in Babylon for over sixty-five years, and the city of Jerusalem had lain in ruins for almost fifty years. The event Daniel narrates occurred about the time of his encounter with the lions; he was at the height of his career serving under Darius. In my opinion, Daniel strengthens the case for the distinction between Darius the Mede and Darius the Persian by emphasizing Darius's ethnic connections at the beginning of this chapter. Darius the Mede was **made ruler over the Babylon kingdom** by Cyrus, who was the monarch over all of the Medo-Persian Empire.

9:2. Here we have one of the great verses in the Book of Daniel. For one thing, it establishes the messages of Jeremiah as **the Scriptures**, certifying the inspiration of Old Testament prophetic text. More specifically, Daniel had been reading about **the desolation of Jerusalem**, so we know the text is Jeremiah 25:11–13:

> This whole country will become a desolate wasteland, and these nations will serve the king of Babylon seventy years. "But when the seventy years are fulfilled, I will punish the king of Babylon and his nation, the land of the Babylonians, for their guilt," declares the LORD, "and will make it desolate forever. I will bring upon that land all the things I have spoken against it, all that are written in this book and prophesied by Jeremiah against all the nations."

In light of everything Daniel knew about the rigid control of the Medes and Persians, including their power that had destroyed the strong grip of Nebuchadnezzar's Babylon, he must have been astonished at this promise of the return of Jewish captives to Jerusalem. Clearly Daniel had no idea when the seventy years began and when they would end, so he decided to pray about the matter. Daniel had access to Jeremiah 29:10–14, which also emphasizes the restoration.

Before we leave this verse, let's remember that Daniel probably had the scrolls of Jeremiah in his possession for some time. He may have read this passage often, but at this point God directed his attention to plunge deeper into the meaning of the text. We have the same experience; we can read a chapter or a verse scores of time, and then on one particular day God uses it to bring encouragement or challenge to our spiritual lives.

9:3. Daniel had walked with the Lord for a long time and had learned not to command God but rather to approach heaven's throne in the deepest humility. The words **I turned to the Lord God** suggest a definitive act of focus, a turning away from all other things to concentrate on talking with the Lord. He came with fasting and with the ancient Jewish ritual of **sackcloth and ashes**. Forget eating. Forget walking around in purple robes of high office. Forget rights and privileges. This is the time to fall on one's face before God.

9:4. This verse begins one of the longest recorded prayers in the Bible—it starts with confession. Surely confession of what Daniel considered to be his own sins and shortcomings, but also a collective confession for his nation in exile from whom he refused to separate himself. Repeatedly throughout this prayer we see the word *we*, indicating that Daniel placed himself squarely in the company of Jehovah's rebellious servants who deserved his punishment.

Verse 4 centers in God's nature of truth and faithfulness. Here again as in verse 2 he used the sacred name Yahweh (see "Deeper Discoveries"). The eternal covenant of a loving God had, however, been broken by sin, and Daniel acknowledged his understanding of that historic fact.

9:5–6. The people of God confess their sins primarily to God, certainly not to some human intermediary, and only rarely to one another when those sins have had some destructive impact on a fellow human being. Israel's sin and rebellion came about because they **turned away from your commands**

and laws. Even though God had sent **prophets, who spoke in your name,** even though these prophets had been heard by **princes . . . fathers . . . and all the people of the land,** still the nation rebelled and the seventy years of exile came upon them. In addition to the Jeremiah text, Daniel may have recalled Psalm 51:4 or Psalm 32:5 and similar passages which portray confessions of David.

We don't often think of King Solomon as a prophet, but he had used virtually the same language years before in identifying the essential attitudes necessary to deliverance by the exiles:

> And if they have a change of heart in the land where they are held captive, and repent and plead with you in the land of their conquerors and say, "We have sinned, we have done wrong, we have acted wickedly"; and if they turn back to you with all their heart and soul in the land of their enemies who took them captive, and pray to you toward the land you gave their fathers, toward the city you have chosen and the temple I have built for your Name; then from heaven, your dwelling place, hear their prayer and their plea, and uphold their cause (1 Kgs. 8:47–49).

Campbell sums it up: "This forceful accumulation of verbs is a thorough confession that they were guilty of all kinds of sins. Further, all levels of God's people are indicated—kings, princes, fathers, and common people—all are guilty. No one can be excused" (Campbell, 138).

B Affirmation in Prayer (9:7–14)

SUPPORTING IDEA: *Biblical praying begins and ends with the humble acknowledgment that a righteous God never makes a mistake.*

9:7–8. The entire Old Testament offers a commentary on this prayer. Many years later the chronicler of Israel would detail as history what Daniel was now offering as prayer (2 Chr. 36:15–21). Israel was indeed **covered with shame** before the eyes of a righteous God. They had been scattered abroad **because of our unfaithfulness,** quite a contrast to the promise of Deuteronomy 28:7: "The LORD will grant that the enemies who rise up against you will be defeated before you." In 609 B.C. the righteous king Josiah had died at Megiddo, and it was all downhill from there.

9:9–11. The prayer continues with its contrast between a God who is **merciful and forgiving** and a people who had **rebelled against him**. They had not kept the laws given through Moses, nor had they listened to the prophets. Notice the switch here from the second to the third person. Daniel recited the facts of history as he described the spiritual condition of Israel. The NIV translates **merciful** and **forgiving** as adverbs, but in the original text they appear as plural nouns, emphasizing the multiple and extensive boundaries of God's great grace.

Daniel expressed no surprise that the conditional covenant has been broken and the appropriate punishment applied. He was fully aware of the record of Deuteronomy 28, itemizing the blessings for obedience and the curses for rebellion. Here is a sampling from that chapter:

> If you do not carefully follow all the words of this law, which are written in this book, and do not revere this glorious and awesome name—the LORD your God—the LORD will send fearful plagues on you and your descendants, harsh and prolonged disasters, and severe and lingering illnesses. . . . Just as it pleased the LORD to make you prosper and increase in number, so it will please him to ruin and destroy you. You will be uprooted from the land you are entering to possess (Deut. 28:58–59,63).

9:12–14. Certainly it is worth noticing that this prayer contains no word of petition yet. That will come in verse 16; but throughout the prayer up to this point Daniel remained on his face, spiritually pleading his recognition and understanding of why **all this disaster has come upon us**. Even after severe punishment (we could say many severe punishments), Israel refused to turn their hearts to God. Even as Daniel prayed this prayer, he knew in his heart that his fellow countrymen had adopted the secular patterns of Babylonian/Persian culture and their hearts rarely burned for the glories of the "Beautiful Land" (8:9; 11:16). Notice that **great disaster** in verse 12 becomes **this disaster** in verse 13 and **the disaster** in verse 14. Surely Daniel referred to the captivity that he had experienced only too well for too long. He did not complain but instead affirmed that God's judgment was deserved because **the LORD our God is righteous in everything he does**.

According to Walvoord:

> Even in the midst of the terrible manifestation of the righteous judgment of God, there was no revival, no turning to God; rulers and people alike persisted in their evil ways. What Daniel is saying is that God had no alternative, even though He was a God of mercy; for when mercy is spurned, judgment is inevitable. . . . Jehovah was being faithful in keeping his word both in blessings and cursing, which must have encouraged Daniel in anticipating the end of the captivity (Walvoord, *Daniel*, p. 210).

C Petition in Prayer (9:15–19)

SUPPORTING IDEA: *Whatever the sins of the past, the God of mercy promises that the future can be better through his forgiveness and restoration. In the Bible, hope quite regularly arises out of recollection of the past.*

9:15. Israel didn't sneak out of Egypt; they were miraculously delivered **with a mighty hand**. In the Old Testament the exodus framed the benchmark for God's power in the world. In the New Testament the resurrection of Christ served the same purpose. Furthermore, that famous dash across the Red Sea made some headlines in the ancient world. The God of the Jews introduced **a name that endures to this day**.

9:16. That reputation for power only carried weight among Jews who still believed and trusted, probably a minority in the captivity. Daniel had spent all of his adult life trying to persuade pagan rulers that the God of heaven is greater than all the gods of earth, and not without some notable success. But if he would only now act in miraculous support of his people by restoring the land and the city, Israel would no longer be **an object of scorn to all those around us**.

As Archer points out:

> Certainly a deity who could not preserve his own temple from Nebuchadnezzar's troops was no match for Marduk or Nebo. It was this reproach that had befallen the name of Yahweh and had tarnished his glory before the idol-worshipping world that so distressed Daniel's heart. Moreover, since God had so freely promised full pardon and restoration to his repentant people, the prophet felt emboldened to press

> the Lord as hard as he could for an early return of the Jewish captives to Palestine, that a new commonwealth of chastened believers might be established there and a testimony set up again for the one true God, the holy Sovereign of the universe (Archer, p. 110).

9:17–19. Daniel's heart was breaking, and the petitions gushed forth like a great flood. He reminded God that Jerusalem is "your city, your holy hill" (9:16), **your desolate sanctuary . . . the city that bears your Name**. In Daniel's view God's reputation was at stake in the pagan world. In this portion of the prayer, Daniel switched from the term *Jehovah* to *Adonai* and *Elohim,* which actually occur at verse 15 and seem to center in Daniel's appeal to God's total sovereignty over his people, his nation, and his world.

As we read these verses, we enter the holy of holies with the aging prophet. We can almost see his tears and hear his breaking voice as he cried out, **O Lord, listen! O Lord, forgive! O Lord, hear and act!** The argument of some critics who claim the prayer forms part of a second-century forgery is hardly worth mentioning here. Anyone who respects the Bible and holds an ounce of commitment to inspiration and inerrancy will hardly be moved by such words. Part of the reason for their confusion rests in a failure to distinguish between the seventy years of Jeremiah and the seventy weeks of Daniel (to be discussed in the second part of this chapter).

Wood points out that Daniel did not ask God to break stride with his own time schedule:

> This plea must be seen in the light of the three periods of Israel's captivity. Daniel and his three friends had been taken in 605 B.C., a second contingent (ten thousand craftsmen) in 591 B.C. and the main group in 586 B.C. The seventy years predicted by Jeremiah were nearly concluded if the beginning date was 605 B.C., but it would be proportionately removed in time if either of the other two dates were employed. Accordingly, what Daniel was really requesting was that God would be pleased not to choose either of the later dates as the starting point for the seventy years rather than Daniel's time of captivity, 605 B.C. (Wood, *Daniel,* p. 115).

If the model prayer of the New Testament is the famous Lord's Prayer of the Gospels, surely we might consider this the model prayer of the Old Testament. Yes, there seems to be minimal thanksgiving, but the tone of the prayer clearly indicates Daniel's appreciation for God's grace and longsuffering in the past. The reverence and awe with which he addressed the heavenly Father stands in sad contrast to the flippancy with which many modern Christians come into the presence of God. We sing songs about the Father and the Son with unidentified pronouns which could refer to a girlfriend or boyfriend. The careless chaos of some modern worship could well profit from an intensive study of this magnificent prayer.

MAIN IDEA REVIEW: *When God's people are mystified by the wonders of his word or his work in the world, the best recourse is always prayer—and sometimes the answer will astound you.*

III. CONCLUSION

God Have Mercy!

One of the most pictorial parables of the New Testament shows us two men at the temple in prayer. One is a religious leader, the other a financial functionary of the Roman government. We find the story in Luke 18 where it follows the parable of persistence, both parables teaching us about prayer. In the first eight verses of that chapter, we learn to persevere in prayer even when it looks as though nothing will happen. In the parable of the Pharisee and the tax collector, we learn humility in prayer and the centrality of God's grace in our lives.

In Daniel 9, we see that the righteousness of God has rubbed off on his prophet. He stands in stark contrast to many Pharisees of the New Testament and particularly to this one who "prayed about himself: 'God, I thank you that I am not like other men—robbers, evildoers, adulterers—or even like this tax collector. I fast twice a week and give a tenth of all I get'" (Luke 18:11–12). Few Bible prayers pinpoint empathy with other people in the humility and brokenness we see in this prayer of Daniel. Self-righteousness is one of the great sins of religious people even though the Bible condemns it repeatedly. In the parable of Luke 18, the Pharisee commended himself to God, offering a mini-resume to demonstrate how righteous and godly he had lived. He addressed God but merely wanted to call attention to himself. He congratulated his own religious efforts, and nowhere in the prayer did he ask anything of God. He offered no petition, sought no pardon, and apparently needed no divine strength or guidance. He did not ask for anything because he did not see himself in need of anything—not even God. In a few short words he *maximized self, minimized God,* and *vaporized grace.*

But the publican, though not a believer when he went to pray, looked much more like Daniel. His heart desperately needed pardon; his soul hungered for grace. He did not refer to himself as *a sinner* but rather *the sinner.* He acknowledged exactly what Daniel claimed for Israel—deserved judgment; yet he believed a gracious God could choose to have mercy on him.

At the end of the Lukan parable, Jesus offered a biblical principle particularly related to prayer: "For everyone who exalts himself will be humbled, and he who humbles himself will be exalted" (Luke 18:14). The Lord surely did not intend to teach the tax collector's words as some formula to produce forgiveness but rather to show us we must have the tax collector's heart. Once again in prayer, attitude holds priority over act. An old British poem has been constructed on the attitudes and spiritual conditions of the two men in the parable.

> Two men went to pray; or rather I say,
> One went to brag, the other to pray;
> One stands up close and treads on high,
> Where the other dares not send his eye.
> One nearer to the altar trod,
> The other, to the altar's God.

PRINCIPLES

- Bible study is always great preparation for prayer.
- A church that wants Christians to pray must be a church that teaches Christians to love and understand their Bibles.
- Before we worry about what the Bible means, we must have a solid knowledge of what the Bible says.
- Humility and brokenness form a significant part of biblical prayer attitude.

APPLICATIONS

- We would do well to follow Daniel's example of praise and confession before petition.

- Knowing that God is going to bring about a certain event certainly does not carry with it the knowledge of when that event will occur.
- Biblical praying is not for emergencies only (Dan. 6:10) but should become a lifestyle.
- When we ask God to do something in our lives, let's remember that we do not deserve it.

IV. LIFE APPLICATION

Raising the Bell

An old story from the Far East tells about a large and beautiful bell in the city of Rangoon, a distinctive pride of the great Buddhist temple Shwee-dagone. During the Anglo-Burman wars, the bell had been sunk in the river that ran through the city, and no effort by engineers could raise it.

One day a clever priest asked permission to make an attempt at rescuing the bell on the condition that the bell would be given to his temple. When authorities agreed, he had his assistants gather a large number of bamboo rods—hollow, light, and very buoyant. Divers took the rods down and fastened them to the bell at the bottom of the river.

After thousands had been securely tied to the bell, that ponderous relic actually began to move, and as more and more rods were added, their accumulated buoyancy was so great that they actually lifted the bronze mass from the river bottom and brought it to the surface.

In this chapter Daniel shows us about the buoyant rods of prayer. Prayer can lift the heaviest of burdens and reach down into the muddiest and deepest rivers. Perhaps not one or two or three, but the accumulated power of multiple prayers by one persevering believer over a long time or a group of believers concentrated together calls forth the power of God. Let's remember that prayer does not change things; God changes things through prayer.

V. PRAYER

Father, may the humility and brokenness of your servant Daniel fall again upon those of us who seek to lead your people in the captivity of our own day. Amen.

VI. DEEPER DISCOVERIES

A. Understanding the Scriptures (9:2)

Christians believe the Bible is *a special revelation,* the message of God in words as well as works. God has also spoken in nature, and we call that *natural revelation* or sometimes *general revelation* (Ps. 19; Acts 14:15–17; Rom. 1–3). The Scriptures came to us through human hands, but both Testaments emphasize the careful guidance God employed to guarantee the accurate recording of his message. This passing reference in Daniel 9 offers dramatic emphasis of the authority of Jeremiah. A godly Jew like Daniel would never use a phrase such as "according to the word of the LORD given to Jeremiah the prophet" (9:2) and link it with the word *Scriptures* unless he was completely committed to the authority of the text. And these words were written some seven hundred years before church councils gathered to develop what we call the canon, the official recognition of inspired Scriptures collected in the Bible. Some evidence for the canon exists in the second century, but not until the fourth century (almost one thousand years after Daniel) did Greek Christians begin to use the word *canon* and the doctrine of *canonicity* arose.

Lightner sums it up:

> Acceptance of the Bible as God's Word, and even a thorough knowledge of it, does not automatically mean a godly life will follow. God's Word must be appropriated personally as the Spirit illuminates it for the believer. Its precepts must be obeyed and its truth lived before it will have its intended effect on our lives. To live according to Scripture one must know what it teaches. But knowing what it teaches is not the same as living in harmony with, or yielding to, the Holy Spirit's teaching in it (Lightner, p. 32).

B. The Yahweh Tetragrammaton (9:4)

Ancient Hebrew used no vowels, so the term that we call *Yahweh* (Jehovah) would appear as YHWH and was known as the sacred Tetragrammaton. In this chapter Daniel uses the word for the first time, and it fits the design of the prayer exactly because it is the covenant name for God (translated "LORD") in verses 2 and 4. We can understand this better when we know that the Hebrews did not pronounce the text since they thought God's name too sacred actually to say. When the vowel system came into use, the vowels for *Adonai* were used to form *Jehovah,* which apparently first appeared in the twelfth century A.D. *Adonai* means "my Lord," the phrase used through the centuries in place of actually pronouncing the Tetragrammaton.

C. Your Name (9:18)

We cannot say for certain which name Daniel had in mind here. Several—as noted above—mean "Lord" or "ruler," emphasizing God's sovereignty, but *Elohim* is the usual Old Testament word for "God," a plural conveying omnipotence. Daniel also calls him *Jehovah Elohim,* the self-existent source of all being. Throughout the passage the name "Lord" (*Adonai*) appears nine times, emphasizing again the central theme of the Book of Daniel: God's complete sovereignty in his world.

Certainly the emphasis and respect to the phrase, "the city that bears your Name" (9:18), centers not so much on a specific name for God as it does on the linkage between his person and his people, his person and his place.

VII. TEACHING OUTLINE

A. INTRODUCTION

1. Lead Story: Prophet Profit
2. Context: This chapter devotes three verses to the historical setting, seventeen verses to Daniel's prayer, and eight verses to the answer to the prayer which forms one of the most comprehensive prophecies in the entire Bible.

3. Transition: As we have noted before, in this portion of the book in which Daniel describes his visions, he identifies the exact time of the vision by noting the era of a certain ruler's reign. The vision of chapter 9 took place in 539 or 538 B.C. The vision of chapter 10 came about four or five years later.

B. COMMENTARY

1. Confession in Prayer (9:1–6)
2. Affirmation in Prayer (9:7–14)
3. Petition in Prayer (9:15–19)

C. CONCLUSION: GOD HAVE MERCY!

VIII. ISSUES FOR DISCUSSION

1. In the light of Daniel's spiritual discipline, evaluate your own Bible study and prayer habits.
2. In what specific ways does a Christian show humility and brokenness in prayer?
3. What role does fasting play in today's church life and worship?

Daniel 9:20–27

The Seventy "Sevens"

I. INTRODUCTION
Finding the Messiah

II. COMMENTARY
A verse-by-verse explanation of the chapter.

III. CONCLUSION
Nicolae Carpathia

An overview of the principles and applications from the chapter.

IV. LIFE APPLICATION
"Old Glory Face"

Melding the chapter to life.

V. PRAYER
Tying the chapter to life with God.

VI. DEEPER DISCOVERIES
Historical, geographical, and grammatical enrichment of the commentary.

VII. TEACHING OUTLINE
Suggested step-by-step group study of the chapter.

VIII. ISSUES FOR DISCUSSION
Zeroing the chapter in on daily life.

Quote

"Never be afraid to trust an unknown future to a known God."

Corrie ten Boom

Daniel 9:20–27

IN A NUTSHELL

God can choose to answer prayer in any way he wishes. Here he sends an angel to his prophet personally to explain the future of Daniel's people, Israel.

The Seventy "Sevens"

I. INTRODUCTION

Finding the Messiah

My friend Don Campbell tells the story of Leopold Cohn, a rabbi who lived in Europe. Apparently Rabbi Cohn studied the passage before us and came to the conclusion (largely based on v. 26) that the Messiah had already come, because clearly his coming was expected before the destruction of Jerusalem in A.D. 70. He began to inquire among his friends where the Messiah might be. A fellow rabbi suggested to him, "Go to New York, and you will find Messiah." That's likely the last place I would look, but nevertheless Cohn sold most of what he owned to buy passage to America and upon arrival wandered the streets of New York looking for Messiah. "One day he heard singing coming from a building, and he went in, only to hear a clear gospel message. That night he received the Lord Jesus Christ as Messiah and Savior. Shortly after Mr. Cohn bought a stable, swept it out, set up some chairs, and began to hold Gospel meetings, the first outreach of what was to become the American Board of Missions to the Jews" (Campbell, p. 112).

This chapter is about the first coming of Messiah. Throughout the years thousands of pages have been written to deal with the seventy "sevens." Sometimes the magnificent prayer of Daniel gets slighted in our quest to satiate our appetites for prophecy and our wrangling with end-time issues. But our attention to the prophecy of the seventy weeks requires allegiance to the hermeneutical principle of proportion. God gives more space to Scripture that he wants to emphasize. So with Daniel's prayer ringing in our hearts, we tackle the tricky text of seventy "sevens."

II. COMMENTARY

The Seventy "Sevens"

MAIN IDEA: *Israel's suffering will not end with release from captivity. Centuries of struggle will pass until the Anointed One comes from heaven.*

A Angelic Voice Mail (9:20–23)

SUPPORTING IDEA: *Christians should never fail to ask the meaning of the Bible; God always honors a prayer for insight and understanding.*

9:20–21. Daniel is still very much in his prayer mode, confessing personal and national sin, **and making my request to the LORD my God for his holy hill**. We should assume that we only have a portion of Daniel's prayer; it may have continued for hours, until **the time of the evening sacrifice**. The prophet was still concerned for God's reputation regarding Jerusalem and Israel. Daniel's homeland was already a "desolate sanctuary" (9:17), and he had reminded God about the "desolation of the city that bears your Name" (9:18). Now he prayed for his **holy hill**.

Gabriel's angelic appearance caused him to look "like a man" (8:15), and his revelation has lent continuity to Daniel's visionary experience since chapter 7. We should not be startled that Daniel referred to the angel here as **the man I had seen in the earlier vision**. Furthermore, the Hebrew could be translated *servant*. When we add verse 23 to the mix, we see that Gabriel actually began his flight at the beginning of the prayer but didn't arrive until some time later. We have no concept of the distance between heaven and earth, nor the speed at which angels travel. But the text requires us to consider the time perspective.

Daniel had been praying about the temple and set the angelic visit as **the time of the evening sacrifice**. Remember, no sacrifice had been offered in Jerusalem for fifty years. Yet this prophet had observed the religious rituals of his people all his adult life and still marked his day by those spiritual disciplines. As we have noted earlier, the behavior of Daniel and his three friends in Babylon provides a model for parents. We all want the children we raise to become godly and responsible adults who practice the faith and values of their parents throughout all their adult years and teach them to the next generation.

9:22–23. Gabriel's quick response to Daniel's prayer came because Daniel was **highly esteemed**, a precious treasure in God's sight. Gabriel's purpose was precisely the matter about which Daniel prayed. When would God restore his people? When would God redeem his name? How long would Israel have to suffer in pagan nations? The angel offered **insight and understanding**, two qualities we all need in handling God's Word.

We often say that God is more willing to answer prayer than we are to pray, and Daniel 9:23 supports that principle in some degree. Apparently, however, one's own holiness and humility play a role in how quickly God responds to prayer. I like what Baldwin says about these verses: "One of the most important contributions of the Book of Daniel is its new insistence on the link between faith and intelligence. *Wisdom* and *understanding* were a gift (22) but he was still told to consider the message and understand the vision (23)" (Baldwin, pp. 167–68).

B Divine Objectives (9:24)

SUPPORTING IDEA: *In serious Bible study almost every word is important, but words often repeated gain even greater importance. Such is the case with the fascinating seventy "sevens."*

9:24. The phrase **seventy "sevens"** literally means seventy units of seven or seventy heptads. Most all conservative commentators take this to be 490 years (thereby immediately distinguishing it from the time of the captivity). We shall see in later verses that it divides into three sections. This verse gives an overview of the prophecy, and the remainder of the chapter specifies more details. Before we get into interpretation, have a look at the verse in *The Message:* "Seventy sevens are set for your people and for your holy city to throttle rebellion, stop sin, wipe out crime, set things right forever, confirm what the prophet saw, and anoint The Holy of Holies" (*The Message*).

Repeatedly we have noted that many interpreters claim Daniel was written in the second century, and therefore texts like this describe history rather than prophecy. Others claim the author (not Daniel, of course) somehow mingled Jeremiah's seventy years and other Old Testament numbers to arrive at a period of time which ended in the persecution of Antiochus Epiphanes.

Even some conservative scholars struggle to fit this passage into their eschatology and end up with some indefinite period of time rather than 490 years. Leupold completely ignores any significance to the numbers themselves and sees the whole passage as a general reference to some symbolical description of God's work in the world.

Since the week of creation, *seven* has always been the mark of divine work in the symbolism of numbers. *Seventy* contains seven multiplied by ten, which, being a round number, signifies perfection, completion. Therefore, "seventy heptads" (7 x 7 x 10) is the period in which the divine work of greatest consequence is brought to perfection. There is nothing fantastic or unusual about this to interpreters who recognize how frequently the symbolism of numbers plays a significant role in the Scriptures.

My own mentor in Daniel, Dr. John C. Whitcomb Jr., observes "that while the Hebrew word *shavuah,* meaning 'unit of seven,' has reference to *days* in most of its Old Testament occurrences because of the demands of context, it has reference to *years* in the ninth chapter of Daniel, likewise because of the demands of context" (Whitcomb, *Daniel's Great Seventy-Week Prophecy: An Exegetical Insight,* unpublished professional paper, p. 4).

To finish transgression: Ultimately human rebellion will end. Archer says of this point, "This seems to require nothing less than the inauguration of the kingdom of God on earth. Certainly the crucifixion of Christ in A.D. 30 did not put an end to man's iniquity or rebellion on earth, as the millennial kingdom of Christ promises to do" (Archer, p. 112).

To put an end to sin: The idea here is not forgiveness but restraint (Gen. 8:2). God will one day seal up the sins of Daniel's people. The biblical concept of sin implies missing the mark of God's standards. In this second objective the text moves from rebellion to immorality. Anyone who believes that this goal was achieved at the first advent apparently has no access to television and newspaper accounts of daily rebellion and anarchy around the globe. The end of sin awaits the eternal state.

To atone for wickedness: Certainly this points to the crucifixion and the central message of the New Testament—that Jesus paid for our sins on Calvary. Daniel had been praying about how the nation could find forgiveness, and Gabriel's answer speaks to that question. Let's remember too that his prayer was initiated by a study of Jeremiah and perhaps Daniel had read, "'In those days, at that time,' declares the LORD, 'search will be made for Israel's guilt, but there will be none, and for the sins of Judea, but none will be found, for I will forgive the remnant I spare'" (Jer. 50:20).

Let's pause here to notice that the first three items are in a sense negative, the cleaning up of the sin problem. The second set will move on to the subject of righteousness and national moral integrity that God wants to restore once again.

To bring in everlasting righteousness: God will transform his people and write his law on their hearts (Jer. 31:33–40). Certainly righteousness results from the cross, but hardly the national righteousness of Israel, so it would seem the fulfillment of this objective waits yet a future time.

To seal up vision and prophecy: Once sin is removed and righteousness is installed, the moral proclamations of the prophets will end. Once again, one could hardly argue that prophets were no longer needed after the cross, since we find several in the New Testament. That set of books culminates in Revelation, one of the greatest prophecies of all time. Possibly **seal up** does not mean complete or finish but rather authenticate and accomplish.

To anoint the most holy: J. Barton Payne offers a full two-page table of interpretation of Daniel 9:24–27, and serious students are encouraged to consult that (Payne, 384–85). For this particular phrase he indicates several possible positions: this refers to the altar cleansed in 165 B.C. (the liberal view); this refers to Christ anointed by the Holy Spirit (traditional); this refers to the consecration of millennial Jews (dispensational); this refers to the consummation of God with man (symbolical).

Interpretation seems to come down to the meaning of **most holy** in this text. Is this a building? A person? A group? Archer says:

> This is not likely a reference to the anointing of Christ (as some writers have suggested) because [this Hebrew expression] nowhere else in Scripture refers to a person. Here the anointing of the **most holy** most likely refers to the consecration of the temple of the Lord, quite conceivably the millennial temple, to which so much attention is given in Ezekiel 40–44 (Archer, p. 113).

Surprisingly, Walvoord suggests caution here: "The six items are not in chronological order and it would not violate the text seriously to have this prophecy fulfilled at any time in relation to the consummation. . . . If the final seven years is still eschatologically future, it broadens the possibility of fulfillment to the Second Advent of Christ and events related to it such as the millennial temple" (Walvoord, *Daniel*, p. 223). As readers struggle with interpretation of this phrase they would do well to consult Old Testament passages like Ezekiel 43:1–7; Isaiah 4:1–5; and Haggai 2:9.

Clearly some of these six items pertain only to the first advent, some seem to spread themselves over both advents, and some seem to find complete fulfillment only in the second advent. Wood summarizes it nicely:

> The purpose of this verse is to state three main truths to the Jews of Daniel's day: first, these coming seventy weeks of years would concern two occasions of the Messiah's appearance on earth; second, at the first appearance He would provide for the riddance of sin, which had necessitated their captivity, and replace it with righteousness; and third, in his second appearance there would be a time of full application of this righteousness to the people, as all vision and prophecy would come to complete fulfillment and the new Temple would be anointed for service, where they as righteous people might worship as God desired (Wood, *Daniel*, p. 118).

C National Destiny (9:25–27)

SUPPORTING IDEA: *Whatever our interpretation of the details of this passage, we cannot deny that the centerpiece of the fulfillment is the Anointed One, Jesus Christ.*

9:25. The beginning of 490 years centers in **the issuing of the decree to restore and rebuild Jerusalem**. At first glance that would seem a rather simple date to determine, but interpretation falls into chaos at this point. Some believe it means the time that God first spoke the word to restore Jerusalem. In the overall context of Daniel, however, the chronological focus is always on human kingdoms and that surely would be our best choice here. However, that only branches out into further complexity, since at least four options could qualify as **the decree to restore and rebuild Jerusalem**.

1. The decree of Cyrus to rebuild the temple (2 Chr. 36:22–23; Ezra 4:1–4; 6:1–5). Of this Baldwin writes: "The starting-point of the interpretation is the command to rebuild the temple, given by Cyrus in 539 B.C. . . . unless a distinction is made between the Temple and the city, in which case the time of Nehemiah would be the starting-point (Neh. 2:5, 445 B.C.). No other alternative seems possible" (Baldwin, pp. 169–70).
2. A decree by Darius confirming the decree of Cyrus (Ezra 6:6–12).

3. The decree of Artaxerxes (Ezra 7:11–26).
4. The decree of Artaxerxes given to Nehemiah authorizing the rebuilding of the city (Neh. 2:1–8).

The key here is to take the text of Daniel 9:25 literally and conclude that rebuilding the temple is not the same as rebuilding Jerusalem. Once we get over that hurdle, we are inclined to option 4 and the date of 445 B.C. issued by Artaxerxes Longimanus and carried out by Nehemiah. So we begin at approximately 445 B.C. Now our passage requires us to fix the ending point of the first two units—**until the Anointed One, the ruler, comes**.

Some have tried to design an exacting calendar to pinpoint the very month of the crucifixion, but the text seems to be less specific. Surely this refers to the first advent of Christ, so we know that it would fall somewhere between 4 B.C. and A.D. 33. This is not to say that Christ was thirty-seven years old when he was crucified, simply that the normally accepted boundaries of Jesus' birth and death adopt those numbers. I personally hold to a birth in 4 B.C. and a crucifixion in A.D. 30. Some have also argued that the phrase refers only to the triumphal entry (Culver, Seiss, Ironside, McClain, and Anderson). This seems more likely than the crucifixion but also appears to argue for a greater specificity than Gabriel's explanation requires. Further elaboration can wait until verse 26.

Still to be established in this verse is the time frame between the two events we have just discussed; it **will be seven "sevens," and sixty-two "sevens."** Without great elaboration we can see that the 7 heptads add up to 49 years, and the 62 heptads equal 434 years, a total of 483. The division is clearly intentional, but we are given no information regarding the gap.

What the verse does tell us strengthens our choice of 445 B.C. because of its relationship to the city rather than just the temple: **it will be rebuilt with streets and a trench, but in times of trouble**. We know historically that Nehemiah rebuilt the city in fifty-two days. I should mention here that Archer takes option three, arguing that the record of Ezra 7 justifies the intent to build the city. He begins counting at 457 B.C. and completes the first 49 years at 408 and immediately begins counting again to arrive at A.D. 26 for the 483 years. He adds a year because of the switchover from 1 B.C. to A.D. 1, arriving finally at A.D. 27 as the fulfillment of the 69 "sevens." He then observes: "This would come out to a remarkably exact fulfillment of the terms of v. 25. Christ's public ministry, from the time of his baptism in the

Jordan until his death and resurrection at Jerusalem, must have taken up about three years. The 483 years from the issuing of the decree of Artaxerxes came to an end in A.D. 27, the year of the 'coming of Messiah as ruler'" (Archer, p. 114).

Sir Robert Anderson, building his chronology on 360-day years, begins at 445 B.C. and culminates just before the death of Christ, though in order to achieve that he dates the crucifixion in A.D. 32 (Anderson, pp. 126–29), a view unacceptable to most contemporary scholars.

Attempting an exact month-to-month time span here strikes me as somewhat rigid. I like McClain's summary:

> From this date [445 B.C.] to the arrival of the Messianic King, according to Daniel, will be 69 weeks or 483 prophetic years. After allowing all due consideration for the various differences in computing these years, the prophecy remains unshaken. Its *terminus ad quem,* within close limits, is fixed and must fall somewhere within the earthly career of Jesus of Nazareth. If He is not the Messianic King of Old Testament prophecy, then prophecy has failed, and we can have no certain hope that there will ever be any such king (McClain, p. 173).

9:26. After the sixty-two heptads, **the Anointed One will be cut off and will have nothing**. Perhaps the most important chronological feature is to recognize that this occurs after the sixty-ninth week and before the seventieth. Gabriel will not return to the seventieth week until verse 27. Our natural reading of this text leads us to conclude a reference to the crucifixion. Some time after the sixty-ninth week, the Messiah will die.

Not only that, but also after the end of the sixty-ninth heptad **the people of the ruler who will come will destroy the city and the sanctuary. . . .War will continue until the end, and desolations have been decreed**. Historically, we can see here the destruction of Jerusalem by the Roman armies of Titus in A.D. 70. Both city and temple were completely destroyed approximately forty years after the crucifixion, so historically the death of Christ and the destruction of Jerusalem usher in **the end** with its wars and desolation. This sounds a great deal like Matthew 24:7–22 and requires that we recognize a difference between the beginning of **the end** and the end of **the end**. In short, the period between the ends becomes the seventieth week.

Please note carefully that **the ruler who will come** does not conduct the destruction of the city but rather **the people of the ruler**. The ruler himself is described in verse 27. Remember the iron image which spreads out to the mixture of iron and clay in the toes (chap. 2) and the terrifying beast of chapter 7. The Romans destroyed Jerusalem in A.D. 70, beginning the end for Israel, but that merely commenced the period between the sixty-ninth and seventieth weeks and the **ruler** himself (arising from some extension of the line of Roman kingdoms) comes against the people of God in the seventieth week. But that takes us into verse 27.

9:27. The premillennial interpretation of Scripture identifies this verse as a prophecy of seven years of tribulation, the seventieth heptad of Gabriel's prophecy. At the beginning of the seven years, the Antichrist **will confirm a covenant with many**. In the middle of the tribulation, **he will put an end to sacrifice and offering**. For the next three and one-half years, he pours out **an abomination that causes desolation** until the end of the tribulation when God destroys him.

So General Titus of Rome in A.D. 70 was merely a prototype of the Antichrist, much in the same way that Antiochus Epiphanes served that purpose among the Greeks. This time frame (seven years) appears three times in Daniel 12 (vv. 7,11–12) and in a variety of ways in Revelation (11:2–3; 12:6,14; 13:5). Three and one-half years appears as 1,260 days or 42 months and becomes a very important point of interpretation in Revelation, standing, as it does, directly on Daniel 9:27. In handling the Revelation passage (12:14), Ken Easley writes: "The mention of time, times and half a time is the only instance that Revelation uses the phrase (but see Dan. 7:25; 12:7). This is the fourth and final reference to a three and a half year period of intense suffering, otherwise called '42 months' (Rev. 11:2) or '1,260 days' (11:3; 12:6). . . . These are all stereotyped references to the final limited time of intense tribulation before Christ returns" (Easley, p. 213).

Let me clearly say that I am willing to press the details of this passage a bit more specifically than Easley does. He argues:

> Whatever Daniel had meant, John may have used what had become a contemporary figure of speech cueing readers or listeners that the period under consideration would be *limited* but *characterized by intense tribulation*. . . . Certainly it is possible that these time references will turn out to be precisely literal, but it is also possible

> that they do not define the exact length of time of the Great Tribulation anymore than the American idiom "seven year itch" defines the duration of that condition (Easley, p. 202).

Perhaps. But the chronological references in Daniel seem more precise than a general expression like "seven-year itch." I certainly don't think this passage offers a time chart for the end of the age. But I do suggest that the precision with which Daniel uses numbers throughout the book, and particularly in chapter 9, directs us to a seven-year tribulation with a distinct middle point at which severe persecution begins. The Hebrew text of verse 27 seems a bit obscure in the third sentence of the verse, but the intent prevails.

Archer says:

> The general sense is beyond dispute. The dictator will hold sway till the wrath of God is poured out in fury on the God-defying world of the Beast (little horn or ruler). That which is poured out may include the vials or bowls of divine wrath mentioned in Revelation 16; but certainly what "is poured out on him" points to the climax at Armageddon, when the blasphemous world ruler will be crushed by the full weight of God's judgment (Archer, pp. 118–119).

It seems that Gabriel has told Daniel that the first advent of Christ will occur at the end of sixty-nine weeks of years (v. 25), and the second advent will end the rule of Antichrist at the end of the seventieth week, which is separated by an indeterminate amount of time from the sixty-ninth. Remember that we interpret Daniel 9 in the light of the New Testament. Daniel could hardly have envisioned more than two thousand years of history occurring between the sixty-ninth and seventieth weeks. But with the addition of information from the prophecies of Jesus (particularly in Matt. 24–25) and notably the Book of Revelation, the picture takes on great specificity.

I intend to be faithful to the hermeneutical principle of proportion. In my opinion, the glitz and glamour of eschatology has led most commentators to place 75 percent of their effort on just over 10 percent of the chapter. But for his own reasons God chose to highlight the prayer and pass over the prophecy of the seventy weeks rather quickly; that certainly does not minimize its importance in the text.

So I close, likely earlier than many readers think I should, with a brief paragraph offered by Culver, who gave most of his adult life to the study of Daniel's prophecies:

> In summation on the prophecy of the seventy weeks, five facts appear: that (1) the seventy weeks are 490 years, which relate wholly to the then future of Israel; (2) the seventy weeks are divided into three periods of seven, sixty-two, and one, which follow one another and run consecutively; (3) the first sixty-nine weeks ran out during the lifetime of Messiah and before His crucifixion; (4) the death of Christ and the destruction of Jerusalem, both mentioned in the prophecy, are events which follow the close of the sixty-ninth week and precede the beginning of the seventieth week, and (5) the seventieth week pertains to a seven-year relationship between Antichrist and Daniel's people Israel, in eschatological times, and concludes with the second advent of Christ (Culver, p. 159).

MAIN IDEA REVIEW: *Israel's suffering will not end with release from captivity. Centuries of struggle will pass until the Anointed One comes from heaven.*

III. CONCLUSION

Nicolae Carpathia

Earlier I referred to the runaway best-seller Left Behind series written by Tim LaHaye and Jerry Jenkins. The stories are fictional, along with all the characters, but having established that, we should recognize that these two men, a highly respected pastor and a former vice president for publishing at Moody Bible Institute, write from a solid theological base. They describe conditions as they might be in the tribulation. For their Antichrist they choose the name Nicolae Carpathia, who vaults from the position of secretary general of the United Nations to world dictatorship as "His Excellency, Potentate Nicolae Carpathia." Along with his sidekick Leon Fortunato (the beast) he rebuilds New Babylon in Iraq from which he runs the world. He also establishes a Global Community assisted by the head of the Enigma Babylon One World Faith, Pontifex Maximus Peter the Second.

Let me immediately disavow any notion that we allow fiction to influence our interpretation of the Book of Daniel. On the other hand, let's recognize that these men are not just creating fantasy, but attempting to put into modern graphic fiction what they really believe about the outcome of the world during the end time. They may not be nationally renowned theologians or eschatologists, but they do their best to make sense of Bible prophecy, and that is exactly what we must do, whether our conclusions find us standing with them or in some other camp.

PRINCIPLES

- Only when we commit ourselves to the authenticity and inspiration of Scripture can we make any sense out of Bible prophecy.
- A recognition that God is not yet finished with Israel seems to be foundational to understanding this passage.
- People who humble themselves before God in prayer are prime candidates for understanding and applying the Word of God.

APPLICATIONS

- When we pray biblically, attitudes change and relationships improve.
- Let's not get so wrapped up in the prophecy of Daniel 9 that we miss the prayer.
- God can answer prayer any way he wishes, even by sending an angel.
- The key to understanding both Old and New Testaments is the life, death, and future coming of the Anointed One.

IV. LIFE APPLICATION

"Old Glory Face"

They called Ed Card "Old Glory Face." The superintendent of the Sunshine Rescue Mission in St. Louis seemed always on the verge of exploding with the joy of the Lord. When he preached, he would often shout "Glory!"

and his prayers frequently ended with the words, "And that will be glory for me!"

When hymnist Charles Gabriel learned about Card's life and ministry, he was inspired to write both the words and music of the much-loved gospel song, "Glory for Me." Appropriately, it made its first appearance in the hymnbook *Make His Praise Glorious,* published in 1900. During the next couple of decades, the Billy Sunday Crusades used the song widely and almost always called it "The Glory Song."

First Thessalonians 4:16 provides a solid biblical backdrop for the song because Gabriel focused on the coming of the Lord and our joy with him in heaven: "For the Lord himself will come down from heaven, with a loud command, with the voice of the archangel and with the trumpet call of God, and the dead in Christ will rise first" (1 Thess. 4:16). Certainly there is glory from knowing Christ now in salvation and walking with him on earth. But the song emphasizes that heaven offers the ultimate glory because Jesus is there.

The link of prayer and prophecy in this wonderful chapter of Daniel calls us to look for the future glory of our Lord's coming. Regardless of how we interpret the details of the book, every sincere Christian believes that Jesus Christ will come again, put an end to sin, and reign eternally in righteousness. Such faith produces both hope and joy.

V. PRAYER

Father, we thank you for revealing in your Word that you are not finished with your world. May we shine brightly for truth and faith until the final days arrive and Jesus comes again. Amen.

VI. DEEPER DISCOVERIES

A. Anointed One (9:25–26)

In Old Testament times, three offices among the Jews required anointing with oil—prophets, priests, and kings. As the "anointed one" Jesus becomes the ultimate fulfillment of all three. In the Old Testament we see people like Samuel, Saul, and David anointed to and for God's service. The very name

Christ (Gr. for *Messiah*) comes from the Greek verb *chrio,* meaning "to anoint." References to Christ as "the anointed one" appear 529 times in the New Testament, 379 of them written by Paul.

As Detzler says:

> All this goes back to the beginning of the Levitical priesthood (Exod. 29; Lev. 4) and moves through the Old Testament kings right on to the prophets and their anointing from God (1 Kings 19). Psalm 2:2 and Isaiah 61:1–2 talk about the coming Messiah as the anointed one and Luke picks up the Isaiah passage in Luke 4:18–19. Early apostolic preaching called Jesus the anointed one (Acts 4:26–27; 10:38). The name of Christ, which means anointed, is then a logical extension of the messianic teaching of God's Anointed One. This powerful proclamation ties Jesus of Nazareth to the Messiah. It is seen in His Gospel: The Good News "of Christ" (Rom. 1:16 KJV), the testimony about Christ (1 Cor. 1:6), Christ's coming and God's grace to defeat death (Rom. 14:9), and the satisfaction of the law by Christ's sacrifice (Gal. 3:13) (Detzler, p. 18).

B. Abomination of Desolation (9:27)

We have already read in Daniel 8:13 about "the rebellion that causes desolation," and we will yet encounter the phrase "the abomination that causes desolation" in Daniel 11:31 and 12:11. In the Olivet Discourse Jesus said, "So when you see standing in the holy place 'the abomination that causes desolation,' spoken of through the prophet Daniel—let the reader understand—then let those who are in Judea flee to the mountains" (Matt. 24:15–16). Clearly Jesus considered the fulfillment of Daniel's prophecy yet future, and therefore the abomination under Antiochus Epiphanes was a type of what the Antichrist will eventually do. The strongest corroboration of Daniel's prophecy rests in the words of Jesus himself rather than archeological evidence. Either Jesus was completely mistaken in his understanding of the Old Testament, or Daniel could actually prophesy the future.

Revelation 13 tells us that the little horn will remain in control of world affairs until the end of the tribulation, forcing his will through violence and profaning the holy city and the temple apparently much like Antiochus did. In his commentary on Matthew 24:15, Stu Weber notes: "Jesus took this phrase from Daniel . . . where it was used to mark a particular turning point in the events of the end times. Specifically, this 'abomination' was some kind of defiling, destructive incident in the temple, which would end the practice of daily sacrifices. Jesus specified that the abomination would be standing in the holy place; that is, the second most sacred room in the temple" (Weber, 400).

And a bit later Weber adds:

> The fact that Israel has reestablished itself as a national political entity and occupied the holy temple site again has many scholars anticipating the end times very soon. No other nation has experienced two thousand years of cultural dispersion and retained their national integrity. God is not yet finished with the Jewish people. And the Great Tribulation to come in the seventieth and final of the "seventy weeks" (periods of seven years) predicted for Israel by the prophet Daniel . . . will see the nation purged and prepared for the return of its Messiah-King (Weber, p. 401).

VII. TEACHING OUTLINE

A. INTRODUCTION

1. Lead Story: Finding the Messiah
2. Context: The latter part of Daniel 9 is important to understanding the continuity of the whole book, particularly with reference to Gabriel, who appeared in chapters 7 and 8. We have already discussed the historical chronology of the chapter in relation to chapters 8 and 10, and the particular context of the prophecy of seventy "sevens" *must* be linked to the prayer of Daniel which deals only with Israel as a people, Jerusalem as a city, and the temple of God. Attempts to apply the prophecies of Daniel 9 to the church in any way violate the context and misdirect the thrust of the book.
3. Transition: As we approach the end of chapter 9 holding our breath, we can only anticipate what Daniel might say next. He is not finished with his visions, and he will now take us to the third year of Cyrus, king of Persia.

B. COMMENTARY

1. Angelic Voice Mail (9:20–23)
2. Divine Objectives (9:24)
3. National Destiny (9:25–27)

C. CONCLUSION: NICHOLAE CARPATHIA

VIII. ISSUES FOR DISCUSSION

1. In what ways might we recognize that God has highly esteemed some Christian leaders in our day?
2. After studying the Bible text and the commentary, what is your opinion on the meaning of the seventy "sevens"?
3. If you were explaining Daniel 9:25–27 to your twelve-year-old child, what would you say?

Daniel 10:1–11:1

Angels in the Outfield

I. INTRODUCTION
Playing with Paderewski

II. COMMENTARY
A verse-by-verse explanation of the chapter.

III. CONCLUSION
Calvin's Prayer

An overview of the principles and applications from the chapter.

IV. LIFE APPLICATION
Spiritual Warfare

Melding the chapter to life.

V. PRAYER
Tying the chapter to life with God.

VI. DEEPER DISCOVERIES
Historical, geographical, and grammatical enrichment of the commentary.

VII. TEACHING OUTLINE
Suggested step-by-step group study of the chapter.

VIII. ISSUES FOR DISCUSSION
Zeroing the chapter in on daily life.

Quote

"We who embrace the Bible as God's inerrant Word have often failed to instruct our people in its extended message about angels, demons, and Satan."

Robert Lightner

Daniel 10:1–11:1

PERSONAL PROFILE: MICHAEL

- A name used for ten different men in the Old Testament
- The name means "Who is like God?"
- Jude calls him the archangel (Jude 9)
- Also mentioned in Daniel 12:1

IN A NUTSHELL

In this chapter, as in many other places in the Bible, the mighty God of heaven appears to a godly man on earth to assure him that amid paganism and idolatry, heaven is in charge.

Angels in the Outfield

I. INTRODUCTION

Playing with Paderewski

An old story which I can neither confirm nor deny tells about a mother who wanted to expand her young son's interest in music by taking him to hear Paderewski in concert. They entered the concert hall and took their seats when the mother saw a friend in another section and remembered she needed to speak with her briefly. She turned to the young boy and told him to stay in his seat until she returned. But as young boys will, he became restless and began to wander about the concert hall and even found his way backstage. In his meanderings he came to a room clearly marked "Do Not Enter," but since he had limited reading ability, he opened the door and went into the room.

The house lights dimmed, the mother returned to her seat and saw the boy was missing. Assuming he had made an urgent trip to the bathroom, she decided to wait for a few minutes before panicking. Then the curtain rose, and everyone in the hall saw a small boy seated on the bench of the Steinway grand piano, carefully picking out the tune "Twinkle, twinkle little star." In an instant Paderewski appeared in the wings and walked quickly across the stage to stand behind the Steinway. Leaning over the child he said quietly, "Keep playing—don't stop, you're doing just fine." Then with his left hand he reached around the boy and added some bass chords while with his right hand he played runs and arpeggios. Together the great pianist and a little boy made beautiful music, delighting the audience who stood in applause after that unscheduled opening song.

To the best of my knowledge, Daniel never played with Paderewski. But in this chapter he has a special experience with one far greater than himself. And like that little boy he found himself helpless and frightened in the face of a watching world.

The last three chapters of Daniel form one section which records the reception and the interpretation of a final vision. Chapter 10 offers the initial vision and some additional information regarding the future of Israel and its relationship with other ancient nations. In its verses we see Daniel move from mourning to peace, from weakness to strength; and once again we find in Daniel a spiritual lesson marching alongside the historical and prophetic message of the text.

II. COMMENTARY

Angels in the Outfield

MAIN IDEA: *God wants us to know that, in addition to the human forces of evil on the earth, demonic forces are constantly at work, sometimes through national leaders. But he also wants us to know that none of those forces, human or demonic, can defeat the forces of heaven.*

A The Secret Mourning (10:1–3)

SUPPORTING IDEA: *When events do not seem to be "working together for good" on earth, let's remember that God has a completely different timetable.*

10:1. By now we are accustomed to Daniel's introduction to visions, and once again he tells us the year of the event—about 535 B.C., **the third year of Cyrus king of Persia**. Experts do not find strong agreement on the date in view here. Some place it as early as 539 B.C. and others as late as 534. Actually Cyrus had begun his reign in 558, but he had no direct relationship to Babylon since Darius the Mede was in charge there. Most scholars count from the end of the reign of Darius (approximately 338 B.C.), arriving at something in the neighborhood of the mid-third decade of the sixth century. Daniel speaks again of **vision**, but this time he begins by telling us that he received **a revelation**. Later the **revelation** which came in the **vision** is called throughout the chapter a **message** (*dabar*). He affirms the truth of the **revelation** and tells us it will be about **a great war**. In actuality the message itself came in a revelation, and the understanding came in a vision—such is the strict wording of the text.

As backdrop, let's remember that the rebuilding of the Jerusalem temple is already underway, but a work stoppage has occurred because of opposition in Palestine. Daniel may have known this. He was probably no longer in public office, although we should not make too big a point of that since Daniel 1:21 suggests that his career may have continued beyond the first year of Cyrus. This verse exemplifies the benefits of the NIV over the KJV which reads "a thing was revealed unto Daniel . . . and the thing was true, but the time appointed was long." Actually, there is some question about the translation of *saba gado* as **great war**, since it could also mean "heavy suffering."

10:2–3. I find no reason why we should not see a chronological flow of the text here; the message was so heavy that Daniel **mourned for three weeks**. He ate, but no gourmet menu—carrots, broccoli, lettuce, and water. Daniel makes a point of this to show that physical asceticism was not his usual lifestyle. But hearing this sad message, he simply refused to eat for the sake of enjoyment, choosing rather the barest sustenance. We see nothing in the text that would cause us to take the word **weeks** in anything other than its literal sense. Daniel used the expression **three weeks** twice, and nowhere indicated heptads in any sense.

But what are we to make of the phrase **I used no lotions at all**? Let's remember that Daniel lived in a desert country. People in Arizona and New Mexico understand the necessity of constantly lubricating their skin in a low humidity climate. Perhaps the point here is that Daniel wanted God to see that both inside and outside he had prepared himself to hear this heavy message. We will talk more about fasting in "Deeper Discoveries."

B The Shining Man (10:4–9)

SUPPORTING IDEA: *God is capable of communicating with us in any way he chooses— dreams, visions, voices, and angels.*

10:4–5. Though not as great as the Euphrates in Old Testament perspective (Gen. 15:18), the **Tigris** was no small river. Some 1,150 miles long (about 500 miles less than the Euphrates), the Tigris carried more water than the Euphrates and actually moved more rapidly. It was called "river of the date palm." Whatever the year, Daniel identifies **the twenty-fourth day of the first month** (Nisan). Quite likely his three weeks of mourning had already concluded. Unlike the vision of 8:2, where Daniel saw himself in the citadel of Susa, it seems apparent here that Daniel actually and literally stood on the bank of the great river. He may have been on business in the eastern region, or he may have been taking a holiday after celebrating Passover ten days earlier.

He looked up and saw **a man dressed in linen, with a belt of the finest gold around his waist**. Possibly the linen signified purity (Exod. 28:42) and the belt some high position of importance. We know only that some righteous figure of possible royal standing appeared before the prophet.

10:6. Daniel goes to great pains to flesh out the image of this being. He tells us **his body was like chrysolite**. Translators and commentators run all over the map describing this substance. Some see it as topaz, others transparent gold, others jasper. Specificity seems unimportant since the text only requires us to recognize some rare and beautiful jewel.

Furthermore, this creature's face shone **like lightning**. Some unusual brilliance flashed from his countenance. And along with facial lightning, his eyes seemed like **flaming torches**, language which reminds us somewhat of John's description of Christ in Revelation 1:14. Daniel likens the arms and legs (clearly not covered with a garment of any kind) to the **gleam of burnished bronze**, suggesting a favorable comparison to the yellow burl of the body in general. And finally we learn that when this creature spoke, his voice carried **the sound of a multitude**.

The entire description could fit any angel, a specific angel such as Michael or Gabriel, or *the angel*, a designation of the preincarnate Christ. Commentators hopelessly divide on the conclusion. Leupold, Archer, and Wood select angel in general; Hengstenberg chooses Michael; Young and Kyle consider this a theophany (an earthly appearance of the Father); Walvoord, Culver, and Campbell choose Christophany (an earthly appearance of the Son).

Admittedly, the description somewhat parallels Revelation 1:12–20, although there seems to be insufficient evidence to establish a clear Christophany here. Is the being of verses 5–9 the same as the being of verses 10–14? We shall address that question when we arrive at the latter verses. At this point in the chapter, I'm inclined to agree with Wood who says, "The most likely identity is that this one was simply another angel, perhaps of parallel importance with Gabriel and Michael, whose name, for some reason, is not recorded" (Wood, *Daniel*, p. 128).

10:7. Rather like the experience of the apostle Paul on the road to Damascus, Daniel alone among his companions **saw the vision**. But the text tells us that something terrorized them so much that they **fled and hid themselves**. If they didn't see the vision, what did they see? Possibly they just sensed that something was, as we would say, "in the air." Also the text certainly allows for the possibility that they heard the voice "like the sound of a multitude" (10:6). Clearly Daniel's response did not send these people into hiding; some kind of paranormal experience took place. The text simply doesn't tell us what it was. Daniel's description of their behavior stabilizes the view that this was an actual experience, not a virtual reality vision like he had of Susa.

10:8. As for Daniel, he again adopts the now famous paleface posture and admits **I was helpless**. We find a great spiritual lesson here. Coming into the presence of God's messenger does not always bring indescribable joy. Daniel was emotionally drained, and all human resistance completely dissipated.

10:9. Apparently the angel spoke again, and as Daniel listened, he fell into a coma, face down on the ground. Now the aging prophet was physically, emotionally, and spiritually ready for God's message.

C The Special Messenger (10:10–14)

SUPPORTING IDEA: *When we are helpless before God, when we recognize our own limitations in the spiritual realm, God may speak to us with an important message.*

10:10–11. At a touch Daniel moved from the prostrate position to one that he described as **trembling on my hands and knees**. Who touched Daniel? Some scholars argue that the hand belonged to a different being than the one described in verses 5–6, but that seems an unnatural handling of the text.

As the angel spoke, he again commended Daniel as being **highly esteemed** (see 9:23) and warned him to **consider carefully the words I am about to speak to you**. Still trembling, Daniel stood up. The angel's description could literally be understood as *man of preciousness*. We know that God loves the entire world (John 3:16), but he also chooses certain godly people to whom he shows himself in special ways. On that list we would certainly find David (1 Sam. 13:14), the apostle John (John 13:23), and many others. We might note that carefully considering words is a wise guideline for the study of prophecy in any era of human history.

10:12. James 5:16 tells us that the "prayer of a righteous man is powerful and effective," and Daniel was a good example of that. What was **the first day**? The beginning of Daniel's three weeks of fasting described in 10:2? If we bring in verse 13 to help us, that answer works since the angel described a twenty-one-day delay in his trip. Certainly the spiritual lesson of this verse reminds us again that God answers the prayers of those who come in proper attitude.

10:13. Fasten your seat belt—spiritual warfare ahead. The angel had "been sent" (10:11) and had come "in response" (10:12) to Daniel's prayers. But he had trouble en route and offered the explanation that **the prince of the Persian kingdom resisted me twenty-one days**. All the time Daniel had been praying and fasting, the angel had waged spiritual warfare beyond the boundaries of earth. Every conservative commentator agrees that this verse and similar references in verses 20–21 indicate that fallen angels, to some extent, control and protect earthly kingdoms. We learn in verse 20 that Greece also had such a "prince," and apparently, as we read in 10:13, Michael may be the guardian angel of Israel. Walvoord describes **the prince** as "a fallen angel under the direction of Satan, in contrast to the angelic prince Michael, who leads and protects Israel" (Walvoord, *Daniel,* p. 246).

While our unknown angel struggled against the Persian prince, Michael arrived to help, since he was **one of the chief princes**. From the Book of Jude, we know that Michael was an archangel. In Revelation 12:7, John saw him leading angelic armies against Satan and his demons. It seems fair to conclude that there may have been more than one archangel and also that angels have different duties. In a passage like this, we want to avoid the extremes of either angelphobia or angelmania. Probably the latter dominates our day. Angels are merely the servants of God who do his work wherever he sends them.

10:14. Having safely arrived, thanks to Michael's help, the angel told Daniel that this vision explained **what will happen to your people in the future . . . a time yet to come**. Leupold offers a helpful paragraph related to this verse:

> Bad angels, called demons in the New Testament, are, without a doubt, referred to here. In the course of time, these demonic powers gained a very strong influence over certain nations and the governments of these nations. They became the controlling power. They used whatever resources they could muster to hamper God's work and to thwart His purposes. . . . We get a rare glimpse behind the scene of world history. There are spiritual forces at work that are far in excess of what men who disregard revelation would suppose.

They struggle behind the struggles that are written on the pages of history (Leupold, pp. 457–59).

The word **future**, rendered in the KJV as "the latter days," forms an important Old Testament concept going all the way back to Genesis 49:1. Certainly it is not an overstatement to suggest that the future of Daniel's people included not only their struggles with the Greeks and Romans, but also the full-orbed picture of end times still future. Culver says of this phrase, "It is a technical term taken out of the previous prophetical literature of Israel, and always in Scripture includes some eschatological reference" (Culver, p. 164).

D The Strengthening Message (10:15–11:1)

SUPPORTING IDEA: *Two strains run side by side in these verses—the insufficiency and weakness of humanity and the authority and power of God.*

10:15–17. Daniel's spiritual and emotional struggle continued as he was rendered **speechless** by this talk about spiritual warfare somewhere in the skies over Persia. But someone **touched** Daniel's lips so he could speak again and he expressed verbally how **helpless** and weak he felt—**I can hardly breathe**. We detract from the spiritual message of the chapter if we waste time trying to determine whether this person was the angel God had sent, a different angel, or God himself. The touch of an angel is, in any instance, a de facto touch from God, and here it granted Daniel once again the power of speech. We should not forget that as a prophet, Daniel would consider speaking a major part of his task (Deut. 18:15–22; Jer. 1:6–9).

10:18–19. At the first touch Daniel regained his voice; then at the second touch he received **strength**. The **highly esteemed** prophet heard a message all of us need with some frequency: **Peace! Be strong now; be strong**. Daniel was immediately **strengthened** and, in this newly invigorated condition, acknowledged his readiness for the vision.

10:20. The angel's question seems rhetorical—**Do you know why I have come to you?** Considering what Daniel had been through there on the bank of the Tigris, this might have been a check of his mental and emotional stability. After a smashing sack which knocked John Elway on his back for several minutes during a Denver Bronco football game, the trainer asked him, "Do you know where you are?" Presumably the answer should have been,

"Yes, I'm in a football game in Mile High Stadium." But Elway responded, "Yeah—I'm fourth and seventeen!"

Daniel was fourth and long too, and the angel wanted to be sure he could handle what was coming in chapter 11. Furthermore, there wasn't much time since the angel had scheduled a rematch **against the prince of Persia**. Then he said a most curious thing—**and when I go, the prince of Greece will come**. We don't have any problem recognizing some demonic being as the **prince of Greece**, but to where was he coming and why? I like the way Baldwin puts it: "The heavenly warfare is to be directed against first Persia and then Greece, because each of these in turn will have power over God's people" (Baldwin, 182). This prophecy didn't only deal with Persia, but also with Greece, so its demonic prince was interested in the discussion as well. In a context like this, we take strong spiritual hold once again on Ephesians 6.

10:21. Before the angel left, he told Daniel **what is written in the Book of Truth**. At first glance we think such words refer to the Bible, but more likely they form a figurative expression for God's will regarding Israel's future. Nevertheless, what the angel reported did end up as part of the Bible, so a connection here is certainly possible. Since the future of Daniel's people is already **written in the Book of Truth**, no amount of activity by demonic powers can change the outcome. Apparently the reporting angel normally worked alone since he seemed to make a point of telling Daniel that in the particular spiritual warfare against his adversaries from Persia and Greece he had the support of Michael **your prince**.

This chapter gives us amazing insight into the behavior of evil spirits in the world and their operations as national representatives under Satan's world control. In the Gospel of John, three times Jesus referred to Satan as "the prince of this world" (John 12:31; 14:30; 16:11). The **your** of 10:21 is plural, indicating that Michael belongs not just to Daniel personally, but to the nation of Israel. Wood says, "Michael's main task was to oversee matters pertaining especially to the Jews; but since Jewish welfare was vitally involved with the dominating empire of the day, it fell to him to assist in that respect as well when the need might arise" (Wood, *Daniel*, p. 134).

11:1. This verse links more closely to chapter 10 than it does to chapter 11 because it reflects the words of the angel rather than the words of Daniel. Surely somewhere along the way a scribe saw the words **the first year of**

Darius the Mede and assumed that would be the first verse of the chapter since Daniel had consistently begun visions with such a chronological reference. The angel reported that he had warred with the princes of Persia and Greece since about 539 B.C. (about four or five years). We now understand that Daniel's good life under Darius was largely due to angelic support of that pagan ruler. That having been said, let us note that the **him** at the end of the verse does not require a grammatical connection in the Hebrew with an antecedent (Darius the Mede) and might refer back to Michael in 10:21.

Archer bridges the chapters for us:

> The occasion for the spiritual warfare was the restoration of the believing remnant of Israel to the Holy Land and their survival there as a commonwealth of the faithful, living in obedience to Holy Scripture. Knowing that such a development could lead to the ultimate appearance of the Son of God as the Messiah for God's redeemed, Satan and all his host were determined to thwart the renewal of Israel and the deliverance of her people from destruction (Archer, p. 127).

MAIN IDEA REVIEW: *God wants us to know that, in addition to the human forces of evil on the earth, demonic forces are constantly at work, sometimes through national leaders. But he also wants us to know that none of those forces, human or demonic, can defeat the forces of heaven.*

III. CONCLUSION

Calvin's Prayer

Born at Noyon, France, in 1509, John Calvin was a student and scholar from the beginning. In Geneva, Switzerland, he championed the cause of reformation and determined to set up in that city a disciplined community of people committed to the covenant of God. He was only twenty-seven when he wrote his famous *Institutes* in 1536. Many consider this work to be one of the most comprehensive statements of Reformed theology in print.

One of Calvin's projects was a two-volume commentary on Daniel in which he made much of the lessons of prayer and godliness to be learned in this book, an emphasis I've tried to follow. It was Calvin's practice as a pastor to conduct a regular Bible study for his congregants in Geneva, a meeting he would always close with prayer. After one of those sessions, perhaps even a study of Daniel 10, he offered the following words: "Grant, Almighty God, as Thou didst formerly appear to Daniel Thy holy servant, and to the other prophets, and by their doctrine did render Thy glory conspicuous to us at this day, that we may reverently approach and behold it. When we have become entirely devoted to Thee, may those mysteries which it has pleased Thee to offer by means of their hand and labours, receive from us their due estimation. May we be cast down in ourselves and raised by hope and faith toward heaven; when prostrate before Thy face, may we so conduct ourselves in the world, as in the interval to become free from all the depraved desires and passions of our flesh, and dwell mentally in heaven" (Calvin, 252).

We may never speak with an angel, but we can know the power of God as Daniel did throughout this chapter. Daniel's reaction to all this reminds us of our own frailty but also strongly confirms God's power to take care of his people as well as his prophet.

PRINCIPLES

- Older retired people, no longer active in regular employment, need be no less active in the business of God.
- Fear may be a good thing when it describes our attitude toward supernatural power in the world.
- Voluntary fasting can often prepare God's people for understanding his Word and his will.

APPLICATIONS

- Never forget that we have no right to command God; we tremble and acknowledge our weakness in his presence.
- When God does give us opportunity to speak to him in any form, we approach him courageously and with confidence (Heb. 11:6).
- The Lord knows our shortcomings and failures and is always ready to listen to our cries (Ps. 145:18–19).

IV. LIFE APPLICATION

Spiritual Warfare

Although some have taken the concept to outlandish extremes, spiritual warfare is very real. The Bible never deals with this at great length, but when we do get a glimpse, we sense the eternal battle that has been waged since just after Creation when Satan led the angelic host into rebellion. We need to establish the absolute futility of idols very carefully yet acknowledge the genuine vitality of the spirits who control them. Paul put it right on the line when he wrote to the Corinthians: "Do I mean then that a sacrifice offered to an idol is anything, or that an idol is anything? No, but the sacrifices of pagans are offered to demons, not to God, and I do not want you to be participants with demons. You cannot drink the cup of the Lord and the cup of demons too; you cannot have a part in both the Lord's table and the table of demons" (1 Cor. 10:19–21).

The people of Assyria, Babylonia, Persia, Greece, and Rome did not worship "gods," as we so often say, but actually demons. Any concept of God apart from the biblical account is not only idolatry but ultimately leads to demon worship whether overtly or covertly. The Old Testament never blames Satan or demons for the sin of humanity but always recognizes the power of Satan and his minions. Daniel offers a striking example of the Old Testament manner of handling such matters and winning the victory—trust God, his Word, and his work.

Lightner expresses some concern for the more modern way of approaching the issue of spiritual warfare:

> What the Old Testament teaches about spiritual warfare contrasts strikingly with what "deliverance ministries" advocate. Although this is certainly not intentional, the spiritual warfare movement today has come perilously close to assuming God's prerogative and relegating Him to watching people bind Satan and confront the power of evil. This is at least how their beliefs and practices appear. But this was never the case in the Old Testament. Satan is not God's equal; he is always subject to God, as are all the demons. This is a great comforting truth for the children of God (Lightner, p. 152).

V. PRAYER

Father, may the presence of the blessed Holy Spirit protect our thoughts, our words, and our deeds and keep us from attack by evil spirits in our world and from their influence in our society. Amen.

VI. DEEPER DISCOVERIES

A. Fasting

The Bible frequently mentions the practice of forgoing food and drink as a means of showing repentance and preparation for prayer. Jesus taught it to his disciples (Matt. 6:16–18; Mark 2:19–20), and the Bible illustrates it in many of the most godly people in its pages (Deut. 9:9,18; 2 Chr. 20:3; Ezra 8:21–23, 10:6; Neh. 1:4; Joel 1:14–16). Fasting is voluntary rather than mandatory, and it is used on special occasions rather than as a regular component of worship.

In commenting on the Matthew 6 passage, Stu Weber offers a suggestion for current practice:

> In fact, we can make a scriptural case that fasting is not a critical discipline for believers today. Moses commanded it only on the Day of Atonement (Lev. 16:29–31; 23:27–32). Most often in the Old Testament it is associated with self-humiliation before God, frequently in connection with confession of sins. . . . Fasting may be a healthy personal practice for Christians, but even the Old Testament warns against its abuse (Is. 58:3–7; Jer. 14:12) (Weber, pp. 83–84).

B. Demons

In Old Testament times people believed that every nation had its own special god. In Isaiah 37:38 the king of Nineveh referred to Nisroch as "his god," and we have already seen in Daniel 4:8 that Nebuchadnezzar chose Daniel's new name "after the name of my god." As we have already seen from the 1 Corinthians 10 passage, evil spirits (demons) represent the power behind gods of the world.

The Old Testament does not always use the term *demons*, but the activity of Satan's angels appears everywhere. Leviticus 17:7 talks about "goat idols," and in the song of Moses (Deut. 32) he describes Israel's rebellion and says, "They sacrificed to demons, which are not God" (32:17). These are spirit beings with personality, Satan's supernatural servants who, since he himself is not omnipresent, carry out his work in the world.

Lightner describes the origin of demons:

> The Bible does not tells us exactly when some of God's angels became Satan's angels. As mentioned earlier, the time of Satan's sin is not revealed either. That all the holy angels had a period of probation during which they were tested as to their obedience to God seems probable. We conclude that a host of holy angels sinned when Satan did and in the same way. Here are the reasons for this belief. First, we know that wicked angels exist and we know God did not create them wicked. They sinned at some point after God created them holy. Second, we know that some of Satan's angels are free to roam in the world and afflict God's people (Eph. 6:11–12). Others of them are confined and therefore restricted because they are bound in chains of darkness until the day of their judgment (2 Pet. 2:4). This fact seems to indicate that some of the angels who followed Satan in his rebellion committed an additional sin for which God bound them (Lightner, p. 89).

VII. TEACHING OUTLINE

A. INTRODUCTION

1. Lead Story: Playing with Paderewski
2. Context: The revelatory experiences of Daniel have grown in intensity and importance throughout the book. Furthermore, the final two chapters will provide even more sweeping information about the future of Daniel's people. Although most commentators focus on the prophecy of the seventy "sevens" in chapter 9, we will yet see a great deal more of God's plan in the two chapters ahead of us.
3. Transition: The blend of Daniel 11:1 with the end of the tenth chapter provides one of the great examples in the Bible of inappropriate

chapter divisions. As we have already noted, Daniel begins these sections with a chronological announcement about the current reigning monarch, so it is easy to see why 11:1 holds the place that it does. Nevertheless, the content is much more important than the structure in Bible study. We do well to remember that chapter divisions were added later by human scribes not necessarily under the control of the Holy Spirit.

B. COMMENTARY

1. The Secret Mourning (10:1–3)
2. The Shining Man (10:4–9)
3. The Special Messenger (10:10–14)
4. The Strengthening Message (10:15–11:1)

C. CONCLUSION: CALVIN'S PRAYER

VIII. ISSUES FOR DISCUSSION

1. What do you believe about the work of demons in the world today?
2. Who is the shining man of Daniel 10:4–6? What difference does his identity make in the interpretation of the chapter?
3. In what specific ways do God's angels differ from Satan's angels?
4. What is the appropriate biblical way of handling spiritual warfare in the church?

Daniel 11:1–45

Wars and Rumors of Wars

I. INTRODUCTION
You Can't Tell the Players Without a Program

II. COMMENTARY
A verse-by-verse explanation of the chapter.

III. CONCLUSION
The Ultimate World War
An overview of the principles and applications from the chapter.

IV. LIFE APPLICATION
"A Waiting World"
Melding the chapter to life.

V. PRAYER
Tying the chapter to life with God.

VI. DEEPER DISCOVERIES
Historical, geographical, and grammatical enrichment of the commentary.

VII. TEACHING OUTLINE
Suggested step-by-step group study of the chapter.

VIII. ISSUES FOR DISCUSSION
Zeroing the chapter in on daily life.

Quote

"History teaches us that when a barbarian race confronts a sleeping culture, the barbarians always win."

Arnold Toynbee

GEOGRAPHICAL PROFILE: AMMON

- The name of one of Lot's sons born of incest (Gen. 19:38)
- Nation located east of the Dead Sea
- Equated today with modern Jordan

GEOGRAPHICAL PROFILE: EDOM

- Nation descended from Edom, the son of Esau
- Located east of the Dead Sea and south of Ammon
- Always at animosity with Israel and rejoiced at the fall of Jerusalem to Babylon
- Disappears from history some time during the seventy years of captivity

GEOGRAPHICAL PROFILE: EGYPT

- One of the most ancient and advanced civilizations of the world
- Civilization goes back to before 3000 B.C.
- By Daniel's time Egypt had already been conquered by the Assyrians and subjected to the rule of Persia and later Greece
- The Romans made Egypt a province in 31 B.C.
- The Bible predicts future blessing for Egypt in Isaiah 19:24–25

GEOGRAPHICAL PROFILE: MOAB

- Son of Lot
- Neighbor of Ammon to the south
- Perpetual enemy of Israel

Daniel 11:1–45

IN A NUTSHELL

Daniel 11, like several other chapters in this book, shows us how history evolves into prophecy along God's linear line of sequential events in his world. Thirty-five verses tell us about ancient empires and their perpetual wars, and ten verses catapult us into the future to show how cruelty and destruction continue right up to the coming of Christ.

Wars and Rumors of Wars

I. INTRODUCTION

You Can't Tell the Players Without a Program

How many times have we heard some version of this line upon entering an athletic arena of some kind? Employees of the home team hawk programs with a description of the teams playing that day; a listing of players by name, number, and position; and a smattering of advertisements from local commercial firms. They do not sell it as a work of art, or a piece of memorabilia you will archive for your great grandchildren, or even a handy tool in case a rain squall should blow over the field during the game. Their argument is very simple: "You can't tell the players without a program."

No chapter in Daniel makes it more difficult to tell the players from one another than this one. Depending on how one views the flow of the text, it covers between 150 and 450 years of history and then—in the view of many Old Testament scholars—projects all that into the future on the strength of something we have already seen in Daniel: Antiochus Epiphanes as the prototypical Antichrist. Daniel achieves this without names but with a plethora of pronouns and such sufficient description that historians and Bible scholars find very little dispute in the first thirty-five verses.

Some will wonder why I chose to divide some earlier chapters into two studies yet take chapter 11 in one. I assure you the decision was made only after great wrestling with the text. Indeed, my original structure called for chapter 11 to be dealt with in three separate studies because of its length and complexity. Why then the present arrangement you now see before you?

I offer three reasons that figured into my decision to handle Daniel 11 this way.

1. Information in the first thirty-five verses is readily available in any Daniel commentary, Old Testament survey books, and even secular history books. Hundreds of titles cover the ground detailed in these verses.
2. Although the chapter offers extensive detail regarding the wars between the time of the prophecy and the reference to "the time of the end" in verse 35, only two titles appear with regularity through-

out the chapter—"the king of the North" and "the king of the South." In other words, this entire chapter centers in how the monarchs of Egypt will consistently conflict with the monarchs of Syria from the time of Daniel's vision to the death of Antiochus Epiphanes.

3. I've been a part of the Holman New Testament Commentary and Holman Old Testament Commentary series from the beginning, and I think I understand the mission well. We're appealing to readers who want serious handling of the text, but in a practical form which centers in exposition, interpretation, and application, not preoccupation with historical detail. Those who feel this current study insufficient in its historical detail may consult the excellent summary in Archer or any competent book of Middle East ancient history.

II. COMMENTARY

Wars and Rumors of Wars

MAIN IDEA: *Kings and nations rise and fall; the constant strain through it all is war, hatred, bloodshed, and conflict, whether in Daniel's time or in ours. And so it will be, says our reporting angel, to the end of time. In those final days before the coming of the Lord, some of the same nations that fought one another in ancient history will again capture headlines in the daily news as the spotlight shines again on the Beautiful Land.*

A Alexander and Friends (530–226 B.C.) (11:1–10)

SUPPORTING IDEA: *History is indeed his-story, the record of God's work in the world to achieve his purposes and protect his people.*

11:1. We dealt with this verse in the last chapter and explained why it appears at the end of chapter 10 in the NIV and why some scribe may have chosen to make it the first verse of chapter 11. Remember the angel is still speaking, not Daniel, and he refers to approximately 539–538 B.C., about four years prior to the vision that occupies chapters 10–12. The angel indicates that Darius's success in defeating Babylon came about through angelic assistance.

Archer speculates further that since Cyrus became God's tool in sending the Jews back to the Holy Land, angelic intervention plays a wider role than just the defeat of Babylon:

> The occasion for the spiritual warfare was the restoration of the believing remnant of Israel to the Holy Land and their survival there as a commonwealth of the faithful, living in obedience to Holy Scripture. Knowing that such a development could lead to the ultimate appearance of the Son of God as the Messiah for God's redeemed, Satan and all his hosts were determined to thwart the renewal of Israel and the deliverance of her people from destruction. The supreme effort to exterminate them all together was to take place some fifty-five years later, in the reign of Ahasuerus (Xerxes) when Haman secured his consent to obliterate the entire Jewish race. The conflict between Michael and the "prince of Persia" (10:30) may have had some bearing on this event, and it may have been Michael's victory over his satanic foes that paved the way for Queen Esther to thwart this genocide (Archer, p. 127).

11:2–4. The **three more kings** yet to appear in Persia refer to Cyrus (539–529 B.C.), Cambyses (529–522 B.C.), and Darius Hystaspes (521–486 B.C.), and a **fourth, who will be far richer than all the others**. The great Xerxes of Ezra and Esther fame (485–465 B.C.) in his wealth and power embarked on a campaign against Greece. The famous feast of Esther 1 describes the grandeur of preparation for that very campaign. He put everything he had into the effort but was unsuccessful in avenging the earlier victories of the Greeks over his father Darius Hystaspes.

The casual reader might think the **mighty king** of verse 3 stands in the Persian line, but in fact the mention of **Greece** at the end of verse 2 leads the angel to zoom ahead to Alexander the Great. The description of verses 3 and 4 fits exactly with what we have seen earlier in our study about this powerful and sometimes reckless monarch. After his early death Alexander's kingdom broke into four parts, but they did not fall **to his descendants**, nor did any retain the power of Alexander himself.

11:5–6. Enter the stars of this drama, **the king of the South** and **the king of the North**. Throughout this chapter these titles flow from one person to another; in verse 5 **the king of the South** is Ptolemy Soter (304–283 B.C.), the Alexander protégé who took control of Egypt. The man identified as **one of his commanders** was Seleucus Nicator (304–281 B.C.), a member of the quartet who ruled Syria and who very quickly becomes **the king of the North**.

The **daughter** mentioned in the passage is Berenice, the granddaughter of Soter and daughter of Philadelphus of the Ptolemy regime. The royal politicians planned for her to marry Antiochus Theos, a grandson of Nicator. In order to make this possible, Antiochus had to divorce his first wife, Laodice—an interesting name in view of the early chapters of Revelation. The idea came to naught since within two years of the marriage Ptolemy died and Antiochus remarried Laodice. In true Greek soap opera style, Laodice retaliated by murdering Antiochus, Berenice, and their infant son. Note the NIV marginal note on verse 6 indicating that "his power" might be translated "his offspring." The ancient Mediterranean world was not exactly Walton's Mountain.

11:7–10. Most likely the **one from her family line** refers to Berenice's brother Ptolemy Euergetus (246–221 B.C.), who attacked Seleucus Callinicus and carried home the spoils of war to Egypt.

But, **then the king of the North will invade the realm of the king of the South**, a retaliation attack by Callinicus in 240 B.C. that failed miserably. Verse 10 introduces a new wrinkle; the sons of Callinicus were Seleucus Ceraunus (227–223 B.C.) and Antiochus the Great (223–187 B.C.). Collectively they gathered enormous forces and charged south to wipe out the Egyptians. Ceraunus, however, was killed in Asia Minor before the invasion, so Antiochus the Great overran Phoenicia and Palestine until he came up against the Egyptians at the Battle of Raphia and was thrashed by Ptolemy IV in about 218 B.C. But I am getting ahead of the text.

B Antiochus the Great (226–175 B.C.) (11:11–20)

SUPPORTING IDEA: *These historical portions of Daniel are not given merely to review past events but to trace the working of God in his world in Daniel's time and to the end of time.*

11:11–13. Full of **rage**, Ptolemy Philopator (221–204 B.C.) had marched out to meet Antiochus the Great. As to the army being **carried off** (v. 12), Wood describes it this way: "The armies of both sides were immense and the battle fierce. This time Ptolemy won. The Hebrew text is not clear, but history shows that 'the multitude' that was given into the other's hand was the army of Syria under Antiochus. The text says that, as a result, Ptolemy would be made proud and this is in keeping with his character; he was a disliked, haughty profligate person" (Wood, *Daniel*, p. 139).

Ptolemy owed no allegiance to the Geneva Convention, of course, so he slaughtered most of the troops he captured.

For the next fourteen years Antiochus busied himself with nailing down all the nations in the eastern Mediterranean area and extending his borders as far as India and north as far as the Caspian Sea. Then in 203 B.C., Ptolemy Philopator and his queen died and Antiochus, sensing another opportunity, headed south **with a huge army fully equipped**.

11:14. We take a smaller bite here because interesting developments now accompany the perpetual battle between the Egyptians and Syrians. First, Antiochus made his move partly because the new Egyptian king was four years old (Ptolemy Epiphanes). And not only did he have "another army, larger than the first" (11:13), but also Daniel learned that the Syrians would be helped by **violent men among your own people**. Apostate Jews joined the Syrians in their attack against Egypt, but we should note that the early battles were fought not on Egyptian soil but also in northern Palestine. That makes it easier for us to understand how the Jews could be involved.

11:15–16. But what did the angel mean by telling Daniel this would happen "in fulfillment of the vision" (11:14)? We cannot be sure, but it is quite possible that this first involvement of Jews with Syrian forces lay the early groundwork for the rise of Antiochus Epiphanes.

The **fortified city** of verse 15 was likely Sidon on the Mediterranean Sea, so Egypt itself was not yet in danger. But the Syrians, having taken control of the east and the north, now moved south with great power and besieged **the Beautiful Land**.

11:17. Antiochus assessed that he might control Egypt politically without having to continue his march south so he made **an alliance with the king of the South**. He offered his daughter to ten-year-old Ptolemy V in hopes that she would control her husband and advance a pro-Syrian agenda in Egypt. Her name was Cleopatra (not to be confused with the more famous queen of that name). Presumably Antiochus anticipated an heir who would then become the legal king of both Egypt and Syria, perhaps uniting those nations under his ultimate control.

Archer tells us about the outcome of this brilliant scheme:

> As it turned out, however, after the marriage finally took place in 195, Cleopatra became completely sympathetic to her husband, Ptolemy V, and the Ptolemaic cause, much to the disappointment of her father, Antiochus. Therefore when she gave birth to a royal heir, who became Ptolemy VI, this gave no particular advantage or political leverage to her father. When Ptolemy V died in 181, Cleopatra was appointed queen regent by the Egyptian government, because they all loved and appreciated her loyalty to their cause. But she herself died not long after, and this meant the end of all possible Seleucid influence on Egyptian affairs. Yet by that time Antiochus himself, who died in 187 B.C., was gone (Archer, pp. 132–33).

11:18–19. But again we're getting ahead of the story. After the marriage was arranged, Antiochus turned **his attention to the coastlands**, meaning that he decided to emulate Alexander the Great by conquering and controlling Greece. But he did not count on the Greeks appealing to Rome for help. In time Antiochus found himself battling Greeks, Romans, and Macedonians. At Thermopylai the confederacy smashed a Syrian command post, and Antiochus went back to Asia Minor. As he retreated east the Romans followed him and with a force of thirty thousand defeated Antiochus's seventy thousand somewhere west of Sardis.

The almost anonymous **commander** of verse 18 was hardly unknown in secular history—Lucius Cornelius Sipio Asiaticus, the brother of the general who had defeated Hannibal in 202 B.C. In the treaty of Apamea (188 B.C.), Antiochus lost all claims to Europe, most of Asia Minor, and agreed to stay east of the Taurus range. To guarantee his compliance, twenty hostages were taken to Rome. These included the king's second son, who will become Antiochus Epiphanes and thereby connect us to the next section of this chapter.

11:20. The **successor** of this verse is Seleucus Philopator (187–176), who faced enormous national debt after all the wars his father had conducted. He also owed the Romans some twenty thousand talents, so he planned to plunder Israel **to maintain the royal splendor**. His **tax collector**, Heliodorus, intended to invade the temple of Yahweh but was stopped by a vision of angels assaulting him. Instead of finishing his mission, he returned home to assassinate Seleucus Philopator.

C Antiochus Epiphanes (175–164 B.C.) (11:21–35)

SUPPORTING IDEA: *When God accomplishes his purposes in the world, he sometimes chooses to do so with the most unlikely and contemptible people.*

11:21. Now we're getting down to business. The rightful heir to the throne of Seleucus IV was his young son Demetrius I. But he was still a hostage to Rome, so Uncle Antiochus took over and through political **intrigue** gained control as king of the north.

11:22–24. In 181 Ptolemy VII (Philometor) had taken the throne at the age of six under control of his mother Cleopatra, who still ran the kingdom. Some time later he moved into Palestine with a huge army and was defeated by Antiochus Epiphanes who **destroyed**, in the process, **a prince of the covenant**. Most commentators believe this refers to the Jewish high priest Onias III who was actually killed by one of his own priests (Menelaus) to gain favor with the new Syrian king. Antiochus employed a Robin Hood policy by attacking and plundering wealthy provinces and distributing the **plunder, loot and wealth** to his own forces and also to poorer subjects, thereby strengthening his control over the empire.

11:25–28. These verses describe the final major conflict of Antiochus Epiphanes against the Egyptians that took place just east of the Nile River delta. Clearly the little horn had marched the full length of Palestine right to the border of Egypt. Ptolemy was betrayed by his own people, and Daniel predicted the phony truce: **the two kings, with their hearts bent on evil, will sit at the same table and lie to each other**. When was war any different from this? After this Antiochus headed back to Syria but on his way squashed a minor rebellion in Jerusalem, plundering the temple in the process. Verse 28 offers the first indication in this chapter of Antiochus's hostilities against the Jews.

11:29–30. In 168 B.C. Antiochus again headed south to face a new coalition government in Egypt. But as the Scripture indicates, this time **the outcome will be different** because the Romans again involved themselves, this time on the side of the Egyptians. As Antiochus approached the city of Alexandria intending to level it, he was handed a letter from the Roman senate telling him to cease and desist. So once again on his way home from Egypt, he plowed through Palestine and began negotiations with apostate Jews. Campbell tells about the moment of truth in the outskirts of Alexandria: "When the Syrian king hesitated, the Roman council drew a circle around Antiochus in the sand and told him he must make a decision before stepping out of the circle. Humiliated, frustrated, and enraged, Antiochus turned back toward Syria, having traveled the long distance to Egypt for nothing" (Campbell, p. 168).

11:31–32. Daniel learned that Antiochus would not be satisfied merely with political power and plunder but would **set up the abomination that causes desolation**. Both Daniel and we have already learned this in 8:23–25, and we know it took place in December 168 B.C. Most Old Testament experts believe the abomination itself was a statue of Jupiter or perhaps Zeus. Second Maccabees 6:2 suggests that the temple was actually renamed the temple of Zeus Olympus. It may be worth mentioning again as we did in connection with chapter 8 that our Lord's only reference to Daniel and his prophecies uses this phrase **abomination that causes desolation** (Matt. 24:15; Mark 13:14).

We cannot leave this section without recognizing the phrase **the people who know their God will firmly resist him**. We have already studied the Maccabees. This phrase doubtless refers to them and their faithful followers. They became the centerpiece of the resistance, not only against Antiochus and his successors, but also against pro-Syrian Jewish apostates. From this group later arose the Pharisees and the Essenes. The former we encounter frequently in the New Testament, and the latter became the people of Qumran who gave us the famous Dead Seas Scrolls.

11:33–35. These spiritual leaders **will instruct many**, and their resistance will be accompanied by the martyrdom of many who **will fall by the sword or be burned or captured or plundered** (see Heb. 11:36–38). The **little help** may refer to some early victories of the Maccabees under Mattathias and his son Judas Maccabeus that led to the rededication of the altar in 165 B.C.

Verse 35 forms a bridge over which some commentators cross into the continuing history of Antiochus Epiphanes while others find Antichrist on the other side. Walvoord writes:

> The purging process is indicated in verse 35 to continue "to the time of the end." It is clear from this reference that the persecutions of Antiochus are not the time of the end, even though they foreshadow them. The mention of "the time of the end" in verse 35 is notice, however, that from verse 36 on, the prophecy leaps the centuries that intervene to the last generation prior to God's judgment to Gentile power and its rulers. Beginning in verse 36, prophecy is unfolded that is yet unfulfilled (Walvoord, *Daniel,* p. 269).

Baldwin takes the opposite position, seeing the remainder of the chapter as an application only to Antiochus Epiphanes. As to the **time of the end**, she says simply, "To the writer of Daniel, as he records the words of the heavenly messenger, the persecution has its purpose in God's plan to refine and He will bring it to an end at the time He has appointed" (Baldwin, p. 197).

D Antichrist (Future) (11:36–45)

SUPPORTING IDEA: *An amazing summary of history, which describes 135 prophecies already fulfilled, now unveils the gateway to the future and the ultimate fulfillment of the little horn in Antichrist.*

11:36. Every premillennial theologian agrees that somewhere between 11:5 and 12:1 of Daniel history changes to prophecy. Exactly where might that point be? Payne finds it in verse 40 saying, "After a historical survey in 11:2–39, extending from 527 to 165 B.C. in its fulfillment, Daniel's 4th great vision shifts at v. 40 to 'the time of the end,' signifying, 'the end of the present age or world'" (Payne, pp. 390–91). Others have selected a switchover as early as 11:4 (Tregelles), and Keil finds the transition at verse 21.

In this study I take the position that the break occurs right here, between verses 35 and 36, although we will attempt to represent the amillennial viewpoint fairly. Readers dissatisfied with the premillennial interpretation of this chapter should look at the InterVarsity Press publication *The Meaning of the Millennium* for a variety of positions on end-time events. The premillennial interpretation is hardly some recent position rising out of prophecy mania developed in twentieth-century fundamentalism.

Jerome said of Daniel 11:36, "The Jews believed that this passage has reference to the Antichrist alleging that after the small help of Julian a king is going to rise up who shall do according to his will and shall lift himself up against all that is called god, and shall speak arrogant words against the God of gods" (Jerome, 136). Jerome does not here indicate his agreement with that position, although the wider treatment of his work indicates that he probably did.

Of significance here is the parallelism between Daniel 11:36–45 and descriptions of Antichrist in 2 Thessalonians and Revelation 13 and 17. Most translations insert a paragraph break between 11:35 and 11:36, although that in itself would hardly be an argument for a switch from history to eschatology (see "Deeper Discoveries").

A more convincing argument appears at the beginning of chapter 12 in the words "at that time." The events of chapter 12 will occur at the same time as the events described in the latter part of chapter 11.

Gleason Archer, whom I have quoted liberally throughout this study, can hardly be accused of eschatological excess in his brilliant and careful handling of the Old Testament text. He begins his commentary on this section by saying:

> With the conclusion of the preceding pericope at v. 35, the predictive material that incontestably applies to the Hellenistic Empires and the contest between the Seleucids and the Jewish patriots ends. This present section (vv. 36–39) contains some features that hardly apply to Antiochus IV, though most of the details could apply to him as well as to his latter-day antitype, "the beast." Both liberal and conservative scholars agree that all of chapter 11 up to this point contains strikingly accurate predictions of the whole sweep of events from the reign of Cyrus (during which Daniel bought his career to a close) to the unsuccessful effort of Antiochus Epiphanes to stamp out the Jewish faith. But the two schools of thought radically differ in the explanation for this phenomenon. Evangelicals find this pattern of prediction and fulfillment compelling evidence of the divine inspiration and authority of the Hebrew Scriptures, since only God could possibly foreknow the future and see to it that his announced plan would be precisely fulfilled (Archer, p. 143).

No one should link amillennial scholars with liberal theology, for the above paragraph makes two different points: that 11:36–45 contains elements which apply to Antichrist as well as Antiochus Epiphanes, and that the record of 11:1–35 was written in the sixth century and therefore evidences the miraculous gift of predictive prophecy rather than a recitation of history written by some anonymous second-century author.

11:37. Some take the text of Daniel 11:37 to indicate that the Antichrist will be a Jew since **he will show no regard for the gods of his fathers**, but in fact we learn that he will not **regard any god**. He breaks any kind of alliance with all previous religious tradition in order to set up his own. Daniel uses *Elohim* here and in the context of either Antiochus Epiphanes or Antichrist, there seems to be no reason to place any ethnic boundary on the passage.

Even more confusing is the statement **he will show no regard . . . for the one desired by women**. Here we find no agreement among commentators. Some explain it as a reference to the goddess Nanania, others Adonis, both deities from the era of Syrian control in the early centuries B.C. Young and Kyle think it refers to homosexuality, suggesting that this king is abnormal in his disinterest in women. Still others see a more direct reference to Jewish women delighting in the thought of becoming the mother of Messiah. Archer suggests, "Perhaps it simply points to the cruelty Antiochus showed toward all women he was sexually involved with" (Archer, p. 144).

11:38–39. This willful king will make war his god—**he will honor a god of fortresses**. At this point the text seems to slip away a bit from Antiochus Epiphanes who, though certainly successful at war, hardly serves as a supreme model of a warrior. One could argue that he lost more battles than he won, beating up on the little people of his world while being forced to retreat by the big boys on the block like Egypt and Rome.

As Walvoord points out:

> Examining all other passages relating to the end time, it becomes evident that the sole confidence of a final world ruler is in military power, personified as "the god of war," or "god of fortresses." In other words, he is a complete materialist in contrast to all previous religions and all previous men who claim divine qualities. This is blasphemy to the ultimate, the exaltation of human power and attainment. He is Satan's masterpiece, a human being who is Satan's substitute for Jesus Christ, hence properly identified as the Antichrist (Walvoord, *Daniel*, p. 276).

Hold on, says Baldwin, let's not jump too fast into that eschatological mode:

> The very introduction of the term Anti-Christ to a text given before the Christ had even come raises the question of *a priori* reasoning. It raises acutely the matter of exegetical method, and it is preferable to avoid a term which occurs first in the epistles of John (1 Jn. 2:18,22f.; 4:3; 2 Jn. 7). Nevertheless there are reasons for thinking that, although the chapter finds its first fulfillment in the character and reign of Antiochus IV, the matter does not stop there (Baldwin, p. 199).

Baldwin doesn't move much further than that, and she ultimately concludes that Antiochus is clearly a prototype for some future demonstration of human pride and atheism and that "escalation of opposition will culminate in a final onslaught in which evil will appear to triumph, and only the intervention of God will prove the contrary. This will be the occasion of final judgment and the setting up of God's kingdom" (Baldwin, p. 201).

The ultimate politicians, both Antiochus and Antichrist know how to manipulate people by rewards (**make them rulers**) and political payoffs (**distribute the land at a price**).

11:40. Staying with the titles of his two characters, the angel described **the king of the South** and **the king of the North** in final conflict. This will take place somewhere in the Middle East and will employ virtually every type of warfare the angel could have described at the time Daniel wrote these words. Precisely at this point too many well-meaning evangelical scholars have gone awry trying to identify these two kings in light of nations prominent and powerful at the time. Egypt and Russia seem likely choices, and proponents introduce Ezekiel 38–39 to bolster that viewpoint. But the flow of Daniel 11:36–39 seems to occur considerably later than Ezekiel 38–39. The **king of the North** could be the same entity, but we should not treat those passages as one event.

Furthermore, the grammar of the verse does not allow us to choose which of the kings **will invade many countries and sweep through them like a flood**. The **he** at the beginning of that phrase has no definable antecedent. Probably the best choice applies **he** to neither the king of the north nor the south, but the great world ruler of verses 36–39. Antiochus Epiphanes cannot be the world ruler of this passage since he was clearly the king of the north in the early part of this chapter. If the angel intends to stay with his imagery from the beginning, the Antichrist may find himself battling Egypt and Syria. But one arriving at such a conclusion with any amount of dogmatism does so only to his or her peril.

11:41. Not all countries will fall before the power of the supreme ruler of the world. He invades Israel and **many countries will fall**, but for some reason, **Edom, Moab and the leaders of Ammon will be delivered from his hand**. An interesting comparison with Isaiah 11 shows some of the same countries controlled by a restored Israel. It's useless to speculate on why Edom, Moab, and Ammon are spared; the angel predicted it because that is precisely what will happen in God's plan.

11:42–43. But North Africa is not as fortunate. If we identify **Egypt** as the "king of the South," the Antichrist then moves through that country, taking control of it and marching on west through Libya and Ethiopia. Premillennial scholars hold the literal fulfillment of all this. Surely this is one of the challenges facing those who believe in a real Antichrist but not a literal and physical future of Israel. They are forced to find mystical symbolism in the names of specific nations very much alive in the twenty-first century.

11:44–45. In North Africa Antichrist receives word from the Middle East that causes him to rush back **in a great rage**. Many believe this describes his advance to the battle of Armageddon since **he will pitch his royal tents between the seas at the beautiful holy mountain**. Premillennial scholars agree that **the seas** are the Dead Sea and the Mediterranean Sea, and the **mountain** is Marah where the temple once stood. Once again, the phraseology evokes a connection with Revelation, this time 16:16: "Then they gathered the kings together to the place that in Hebrew is called Armageddon."

Megiddo, mentioned twelve times in the Old Testament (Josh. 12:21; 17:11; Judg. 1:27; 5:19; 1 Kgs. 4:12; 9:15; 2 Kgs. 9:27; 23:29–30; 1 Chr. 7:29; 2 Chr. 35:22; Zech. 12:11), lies on a major highway connecting Egypt with Syria. No one can say with certainty that Daniel 11:45 and Revelation 16:16 indicate the exact geographical site of the final battle between good and evil, but no interpretation makes any better sense. Daniel's angel seems to say that the great world leader finds his final defeat right there: **Yet he will come to his end, and no one will help him**.

But let us not get so awash with eschatological detail that we forget the message of the Book of Daniel—*God is in control.* As McClain puts it, "In all these events, for those who have eyes to see, the great rebel is acting only under the permission of the heavenly court" (McClain, p. 184).

MAIN IDEA REVIEW: *Kings and nations rise and fall; the constant strain through it all is war, hatred, bloodshed, and conflict, whether in Daniel's time or in ours. And so it will be, says our reporting angel, to the end of time. In those final days before the coming of the Lord, some of the same nations that fought one another in ancient history will again capture headlines in the daily news as the spotlight shines again on the Beautiful Land.*

III. CONCLUSION

The Ultimate World War

The United States likes to think of itself as a peaceful nation, one that has now taken on the role of "peacekeeping" in the more warlike nations of the world. As I write these words, blue-helmeted UN peacekeeping forces patrol the streets, deserts, and jungles of numerous countries, and a significant portion of the money and manpower comes from the United States. Yet we ourselves have been something of a warlike people. In two and a quarter centuries we have lost thirteen million lives in declared war and spent a half trillion dollars supporting the efforts of war. This has been the pattern of sinful humankind, a condition which will persist and inflame toward the end of time. The Gospels record the Lord's words of warning: "You will hear of wars and rumors of wars, but see to it that you are not alarmed. Such things must happen, but the end is still to come. Nation will rise against nation, and kingdom against kingdom. There will be famines and earthquakes in various places. All these are the beginning of birth pains" (Matt. 24:6–8). Matthew's record is echoed in Mark 13:5–8 and Luke 21:8–11.

Every time Christians read a headline about another war, they should remember the lawless one, who "will honor a god of fortresses" (11:38). Despite all the talk of peace, war prevails within, between, and among the nations of the world. A huge financial commitment of any modern country is dedicated to supporting military efforts, both defensive and offensive.

Christians divide over whether they will actually see Antichrist in power and experience the suffering of the time, but one thing is clear from the end of this chapter: "He will come to his end, and no one will help him" (11:45).

PRINCIPLES

- Since Christians struggle against demonic forces of darkness, we must understand why our weapons are not of our own making.
- As we read about the constant struggles of nations, it reminds us to pray for our own national leaders and for peace.
- The secular godlessness of our own age gives us some hint of the climate that could give birth to the ultimate lawless one.

APPLICATIONS

- During the struggles against Antiochus Epiphanes, only "the people who know their god" were able to resist his terror.
- The idea "might makes right," wherever and however it is applied, fits right into the spirit of Antichrist.
- Whatever the particulars, it seems clear from Old Testament prophecy that Israel will be a spotlight location for end-time events.

IV. LIFE APPLICATION

"A Waiting World"

Exactly twenty-four hours before I began writing this chapter, I sang in a Christmas cantata composed and directed by our church music director, James Stewart. James is a brilliant young man who has an excellent future in Christian music. Not all the songs in our cantata were original, but the setting played on the idea of both advents of Christ, emphasizing how desperately the world needed his coming at the time of the Incarnation and how desperately we need it today.

As we read passages like Daniel 11, we understand how our society is mired in hate, anger, cruelty, bitterness, and war, all behaviors antithetical to the nature of Christ. Like ancient Israel, contemporary Christians live as remnant believers in an alien society that would do them in if it could but, restrained by the power of heaven, settles for constant scorn instead. Paul told the Thessalonian believers that Jesus would come back again and that ignorance or grieving was not the proper posture of expectation. Instead, hope and encouragement should characterize Christians in this waiting world.

A restless world in darkness waiting for a light,
Centuries of silence like a cold and frozen night,
A worn and angry people held beneath oppression's hand,
A praying generation for a healing in their land.

Every tribe and nation has been looking for a sign,
Waiting for a promise of long, long ago time;
Staring into starlight asking, "When will He come?"
Deliverer, Messiah, God's one and only Son.

No one had predicted this coming of a king,
Expecting a hero, not a tiny little thing,
Waiting for a Savior with a sword held in His hand,
Not seeing God Himself in the form of a man.

Two thousand years of waiting, we now stare toward the sky,
For Jesus Christ has promised to return for His bride;
And we hold within us this bright and burning flame,
A waiting world, ready for the Son.

Come and bring the dawn.
And end the night of a thousand lifetimes.
A waiting world, ready to be reborn, crying to be shown
What their hearts have been hoping for—a waiting world.

V. PRAYER

Father, deliver your people from the evil all around us and keep us steadfast and secure through whatever darkness lies ahead until Jesus comes again. Amen.

VI. DEEPER DISCOVERIES

A. Why This Chapter?

Casual Bible readers stumbling upon Daniel 11 might wonder why the Holy Spirit directed the prophet to such historical detail in the first thirty-five verses. Verses 36–45 seem to fit well with what we have read earlier, and when applied to both Antiochus Epiphanes and the Antichrist, certainly blend with the overall message of Daniel. But do we really need to know everything that happened between the sixth and second centuries B.C.? If so, why not spell out the names rather than using figurative language?

I have asked that question myself frequently down through the years, and never more intently than when preparing this commentary. Although I offer no brilliant revelatory solutions, let me suggest a few things to keep in mind.

- Prophecy is grounded in history. That axiom plays out in virtually every prophetic book, particularly in the Old Testament. Isaiah, Jeremiah, Ezekiel, and Daniel all lay out details of how God will handle Israel in the years following the prophecies.
- We tend to lack a sense of history in our country, always looking forward rather than behind. Fifty-one years after World War II, we finally broke ground for a monument to the multiple thousands of men and women who died in those battles. Many Americans seem far more interested in what the stock market will do next week than in the history of their own country. Someone once said that those who ignore history are doomed to repeat its mistakes, and Daniel 11 certainly bears that out. This is no fortune-cookie prediction; it clearly links end-time events with those grounded in the history of Daniel's time and the centuries immediately following.
- One of the major issues in interpretation is the recognition of what Bible scholars often called *authorial intent*. We ask ourselves, what did the author intend when he wrote these words? Even though Daniel received the visions, we would know nothing unless he had written them down and passed them on. Nothing in the angel's words requires a written record of what Daniel

heard and saw. But the Holy Spirit directed the prophets to record the message accurately so that we may profit from it. Daniel surely stayed focused throughout the entire book on what was happening in Israel, although it lay in tattered ruin during most of his adult life. Certainly he had a vast interest in who would follow Cyrus, the benefactor of Daniel's people, and how all this would end.

B. Eschatology

It is nearly impossible to deal with the Book of Daniel without using this five-syllable word so common to theologians and yet so mysterious to many others. It describes a branch of theology that deals with the last things. The term is transliterated from the Greek work *eschatos,* which means "last" or "last thing." The second part of the word comes from the Greek word *logos,* the term for "word," so eschatology is the word about the last things.

In a study of systematic theology, eschatology refers to events just preceding the second advent of Christ, the intermediate state between human death and resurrection, resurrection, judgment, heaven, hell, and all matters regarding the future of the human race.

Eschatology is not as popular today as it was sixty years ago when prophecy conferences dotted North America and people were quick to name antichrists right and left, with Hitler, Mussolini, and Stalin making everybody's top ten list. Many evangelical Bible teachers learned the hard way to avoid dogmatism about Bible prophecy as they found themselves burying antichrists from one decade to the next.

Lightner entitles his chapter on eschatology "God's Plan for the Future" and concludes it with some practical observations:

> Belief that Christ could come at any moment brings an added dimension to Christian living. If you really believe the Savior could return to take His own to be with Him today, or before you finish reading this chapter, life should take on a vital new urgency for you. I submit that if what we believe does not affect our behavior, we are either believing the wrong thing or behaving in the wrong way, or both. How should we then live in view of the biblical message about the future? We should live according to Scripture, live as those who would appear before the Lord in a matter of minutes or hours. As we

so live, we should view every opportunity as though it might be the last one we will ever have. The Bible does not teach God's believers to fold their hands and wait idly for Christ to return. Rather, it emphasizes the need to be actively serving while we wait for God's Son from heaven (Lightner, *Evangelical Theology,* p. 279).

Dr. John Walvoord, the longtime president of Dallas Seminary, was my friend and colleague for fifteen years during the latter part of my own career. For fifty years he was considered one of America's prominent eschatologists, and in his commentary on Daniel, he offers a paragraph good enough for Archer to reproduce:

> The entire section from Daniel 11:36 to 12:3 constitutes a revelation of the major factors of the times of the end which may be summarized as follows: (1) a world ruler, (2) a world religion, (3) a world war, (4) a time of great tribulation for Israel, (5) deliverance for the people of God at the end of the tribulation, (6) resurrection and judgment, and (7) reward of the righteous. All of these factors are introduced in this section. Added elsewhere in the Scriptures are the additional facts that this time of the end begins with the breaking of the covenant by "the prince that shall come" (Dan 9:26–27); that "the time of the end" will last for three and one-half years (Dan 7:25; 12:7; Rev 13:5); and that the time of the end is the same as the time of Jacob's trouble and the Great Tribulation (Jer 30:7; Mt 24:21). Many additional details are supplied in Revelation 6–19 (Archer, *Daniel,* pp. 281–82).

VII. TEACHING OUTLINE

A. INTRODUCTION

1. Lead Story: You Can't Tell the Players Without a Program
2. Context: Although it flows immediately from Daniel 10, chapter 11 is linked closely in content with chapter 8. Both of these chapters show us the historical narrative in general terms until it reaches Antiochus Epiphanes, who then becomes the primary figure of the chapter and leads to an analysis of Antichrist.

3. Transition: The subject matter does not change between Daniel 11 and 12. The angelic message continues without break right up to 12:4. It actually extends from 10:20–12:4. As we have observed earlier, the last three chapters of Daniel must be read as a unit.

B. COMMENTARY

1. Alexander and Friends (530–226 B.C.) (11:1–10)
2. Antiochus the Great (226–175 B.C.) (11:11–20)
3. Antiochus Epiphanes (175–164 B.C.) (11:21–35)
4. Antichrist (Future) (11:36–45)

C. CONCLUSION: THE ULTIMATE WORLD WAR

VIII. ISSUES FOR DISCUSSION

1. Read Daniel 11 in a modern language translation like *The Living Bible* or *The Message*.
2. How does your understanding of this chapter differ from the interpretation put forth in this study?
3. Identify at least three spiritual lessons for practical everyday living which you have derived from Daniel 11.

Daniel 12:1–13

Back to the Future

I. INTRODUCTION
Questions About Qumran

II. COMMENTARY
A verse-by-verse explanation of the chapter.

III. CONCLUSION
Prophecy and Miracles
An overview of the principles and applications from the chapter.

IV. LIFE APPLICATION
The Center of the Bible
Melding the chapter to life.

V. PRAYER
Tying the chapter to life with God.

VI. DEEPER DISCOVERIES
Historical, geographical, and grammatical enrichment of the commentary.

VII. TEACHING OUTLINE
Suggested step-by-step group study of the chapter.

VIII. ISSUES FOR DISCUSSION
Zeroing the chapter in on daily life.

Quote

"Every tomorrow has two handles; we can take hold by the handle of anxiety or by the handle of faith."

Southern Baptist Brotherhood Journal

Daniel 12:1–13

IN A NUTSHELL

As the old spiritual says, "There's a great day coming by and by." Although Matthew 24, 1 Thessalonians 4, and the Book of Revelation fill in more detail, from Daniel 12 we understand clearly that God will wrap up human history in some future day.

Back to the Future

I. INTRODUCTION

Questions About Qumran

The year 2001 will see the final publication of the complete translation of the Dead Seas Scrolls, headed by Dr. Eugene Ulrich of Notre Dame, chief editor of the material. The scrolls were written between 200 B.C. and A.D. 70, and they have added a great deal to our understanding of the Old Testament. The texts were retained by the Essene community arising from Matathias and the Maccabean family. We do not know their theological persuasion, so conservative scholars will not abandon the Masoretic text in favor of the multiple-option *Dead Sea Scrolls Bible* that will culminate Ulrich's work.

The scrolls were found in 1947 by a shepherd called Muhammed el-Hamed, nicknamed edh-Dhib, which means "the wolf." He was tending goats in the desert near the northwest corner of the Dead Sea when one of the animals disappeared from the herd. Edh-Dhib climbed the mountain to search for it and came upon a cave. Hoping to frighten the animal out of the cave, he threw in a rock and was surprised to hear it breaking a piece of pottery. When he returned with his friends they discovered several pottery jars containing ancient scrolls with 230 texts of Old Testament books. These texts are considered one of the greatest archeological finds of the twentieth century.

One major mark of Essenian theology centered in the eager anticipation of the Messiah's coming. Jewish people all over the Mediterranean world knew he would be born in Bethlehem from David's line and that he would bring peace to the world. As we come to Daniel 12, we see again the hope and expectation of the Messiah's coming. But this time he will appear at the second advent to provide resurrection and justice for a world that has suffered in sin and death for so long.

II. COMMENTARY

Back to the Future

MAIN IDEA: *After the dreary sadness of warfare in chapter 11, the angel tells the prophet, those who are wise will shine like the brightness of the heavens, and those who lead many to righteousness, like the stars for ever and ever.*

A Resurrection of the Righteous (12:1–4)

SUPPORTING IDEA: *The climax of the world comes about not only with cruel warfare and intense suffering, but also in resurrection to an eternal state.*

12:1. We have already met **Michael, the great prince** in 10:13,21; now we have solid confirmation of the suggestion made earlier that Michael serves as the guardian angel of Israel. Although he is not always named, we see angelic involvement in Israel's behalf in Joshua 5:13–15; 2 Kings 6:15–17; Isaiah 37:35–36; and in the final conflict of Revelation 12 where Michael is clearly identified: "And there was war in heaven. Michael and his angels fought against the dragon, and the dragon and his angels fought back. But he was not strong enough, and they lost their place in heaven. The great dragon was hurled down—that ancient serpent called the devil, or Satan, who leads the whole world astray. He was hurled to the earth, and his angels with him" (Rev. 12:7–9).

Daniel learned that the future held **a time of distress such as has not happened from the beginning of nations until then**. We have noted repeatedly how the rejection of prophecy in this book leads some scholars to conclude a fulfillment of this persecution during the time of Antiochus Epiphanes. Jeremiah also describes this period of time we have come to call the *tribulation* (Jer. 30:4–6). The prophecy primarily aims at Israel; no other inference is possible from the way Daniel words this verse.

Revelation 16 describes these "seven bowls of God's wrath on the earth." The wording of Daniel 12:1 sounds much like Matthew 24:21. Archer concludes, "Quite evidently Jesus took this prophecy in Daniel as relating to the Last Days and particularly to the Great Tribulation with which our present church age is destined to close" (Archer, p. 149). The protection of Israel during the great tribulation (considered by most premillennial scholars to be the second half of Daniel's seventieth week) has been assigned to Michael, and all genuine believers will persevere through this time of great suffering.

Among Daniel's people there will be those whose names are **found written in the book**, and they **will be delivered**. This is likely the book of life that the Bible first mentions in Exodus 32:33 and various times right up to the end of the Bible in Revelation 20:12. We will discuss this further in "Deeper Discoveries." Notice that apostates and unbelievers are excluded from this deliverance; only those whose names are written in the book will greet the Messiah when he returns.

12:2–3. At the time of this deliverance, there will be a great resurrection of **multitudes who sleep in the dust of the earth**. The participants are headed toward **everlasting life** or **everlasting contempt**. If we had any doubt about this passage being yet future, it should be put to rest here. Certainly nothing like this occurred during the time of Antiochus. Resurrection represents a great ancient hope among the Jews (Isa. 26:19). Yet even among conservative premillennarians we find confusion. In their zeal to protect a pretribulation rapture, good and godly men like Gaebelein, Kelly, and Ironside argue that this verse describes some spiritual form of resurrection. But this seems unnecessary and, indeed, a mishandling of the text.

Walvoord attacks the issue head on:

> The thing so utterly unacceptable about this is that Gaebelein adopts the very "spiritualizing" or "symbolizing" principle of interpretation which our opponents adopt—and that in the midst of a passage where everything else is esteemed . . . to be literal, not figurative. He does with this passage precisely what the Postmillennialist and Amillennialist do with the reference to a first resurrection in Revelation 20. Thus he throws away the hermeneutical advantage of premillennialism (Walvoord, p. 172).

When will this event occur? Clearly at the end of the tribulation when Jews delivered from that curse are united with Old Testament saints raised from the dead (Rom. 11:26). We will deal with the rapture in "Deeper Discoveries," but here we should say that no scriptural passage actually teaches that Old Testament saints will be raised at the same time believers in Christ are taken to heaven before the tribulation. Note carefully that this is not the final resurrection of the dead described in Revelation 20:4–6.

Walvoord reminds us that

> Old Testament prophecy includes events separated by a considerable span of time as if they concurred in immediate relation to each other. The passing over of the entire present age—the period between the first and second advents of Christ—in such passages as Isaiah 61:1–2 is familiar to all expositors of the Old Testament. Here is another illustration. The righteous will be raised according to this interpretation as a reward for their faith and faithfulness, but the wicked who die are warned concerning their final judgment. The setting off of the many who await into two classes by inference assumes that there will be two resurrections with different destinies. Although this passage does not teach premillennialism expressly, it is not out of harmony with the premillennial interpretation (Walvoord, *Daniel,* p. 289).

Having assumed the dual resurrection, the angel next focused only on the righteous, those who were wise enough to hold on to the truth in the most difficult of surroundings. Now they **shine like the brightness of the heavens**. Criswell reminds us of the great light of this verse: "The beauty, the poetic flow of those words is magnificent. The reason that I notice it so much is because of the context where the verse is found. It is found in one of the darkest visions in the Bible. Shining in that darkness is this glorious, diamond-like beautiful promise. Is that not an unusual thing? But the Scriptures always present the promises against the darkest backgrounds" (Criswell, p. 178).

12:4. The Old Testament talks a lot about sealing books, emphasizing their authority and authenticity as well as the preservation of their integrity. We have the Book of Daniel in our hands today because God has preserved it until the end times in which we live.

Some interpreters have pushed this verse to outlandish extremes by referring the last phrase (**many will go here and there to increase knowledge**) to modern travel and the advances of scientific learning. Nothing justifies such handling of the text. Yes, we do live in an era of knowledge explosion, but one would be hard-pressed to argue that the message of Daniel is any less relevant in the twenty-first century than it was twenty-five hundred years ago when Daniel wrote it. Certainly in the light of history and the New Testament (particularly Revelation) we know more about Daniel's prophecies than he did and therefore bear greater responsibility to understand them. Furthermore, it seems highly likely that those who will actually live through the events described in this book will grasp their meaning even better than we can now.

Campbell says: "This cryptic expression [many will go here and there] is best understood to mean that people in the Tribulation will run about seeking answers to questions about the climatic events of their times and that they will find those answers through increased knowledge of the Book of Daniel" (Campbell, p. 182).

B Revelation of the Schedule (12:5–8)

SUPPORTING IDEA: *Although the details are fuzzy at times, God clearly wants Bible readers to understand that he has a definitive timetable for the manner in which he will wrap up the world.*

12:5–6. Remember Daniel is still describing what happened on the banks of the Tigris (10:4), still speaking with angels. One of them voiced a question already well entrenched in Daniel's mind: **How long will it be before these astonishing things are fulfilled?**

The **man clothed in linen** is surely the same being of 10:5–6 who has moved from the bank to a position **above the waters of the river**. This business of standing on water has led some to emphasize that this linen-clad figure must be the preincarnate Christ. But standing over water seems a simple trick for an angel, so interpretation here probably comes down to whatever readers concluded in chapter 10.

12:7. The ancient Hebrews held up a hand to signify an oath as a gesture of affirmation and guarantee (Gen. 14:22; Deut. 32:40). Apparently this prophecy takes on greater significance since the angel lifted two hands, in effect doubling the impact of confirmation.

Daniel heard the answer, sworn **by him who lives forever . . . "It will be for a time, times and half a time."** We have already noticed this expression and commented on it in connection with 7:25. Archer says: "Three and a half years is exactly one-half the full seven years of the seventieth week referred to in 9:27. It would be the second half that is intended by 'a time, times and half time,' since it ends (in all probability) with the destruction of the Beast at the Battle of Armageddon" (Archer, p. 155).

That leaves us with one phrase to ponder: **When the power of the holy people has been finally broken, all these things will be completed**. This refers again to the impact of the tribulation and the suffering of Israel during the three and one-half years. The resurrection and restoration will occur, and God will wind up human history at that time. Comparison of this brief statement with Zechariah (12:7–10; 13:8–9) shows us that God needs to break the Jews until they are willing to accept the Messiah.

12:8. Daniel found himself still confused and wondering how all this would turn out. All who find some difficulty in interpreting prophecy should be encouraged by Daniel's honest statement: **I heard, but I did not understand**.

 Restoration of the Kingdom (12:9–13)

SUPPORTING IDEA: *When we ask for understanding in a spirit of humility and faith, God provides adequate answers.*

12:9. Some interpreters find a mild rebuke in the angelic answer and suggest the angel's answer meant that Daniel already knew enough. The angel emphasized again that this message was completely protected, **closed up and sealed until the time of the end**. People who really need this message in the future time of trouble will have access to it, and Daniel should rest in the assurance of that promise.

12:10. Now we learn that the end times will refine and purify, **but the wicked will continue to be wicked**. Furthermore, **none of the wicked will understand, but those who are wise will understand**. This reminds us of Daniel 11:35 and its reference to the time of suffering under Antiochus Epiphanes. This common theme appears throughout the Bible, especially early in Jesus' teaching. The disciples asked him why he used parables so frequently in teaching the people, and Jesus said, "The knowledge of the secrets of the kingdom of heaven has been given to you, but not to them. Whoever has will be given more, and he will have an abundance. Whoever does not have, even what he has will be taken from him" (Matt. 13:11–12). His answer draws from Isaiah 6:9–10.

In commenting on the Matthew passage, Stu Weber says:

> Those who already had some knowledge—because they responded with humble faith to what had already been revealed—

had been good stewards of this information. They would be entrusted with more (particularly through their understanding of the parables). These people, because of their faith, had received God's gracious favor. However, those who had consciously rejected the Messiah would receive only judgment, beginning with Jesus' withholding of insight by the use of parables. These outsiders had enough knowledge of the truth to be hostile against Jesus, but even that insight would be further clouded by their disbelief. Jesus' teaching style was designed to give them little help as long as they persisted in their rebellion (Weber, p. 193).

12:11–12. Once again we see parallels between Antiochus Epiphanes and Antichrist. The phrase **the abomination that causes desolation** has appeared in Daniel 9:27 and 11:31. But it will happen again as Jesus tells us in Matthew 24:15. This very specific answer to Daniel's question establishes the time between the setting up of the pagan image in the temple in the middle of the tribulation to the end of the tribulation, **1,290 days**.

We have a chronological problem here. The three and one-half (time, times, and half a time) are normally taken to be 42 months of 30 days each, which would total 1,260 days. Not 1,290. When we add the **1,335 days**, we have two numbers which seem to represent either 30 days or 45 days beyond the exact three and one-half years in the second half of Daniel's seventieth week.

According to Walvoord:

> A clue comes from Matthew 25:31–46, which describes a time of judgment by Christ immediately after he comes to power at the close of this period. The purpose of this judgment is to determine who will be permitted to enter and enjoy the millennial period. But such an act of judgment will take a little time, and the added 30 days here in view would seem appropriate for that period. This would mean that the full time in view of these 1,290 days would be from the middle of the tribulation week until the completion of this time of judgment (Walvoord, *Daniel*, p. 157).

Most scholars begin the count from the establishment of the millennial government, Christ's thousand-year reign on earth. Pentecost, however, sees this as an additional time of judgment and says, "It is suggested that the forty-five day period is the period in which the judgments associated with the second advent of Christ are poured out on the earth. And that entire forty-five day period, then, could be called the second advent of Christ" (Pentecost, p. 301).

In all fairness we should note that not everyone takes these numbers literally. Baldwin says, "All attempts to find an exact application of the literal numbers break down. We turn next to the symbolic interpretation, keeping in mind that there have already been indications of symbolic numbers in the book, notably the seventy sevens of years in 9:24–27" (Baldwin, p. 210). Some see the time as a general and symbolic call for perseverance among people who are trying to follow Jesus in persecution.

12:13. The angel repeated his command to the prophet, **go your way**, but this time the word seems more permanent. Daniel **will rest, and then at the end of the days** would be resurrected to receive his **allotted inheritance** (Judg. 1:3; Col. 1:12). Wood picks up on the obvious but important point: "If Daniel is to be resurrected at this time, then other Old Testament saints will likely be resurrected at the same time, thus giving evidence regarding the probable time for the resurrection of Old Testament saints" (Wood, *Daniel*, p. 158).

MAIN IDEA REVIEW: *After the dreary sadness of warfare in chapter 11, the angel tells the prophet, those who are wise will shine like the brightness of the heavens, and those who lead many to righteousness, like the stars for ever and ever.*

III. CONCLUSION

Prophecy and Miracles

Despite the efforts of critics through the years to discredit the prophetic element in Daniel, belief in miracles has hardly gone out of style among modern peoples. I make this connection since prophecy is a miraculous act of God to send messages of the future through some means to people whom he selects. Generally, those who refuse the prophetic element in the Bible also deny miracles. But the popularity of the Left Behind series (which we have already mentioned), and the prime-time appearance of *Touched by an Angel* remind us that Americans are not completely secular.

In his new work entitled *The Book of Miracles,* Kenneth Woodward, the respected religion editor of *Newsweek,* claims that 84 percent of adult Americans believe that God performs miracles and 48 percent believe they have experienced a miracle in their own lives. Eighty-one percent of evangelicals, 75 percent of American Catholics, 54 percent of nonevangelical Protestants and 43 percent of non-Christians all say they have prayed at one time or another for a miracle.

There will always be skeptics, but well-meaning people who read the Bible naturally and literally should have no problem with the text of Daniel. The premillennial position arises from a natural, literal handling of the text, denying all attempts to make it mystical, symbolic, or merely historical. Veldkamp ends his devotional treatment of Daniel by reminding us: "The angel's instructions to Daniel also apply to us . . . whatever trials and struggles we may face in the future, the study of the Book of Daniel should leave us convinced that the Word of God will abide forever. Jesus Christ is the same yesterday, today, and forever. Amen" (Veldkamp, pp. 250–51).

PRINCIPLES

- This demonstration of God's great control of the past, the present, and the future should bring rest to the hearts of all who study Daniel.
- Selfless and diligent service for God always pays off in the end—the very end.
- Angels may be invisible, but they are very real and very much involved in the lives of believers.
- God cares about his truth and wants it preserved and presented to those who need to hear it.

APPLICATIONS

- Even when we find Bible passages difficult to understand, it is important to persist to some kind of interpretation that fits the context.
- Sharing the message of the gospel and leading "many to righteousness" produces a shining and eternal reward.

- As we wrestle with the truth of the Book of Daniel, we must remember to apply its values to our lives.
- We should never make interpretation of some details of a prophetic passage a test of faith and fellowship with other believers.

IV. LIFE APPLICATION

The Center of the Bible

Psalm 118 stands in a very interesting position in Scripture. I do not mean to suggest that God has placed it there for any special reason, but certainly its message anchors the ship of our theology. Psalm 117 is the shortest chapter in the Bible and Psalm 119 the longest. The Bible has 594 chapters before Psalm 118 and 594 chapters after Psalm 118. Within the psalm itself, one could say that verse 8 is the middle verse of the entire Bible, and it proclaims the axiom, "It is better to take refuge in the LORD than to trust in man."

That's the way Daniel lived. He had every reason to abandon his faith in the God of Israel when the kingdom of Judah fell and he was taken captive to a foreign land. But God constantly strengthened him through dreams and visions, and Daniel never wavered in his constant faith.

Samuel Rutherford was born in Scotland in 1600. As a young adult he became a pastor and was arrested when Scottish Calvinism was banished by Charles I in 1638. During the next two years he wrote 220 letters. After his release, his strong covenanter stance pitted him against the Catholic hierarchy of his country throughout most of his life. Indeed, he would have lost his head on the block in 1661 had he not been seriously ill. Among his final words he uttered the phrase, "Glory, glory dwelleth in Emmanuel's land."

In 1857, Anne Ross Cousin, a pastor's wife in Irvine, Scotland, read Rutherford's letters and wrote a hymn using fragments of his sentences and focusing on that dramatic final line. The first verse looks like this:

The sands of times are sinking, the dawn of heaven breaks;
The summer morn I've sighed for, the fair, sweet morn awaits.
Dark, dark hath been the midnight, but dayspring is at hand,
And glory, glory dwelleth in Emmanuel's land.

Our relationship in the church as the bride of Christ our bridegroom finds expression in Scripture from the Gospels to Revelation. When John the Baptist heard that his disciples were defecting to Jesus, he said, "The bride belongs to the bridegroom. The friend who attends the bridegroom waits and listens for him, and is full of joy when he hears the bridegroom's voice . . . he must become greater; I must become less" (John 3:29–30).

I can imagine Daniel and John having a discussion in heaven in which John expresses his appreciation for Daniel's wonderful model and for his book of prophecies. Daniel responds by commending John for his role in the early days of the new covenant people and wanting to know what it was like to be taught personally by Jesus for three and one-half years.

V. PRAYER

Father, thank you for the hope that lies before us. May we be like those who are wise and like those who lead many to righteousness. Amen.

VI. DEEPER DISCOVERIES

A. Book of Life (12:1)

Although the words *of life* are not added in Daniel 12:1, surely this is a reference to the famous "book of life" that appears throughout the Scripture. Exodus 32:33 describes people who have made a covenant with God; in Psalm 69:28 we find a curse against those who fight against the people of the Lord with a very specific prayer request: "Charge them with crime upon crime; do not let them share in your salvation. May they be blotted out of the book of life and not be listed with the righteous" (Ps. 69:27–28). Malachi 3:16 says, "Then those who feared the LORD talked with each other, and the LORD listened and heard. A scroll of remembrance was written in his presence concerning those who feared the LORD and honored his name." In Luke 10:20 Jesus said to his disciples, "However, do not rejoice that the spirits submit to you, but rejoice that your names are written in heaven."

When we come to Revelation 13:8, we learn that "all inhabitants of the earth will worship the beast—all whose names have not been written in the book of life belonging to the Lamb that was slain from the creation of the world." The book is mentioned again in Revelation 17:8. Finally in Revelation 20 we read, "Another book was opened, which is the book of life. . . . If anyone's name was not found written in the book of life, he was thrown into the lake of fire" (Rev. 20:12,15).

B. Resurrection (12:2–3,13)

The resurrection of Daniel 12 is commonly called the first resurrection (Rev. 20:5–6) because it takes place before the millennial kingdom and because that wording appears in the Revelation text. But it is really the fifth resurrection if we count the resurrection of Jesus (John 20:1–18); the resurrection of those who came out of their graves at the time of Christ's resurrection (Matt. 27:50–53); the resurrection which will take place at the time of the rapture of the church (1 Thess. 4:13–18); and the resurrection of the two witnesses (Rev. 11:11–12).

The resurrection in our text deals with the righteous martyrs of the great tribulation. To be more precise, the resurrection at the beginning of the tribulation (the rapture) applies to people of the new covenant—Christians who have died between the cross and the rapture. The resurrection seven years later will bring back tribulation martyrs, who will then be joined at the final resurrection with all the Old Testament saints from Adam to the cross, mentioned here in Daniel 12:2.

As Walvoord says:

> The doctrine of resurrection falls into place when one recognizes that there is a series of resurrections in Scripture, beginning with the resurrection of Christ and ending with the resurrection of the wicked [following the millennial kingdom]. In this series the resurrection of the martyred dead of the great tribulation is resurrection number five and is probably followed by the resurrection of the Old Testament saints. The resurrection of the wicked is the last resurrection (Walvoord, *Major Bible Prophecies,* pp. 379–80).

C. The Rapture

We've spent very little time in our discussion of Daniel talking about the rapture because it is not mentioned in this book. But since Daniel talks about the tribulation, it is only fair to ask whether Christian believers will be on earth during all or a portion of that time. If so, many of the things Daniel says about Jewish believers will also apply to Christian believers. Christians who maintain that believers will be taken to heaven before the tribulation target passages like Revelation 3:10 and John 5:24. Those who expect the church to go through the tribulation emphasize that 2 Thessalonians 2 seems to place the appearance of the Antichrist before the second coming of Christ. They also emphasize that the great commission requires Christians to proclaim the gospel until the end of the age.

Although I do not consider it important in the interpretation of Daniel, I adhere to the pretribulation rapture position. It seems to have adequate scriptural support, and it makes a very important distinction between old covenant and new covenant relationships with God. One of the crucial elements in the interpretation of Daniel requires us to recognize that his prophecies relate to Israel and not to redeemed Gentiles in the church. The resurrection of Daniel 12:2 fits very well into the scheme that premillennial scholars hold.

Walvoord is certainly a champion in that camp, and he puts it this way:

> From the standpoint of the pre-tribulational interpretation of prophecy, which holds to a resurrection of the church before the tribulation and therefore as preceding this resurrection, this passage can be taken quite literally. As a matter of fact, if the pre-tribulationists are correct, there will be an extensive resurrection of the righteous at this point when Christ returns to reign. Although it would be too much to say that this confirms pre-tribulationism, it harmonizes with this interpretation" (Walvoord, *Daniel*, p. 290).

VII. TEACHING OUTLINE

A. INTRODUCTION

1. Lead Story: Questions About Qumran
2. Context: Once again students of Daniel must remember that the last three chapters form a seamless garment of prophetic information. The context of chapter 12 rests in chapters 10–11, and the conclusion of chapters 10–11 can only be found in chapter 12.

3. Transition: Daniel transitions between chapters 11 and 12 by using the words "at that time," a direct reference to the dominance of Antichrist described at the end of chapter 11. There is no logical transition between Daniel and Hosea, the first of the minor prophets, since Hosea's work was written some two hundred years before Daniel lived.

B. COMMENTARY

1. Resurrection of the Righteous (12:1–4)
2. Revelation of the Schedule (12:5–8)
3. Restoration of the Kingdom (12:9–13)

C. CONCLUSION: PROPHECY AND MIRACLES

VIII. ISSUES FOR DISCUSSION

1. How do you respond to the suggestion of three different resurrections yet to come?
2. If you were to select a key verse for Daniel 12, which verse would it be?
3. How should the expectation of resurrection affect believers? How should it affect unbelievers?
4. What difference does it make if we believe the rapture of the church will occur before the tribulation or take the view that the church will go through the tribulation?

Glossary

angel—A messenger from God who delivers God's message of instruction, warning, or hope

Antichrist—Anyone who opposes God or Christ, but especially the evil leader at the end of the age whom Christ will defeat at his second coming

apocalyptic—Symbolic language reflecting belief in two opposing universal powers (God and Satan); two ages of universal history (present age dominated by evil and Satan and age to come under God's rule); and a future judgment giving rewards to the people of God and eternal punishment to the wicked

Babylon—Name of an evil city and empire in the sixth century B.C.; a code name for another evil city in Revelation

eschatology—The study of last things or the end time when Christ returns

evil—Anyone or anything that opposes the plan of God

exile—Israel's life in the Assyrian kingdom after 722 B.C. and Judah's life in Babylon after 587 B.C.

glorification—God's action in the lives of believers, making them able to share the glory and reward of heaven

idolatry—The worship of that which is not God

Messiah—The coming king promised by the prophets; Jesus Christ who fulfilled the prophetic promises; Christ represents the Greek translation of the Hebrew word *messiah*

miracle—A supernatural act of God that inspires wonder, displays God's greatness, and leads people to recognize God at work in the world

monotheism—Belief in only one God

omnipotent—God's unlimited power to do that which is within his holy and righteous character

pagans—Those who worship a god or gods other than the living God to whom the Bible witnesses

polytheism—Belief in more than one god; a heresy prevalent in biblical times

prayer—Communication with God

prophet—One who speaks for God

providence—God's care for and guidance of his creation against all opposition

revelation—Making known that which has been hidden; God making known his nature and purpose through the natural world, history, prophets, and most completely through Jesus Christ

sovereignty—God's freedom from outward restraint; his unlimited rule of and control over his creation

trials—Afflictions and hardships permitted in our lives by God to develop spiritual strength and endurance in us

worship—Reverence, honor, praise, and service shown to God

Bibliography

Anderson, Robert. *Daniel in the Critics' Den.* Grand Rapids, Mich.: Kregel Publications, 1990 (reprint).

_________. *The Coming Prince.* London: Hodder and Stoughton, 1903.

Archer, Gleason L., Jr. "Daniel." In *The Expositor's Bible Commentary.* Vol. 7. Grand Rapids, Mich.: Zondervan Publishing House, 1985.

Baldwin, Joyce G. *Daniel.* Downers Grove, Ill.: InterVarsity Press, 1978.

Beers, V. Gilbert. *The Victor Handbook of Bible Knowledge.* Wheaton, Ill.: Victor Books, 1981.

Bock, Darrell L., "The Son of Man in Daniel and the Messiah." Unpublished Master of Theology thesis. Dallas Theological Seminary (1979).

Boice, James M. *The Sovereign God.* Vol. 1. Downers Grove, Ill.: InterVarsity Press, 1978.

Boutflower, Charles. *In and Around the Book of Daniel.* Grand Rapids, Mich.: Kregel, 1977.

Braden, Charles S. *The World's Religions.* New York: Abingdon, 1939.

Calvin, John. *Commentaries on the Book of the Prophet Daniel.* Translated by Thomas Nyers. Vols. 1 and 2. Grand Rapids, Mich.: Eerdmans Publishing Co., 1561, 1948.

Campbell, Donald K. *Daniel: God's Man in a Secular Society.* Grand Rapids, Mich.: Discovery House, 1988.

Campbell, Donald K., and Jeffrey L. Townsend, eds. *A Case for Premillennialism.* Chicago: Moody Press, 1992.

Cedar, Paul. *A Life of Prayer.* Nashville, Tenn.: Word, 1998.

Clouse, Robert G., ed. *The Meaning of the Millennium.* Downers Grove, Ill.: InterVarsity Press, 1977.

Criswell, W. A. *Expository Sermons on the Book of Daniel.* Grand Rapids, Mich.: Zondervan, 1976.

Culver, Robert D. *Daniel and the Latter Days.* Westwood, N.J.: Fleming H. Revell, 1954.

Detzler, Wayne. *New Testament Words in Today's Language.* Wheaton, Ill.: Victor Books, 1986.

Easley, Ken. "Revelation." In the *Holman New Testament Commentary.* Nashville, Tenn.: Broadman & Holman, 1998.

Flynn, Leslie B. *Come Alive with Illustrations.* Grand Rapids, Mich.: Baker Book House, 1988.

Gariepy, Henry. *Portraits of Perseverance.* Wheaton, Ill.: Victor Books, 1989.

Girdlestone, Robert B. *Synonyms of the Old Testament.* Grand Rapids, Mich.: Baker Book House, 1991.

Hanhart, K. "The Four Beasts of Daniel's Vision in the Night in the Light of Rev. 13:2." *New Testament Studies*, 27:4 (July 1981).

Henry, Carl F. H. *Twilight of a Great Civilization.* West Chester, Ill.: Crossway Books, 1988.

Hoehner, Harold W. "Between the Testaments." In *The Expositor's Bible Commentary.* Vol. 1. Grand Rapids, Mich.: Zondervan, 1979.

Jerome's Commentary on Daniel. Translated by Gleason L. Archer, Jr. Grand Rapids, Mich.: Baker Book House, 1958.

Kaiser, Walter C., Jr. *The Uses of the Old Testament in the New.* Chicago: Moody Press, 1985.

Kraeling, Emil G. *Rand McNally Bible Atlas.* New York: Rand McNally and Co., 1956.

Kyle, C. F. *Biblical Commentary on the Book of Daniel.* Translated by M. G. Easton. Grand Rapids, Mich.: Eerdmans Publishing Co., 1949.

Ladd, George E. *A Commentary of the Revelation of John.* Grand Rapids, Mich.: Eerdmans, 1972.

Lang, G. H. *The Histories and Prophecies of Daniel.* Grand Rapids, Mich.: Kregel Publications, 1973.

Laney, J. Carl. *God.* Nashville, Tenn.: Word Publishing, 1999.

Leupold, Herbert C. *Exposition of Daniel.* Grand Rapids, Mich.: Baker Book House, 1969 (reprint).

Lightner, Robert. *Angels, Satan and Demons.* Nashville, Tenn.: Word, 1998.

Lightner, Robert P. *Evangelical Theology.* Grand Rapids, Mich.: Baker, 1986.

McClain, Alva J. *The Greatness of the Kingdom.* Grand Rapids, Mich.: Zondervan, 1959.

Miller, Stephen R. "Daniel." In *The New American Commentary.* Vol. 18. Nashville, Tenn.: Broadman & Holman, 1994.

Packer, J. I. *Knowing God.* Downers Grove, Ill.: InterVarsity Press, 1973.

Payne, Donna W., and Fran Lenzo. *The Handel's Messiah Family Advent Reader.* Chicago: Moody Press, 1999.

Payne, J. Barton. *Encyclopedia of Biblical Prophecy.* New York: Harper & Row, 1973.

Pentecost, J. Dwight. *Thy Kingdom Come.* Wheaton, Ill.: Victor Books, 1990.

Peterson, Eugene H. *The Message—The Old Testament Prophets.* Colorado Springs, Colo.: NavPress, 2000.

Robertson, James D. *Handbook of Preaching Resources from English Literature.* New York: The Macmillan Company, 1962.

Ryrie, Charles C. *Basic Theology.* Wheaton, Ill.: Victor Books, 1981.

Seiss, J. A. *The Apocalypse.* Grand Rapids, Mich.: Zondervan, 1957.

Seiss, Joseph. *Voices from Babylon.* Philadelphia: The Castle Press, 1879.

Tenney, Merrill C. *The Zondervan Pictorial Bible Dictionary.* Grand Rapids, Mich.: Zondervan, 1963.

The NIV Study Bible. Kenneth Baker, general ed. Grand Rapids, Mich.: Zondervan Bible Publishers, 1985.

The Works of Flavius Josephus. Translated by William Whiston. London: William P. Nimmo, n.d.

Tozer, A. W. *The Knowledge of the Holy.* New York: Harper & Row, 1961.

Veldkamp, Herman. *Dreams and Dictators.* St. Catharines, ON, Canada: Paideia Press, 1978.

Walvoord, John F. *Daniel: The Key to Prophetic Revelation.* Chicago: Moody Press, 1971.

_________. *End Times.* Nashville, Tenn.: Word, 1998.

_________. *Major Bible Prophecies.* Grand Rapids, Mich.: Zondervan, 1991.

_________. *The Prophecy Knowledge Handbook.* Wheaton, Ill.: Victor Books, 1990.

Wallace, Ronald S. *The Message of Daniel.* Leicester, England: InterVarsity Press, 1984.

Weber, Stuart K. "Matthew." In the *Holman New Testament Commentary.* Nashville, Tenn.: Broadman & Holman, 2000.

Whitcomb, John C., Jr. *Daniel.* Chicago: Moody Press, 1985.

_________. *Darius the Mede.* Grand Rapids, Mich.: Eerdmans Publishing Co., 1959.

Williams, Oscar, ed. *Immortal Poems of the English Language.* New York: Washington Square Press, 1952.

Wilmington, Harold L. *Wilmington's Survey of the Old Testament.* Wheaton, Ill.: Victor Books, 1987.

Wilson, Robert Dick. *Studies in the Book of Daniel* (four volumes). Grand Rapids, Mich.: Baker Book House, 1972.

Wood, Leon J. *A Survey of Israel's History.* Grand Rapids, Mich.: Zondervan, 1970.

_________. *Daniel.* Grand Rapids, Mich.: Zondervan, 1975.

_________. *The Prophets of Israel.* Grand Rapids, Mich.: Baker Book House, 1979.

Woodward, Kenneth L. *The Book of Miracles.* New York: Simon and Schuster, 2001.

Würthwein, Ernst. *The Text of the Old Testament.* Grand Rapids, Mich.: Eerdmans Publishing Co., 1979.

Young, Edward J. *The Prophecy of Daniel.* Grand Rapids, Mich.: Eerdmans Publishing Co., 1949.